D1563497

Immigrants, Progressives, and Exclusion Politics

Immigrants, Progressives, and Exclusion Politics

The Dillingham Commission,

1900–1927

Robert F. Zeidel

Northern Illinois University Press / DeKalb

Material in chapter 1 appeared in different form in Robert F. Zeidel, "Hayseed Immigration Policy: 'Uncle Joe' Cannon and the Immigration Question" *Illinois Historical Journal* 88 (autumn 1995): 173–88.

Library of Congress Cataloging-in-Publication Data

Zeidel, Robert F.

Immigrants, Progressives, and exclusion politics : the Dillingham Commission, 1900–1927 / Robert F. Zeidel.

   p.   cm.

Includes bibliographical references and index.

ISBN 0-87580-323-7 (alk. paper)

1. United States—Emigration and immigration—Government policy—History.

2. Dillingham, William P. (William Paul), 1843–1923. 3. United States—Immigration Commission (1907–1910). 4. Nativism. 5. Progressivism (United States politics).

6. United States—Politics and government—1901–1953. I. Title.

JV6483.Z45 2004

325.73'09'041—dc22

 2003066162

For the Zeidels

Bill and Peg, for who they were

Tom and Betty, for who they have been

Julie and Maggie, for who they are

CONTENTS

ACKNOWLEDGMENTS

WITHOUT THE SUPPORT of many institutions, colleagues, and friends, I never could have completed the task. My heartfelt appreciation goes out to all of you for your considerable assistance.

Numerous institutions and agencies have provided funding or other support. Research grants from the National Endowment for the Humanities, the Dirksen Center for the Study of the United States Congress, the University of Wisconsin Institute on Race and Ethnicity, and the University of Wisconsin—Stout Development Grant Program allowed me to visit several depositories. Friendly staffs at the Massachusetts Historical Society, the Harvard Houghton Library, the Chicago Historical Society, the Illinois State Historical Library, the Syracuse University Special Collections Research Center, and the University of Virginia Special Collections Library graciously assisted in the location of pertinent collections and other research requests. Many other depositories responded to my queries or provided photocopies, and the University of Minnesota Wilson Library gave me borrowing privileges as a visiting scholar. My academic home, the University of Wisconsin—Stout, provided institutional support and encouragement.

A number of conferences and forums allowed me to present different parts of my work, and the participant and audience comments helped me to evaluate and focus my ideas. Presentations took place at the Northern Great Plains History Conference, the Great Lakes History Conference, and the American Historical Association Pacific Coast Branch Conference. I also gave an overview of my project at an Immigration History Research Center Research in Progress session.

In addition, innumerable colleagues contributed immeasurably to my work. My study of the American reaction to the arrival of Progressive Era immigrants began with my doctoral studies at Marquette University, and I owe a special debt of gratitude to my mentor, Professor Emeritus Karel D. Bicha, for all of his help and guidance. Special thanks go also to departmental colleagues and support staffers at St. Cloud State University, University of St. Thomas, and University of Wisconsin—Stout. Scholars too numerous to name read and commented on parts of the manuscript, but the three who read and evaluated it in its entirety—Keith P. Dyrud, Julieanne Phillips, and especially

George Lankevich—warrant special mention. Leonard Dinnerstein patiently answered my numerous email queries, and Fred Jaher spent an evening at the AP-US History Reading talking about the project and offering keen observations and suggestions. Anonymous readers caught numerous mistakes and indicated several places that needed revision.

Northern Illinois University Press has been a joy with which to work, and the superb editorial staff—specially Martin Johnson, Melody Herr, and Susan Bean—provided much appreciated help in polishing the manuscript and making it worthy of publication. Of course, I alone bear responsibility for all statements of fact, interpretation, and opinion, and for any errors or other failings.

Like myriad other writers, friends and family have helped me through this arduous task, and I herewith acknowledge their considerable support. Those with whom I have run a few miles and shared a few beers include Joe and Jan Hallman, Winston Chrislock, Joe Fitzharris, Paul Duff, Joe and Jan Perske, Kurt and Karen Leichtle, Bruce and Patty Pettit, a whole bunch of AP Exam Readers, and many more. Most important, my family has been my inspiration and foundation, and it is to them that I dedicate this book. My late parents, Bill and Peg Zeidel, encouraged their son to pursue a scholastic career, and I only wish that they were here to share in this accomplishment. My brother, Tom, and sister-in-law, Betty, long have been good friends and trusted advisors, and I could not begin to repay them for their years of warm hospitality and sage advice. My wife, Julie, is my best friend, closest confidant, and greatest motivator. Over the last ten years, as I have worked on this book, she has prodded me with lots of love and occasionally has given me a much needed kick in the pants, and along the way she has given me the greatest gift for which a man could ask, our daughter, Maggie, the apple of her dad's eye. Thanks to you all for all that you have done.

Immigrants, Progressives, and Exclusion Politics

INTRODUCTION

The Dillingham Commission
and Progressive Reform

AS PART OF THE PROGRESSIVE ERA quest for social betterment, Congress created the Dillingham Commission, a body that
would have substantial influence on the formation of a half-cen-
tury of U.S. immigration policy. During the Theodore Roosevelt
administration the large number of immigrants was challenging
the nation's powers of assimilation and convincing some that
the time had come for more restriction on entry into the United
States. Section 39 of the Immigration Act of 1907 created the
nine-member commission, made up equally of senators, representatives, and presidential appointees, and directed it to make a
"full inquiry, examination, and investigation . . . into the subject
of immigration." The commission would then report to Congress
its findings and such recommendations "as in its judgment may
seem proper."[1] Among the commission's legacies were the literacy requirement and the quota system.

The commission and its work should be understood in the
context of the progressive movement of the early 1900s, in
which Americans made wide-ranging efforts to improve socioeconomic conditions. Although this diffuse movement had multiple layers and its reforms were complex and often contradictory,
it did possess some overarching characteristics. Progressives exhibited an almost religious faith in their ability to engender social betterment, a resolute trust in what they considered to be scientific objectivity, and an unflagging commitment to
government intervention. They believed that investigation and
analysis carried out by properly trained experts would equip policy makers with the means to eradicate social blight. Backed by
statistical studies that provided the requisite certainty, reformers
could ascertain the "true" nature of a problem and then find and
implement the right solution.[2]

Immigration presented one such problem. As previous studies
of the Progressive Era have emphasized, many American feared

the growing number of immigrants; historian William O'Neill has noted that immigration trailed only business consolidation and political corruption as a matter evoking public concern. Arthur Link defines immigration restriction as a "progressive goal," warning us that its racist, nativist, and anti-Semitic aspects "should not blind us to the fact that it was also progressive." Similarly, Morton Keller labels restriction "a paradigmatic Progressive cause," which in its efforts "to preserve a core national identity in the face of social change . . . called for massive fact gathering and complex regulation." Congress thus acted "in typical Progressive fashion" by creating the Dillingham Commission.[3]

Perhaps because they have not wanted to equate any form of xenophobia with progress, most immigration historians have ignored the Dillingham Commission's origins within the reform movement of the early 1900s and its contributions to that movement. Stressing instead the commission's part in the enactment of biased and prejudicial legislation, these scholars generally have agreed with Oscar Handlin's conclusion that "the commission's report was neither impartial nor scientific, and the confidence in it was not altogether justified." Handlin and other critics lament the commission's neglect of valuable information, its failure to consider various groups' duration of settlement, and its manipulation of findings to validate a predetermined belief that newer immigrants were incapable of being assimilated. Other commentators have contended that this bias was either the first step toward the passage of restrictive legislation or was an integral part of its eventual enactment. Even those who have recognized the breadth of the commission's investigation have criticized its methodology, asserting that it was intended to show the so-called new immigrants at their worst.[4]

Such assessments place the commission squarely within the context of nativism, defined by John Higham in his seminal *Strangers in the Land* as "intense opposition to an internal minority on the ground of its foreign (i.e., 'Un-American') connections." Even some historical surveys of the Progressive Era, such as one by Lewis Gould, associate the response to immigration with "heightened cultural and racial fears among the white middle-class" and describe immigration restriction as "usually justified on grounds of racial, religious, or ethno-cultural prejudice." Reliance on this interpretation is not surprising, given the prevalence of xenophobia in the late nineteenth and early twentieth centuries. Southern and eastern Europeans were called "new immigrants," an appellation that suggests their foreignness, and much Progressive Era rhetoric illustrates the popular hostility toward and denigration of these newcomers. *Yale Review* editor William F. Blackman spoke for many of his contemporaries when he wrote in 1902 that southern and eastern European immigrants were "in several respects, at least, a less desirable element of the population than those from the northern countries, . . . alien in blood, in language, and in political and social tradition." Such sentiments give credence to historians' interpretation of the restrictionist movement as having been primarily nativist.[5]

Yet, nativism's considerable presence notwithstanding, the nation's turn-of-the-century response to immigration was more than simply a matter of institutionalization of national bigotry. Some who were concerned about the large number of new arrivals, including many of those who supported more stringent restriction, failed to exhibit hostility toward the foreign-born. Immigrants, by definition, were different from Americans, but not all restrictionists found their foreignness inherently detrimental to the United States. Instead, many non-nativists, including members of the Dillingham Commission, questioned immigration's value in an increasingly urban and industrialized nation. Most of the commission's study focused not on immigrants themselves, but on how they lived and labored in the United States. Field investigators collected enormous amounts of information about immigrant workers—their occupations, wages, and living conditions—and the commissioners then assessed how new arrivals affected communities and industries.[6] This rational and statistically driven approach is not indicative of the work of nativists.

The Dillingham Commission deserves to be accorded not just a cultural interpretation but also a policy-oriented interpretation. Anthropologist Bruce G. Trigger calls these two approaches the romantic and the rationalist. Romantics, he contends, tend to see that indigenous peoples use their culture to define the "other." Leading historians have contended that nativistic Americans focused on what made the immigrants different, saw those differences as negative, and then used those differences as justification for exclusion. Rationalists, conversely, believe that the relations that develop between hosts and newcomers "can be accounted for more effectively in terms of economic and political consideration."[7] In the case of early-twentieth-century immigrants, their putative pernicious effects on labor and politics were of greater concern to many Americans than were their foreign characteristics.

A rationalist interpretation provides the best means for assessing and understanding the Dillingham Commission, and it allows for the connection between progressivism and the formation of U.S. immigration policy. When policy makers could not agree on a proper answer to the nation's "immigration question," they set up the expert commission to carry out a detailed investigation. The scope of its inquiry, the breadth its reports, and even its rationale for restrictive recommendations bear witness to the commissioners' concern for thoroughness and objectivity. Conversely, the commission made few negative references to immigrants on the basis of their physical, social, or cultural characteristics.

An understanding of the commission's phraseology, particularly of the terms it used to describe immigrants, also enables fuller comprehension of its work. Misconceptions about terminology, especially about the use of *race* as a synonym for *ethnicity*, have led some historians to make unwarranted negative assessments of the commission. It is true that turn-of-the-century social scientists believed in much more rigid and inherent differences between ethnic or national groups than did their latter-day counterparts, but this did not preclude the study of the various groups' historical, social, and cultural backgrounds. Matthew Jacobson, in his study of "whiteness," notes the widespread recognition of "biologically based 'races' rather than culturally based 'ethnicities,'" but he also discusses the extent to which the Dillingham Commission's *Dictionary of Races and Peoples* combined physiological and cultural characteristics in its definitions of immigrant groups.[8]

The commission did emphasize its intent to study "the various races, or at least the principal races," of American immigrants, and it consistently used that terminology in its reports, but what it called racial classifications in its *Dictionary of Races and Peoples* were essentially what subsequent investigators (such as members of the 1978 Hesburgh Commission) would call ethnic groups. Their use of the term *race*, then, did not make the Dillingham Commissioners virulent racists in any more modern sense. Even immigrant-friendly historians, such as Theodore Blegen in his 1931 study of Norwegian Americans, referred to nationality using the phrase *racial group*.[9]

Use of the term *Anglo Saxon* also poses problems. Turn-of-the-century Americans used this designation with regularity, but scholars subsequently have made clear that, except perhaps in medieval England, it was never a precise ethnic category or designation. In the sage words of Mr. Dooley, "An Anglo Saxon, Hinnissy, is a German that's forgot who was his parents." Scholars tend to resolve the matter by putting the phrase in quotations to show its artificial, social construction, but I have decided not to use this convention unless the phrase is part of a direct quote. Readers must understand that when Americans in the era of the Dillingham Commission used the term, they did so in nativist fashion, as a way to distinguish themselves from others, mainly immigrants, who were different. In their understanding, *Anglo Saxon* denoted Protestant whites whose ancestors had come to America before the immigrants of their own era, and who were, in some vaguely defined manner, of distinguished ethnic stock. The fact that the United States and its colonial antecedents had always had an ethnically diverse population was of little consequence to those who wanted to set themselves apart.[10]

Clarification is also needed regarding the commission's use of *old* and *new* to designate immigrant groups that predominated before and after 1890 and came from western and eastern Europe, respectively. Given the numerous waves of immigrants who have come to the United States, it is no doubt time for historians to heed Roger Daniels's advice and "retire that hoary concept" of old and new immigrants when writing about the immigrants themselves. Yet, in helping us to understand how Progressive Era Americans responded to immigrants, the terms *old* and *new* retain value. The Dillingham Commission used these then-popular designations to direct "its efforts almost entirely to an inquiry relative to the general status of the newer immigrants as residents in the United States." Their relatively recent and increasing prominence, admittedly along with their differences from earlier immigrants, ensured that these new immigrants would receive most of the commission's scrutiny. By focusing on these more recent newcomers, the commission sought to test many of the assumptions that underlay such people's bad reputations.[11]

Problems with sources have made it difficult to assess the Dillingham Commission properly. The commission's forty-one volumes of reports, as well as other government documents, provide a wealth of information about what the investigators found and have been used as basic source material for previous studies of the commission. Unfortunately, these documents provide only limited insight into how the inquiry proceeded and why it unfolded as it did. During World War I, under authority of Congress, the Department of Labor destroyed most of the commission's quotidian records and papers, which could have shed more light on the commission's internal workings; relatively few files survive in the records of the Immigration and Naturalization Service.[12] These sources, then, must be augmented with materials from other manuscript collections, especially the papers of those who worked for the commission or who had significant involvement in the immigration debate of the early 1900s.

Today at the beginning of the twenty-first century, that debate has begun anew. Yet another wave of new arrivals is adding to the nation's cultural and ethnic diversity and renewing its fear of and fascination with immigrants. As the percentage of foreign-born in the U.S. population approaches that of the Dillingham Commission era, Americans once again are worried about immigration's detrimental effects. Conversely, the recently refurbished Statue of Liberty and the partially restored Ellis Island Immigration Station stand as iconic testaments to the nation's immigrant forebears and are visited every year by millions of their descendants. Those visitors, too, have reached Oscar Handlin's famous conclusion "that the immigrants *were* American history." Yet especially in the context of the arrival of our own era's "new" immigrants, it is important to understand that immigration has had a problematic history and that the acceptance of foreign newcomers, even when most of them were white and European, has not been easy.[13]

DEFINING THE QUESTION OF IMMIGRATION, 1890–1900

"We have got to do something with this question of immigration," bemoaned Minnesota senator Cushman K. Davis in 1894. As the nineteenth century came to a close, many others were reaching the same conclusion. Calls for more rigid controls on the number and types of immigrants were heard across the nation. The Immigration Restriction League (IRL) of Boston, organized in 1894–1895 by three Harvard University graduates, identified over three hundred pro-restriction newspapers. "In my judgment," concluded League founder Robert Ward, "there is no less danger

[than] in the negro problem; there is less importance in the tariff; there is less real critical moment in any National question than there is in this immigration question: *The Great American Problem.*"[14]

A complex web of interconnected developments that were indicative of fundamental national changes made up this so-called immigration problem and spurred myriad calls for its eradication. Since the end of the Civil War, the United States had experienced both a precipitous rise in the number of immigrants and a noticeable shift in their places of origin. Concurrently, the largely rural-agrarian milieu, with its attendant cultural values dating from the early republic, was giving way to industrialization and urbanization, replete with slums, new employment conditions, and class-based social unrest. The combination of a larger number of immigrants, greater ethnic diversity, a perceived connection between aliens and social decay, and a growing fear of imported radicalism convinced many Americans that immigration threatened their quality of life. During the 1890s, at the height of the Gilded Age, perceptions of immigrants' malfeasance engendered impassioned calls on the part of some for restrictions on immigration, but uncertainty convinced others of the need for more objective information.

Indications of a greater immigrant presence were readily apparent. Construction of a new processing station at New York's Ellis Island, begun in 1890, bore witness to the increased volume of immigration, as did the proliferation of ethnic enclaves. Because immigrants tended to congregate among others from their homeland and near places of ready employment, virtually every urban area and industrial center contained at least one "little" community filled with people of a particular ethnic group. In New York City, writer-photographer Jacob Riis observed, "One may find for the asking an Italian, a German, a French, African, Spanish, Bohemian, Russian, Scandinavian, Jewish, and Chinese colony." A "distinctively American" community, however, was notably absent. Although the actual number of new arrivals varied considerably from year to year and declined significantly during the periodic depressions, this neither reduced the immigrants' visibility nor placated their critics.[15]

Ethnic differences also fueled natives' concerns. Over time larger and larger numbers of southern and eastern Europeans were coming to the United States, and their proportion relative to members of traditional immigrant groups was growing as well. In 1870 they numbered fewer than 10,000 and made up only 2.5 percent of all immigrants, and by 1890, these figures had risen to almost 160,000 and 35 percent. "In recent years," concluded one contemporary observer, "a class has come, accustomed to a distinctly lower standard, with no notion of anything else, perfectly content to live as at home, and whose only ambition has been to save enough to return to the old country." IRL spokesman Robert Ward went further, describing these "new" European immigrants as "without question the most illiterate and the most depraved people of that continent" and calling for quick action to ensure their exclusion. On the Pacific Coast, the growing number of Chinese and then Japanese immigrants aroused concern about the so-called Asian menace.[16]

Immigrants who were most different from the mythical Anglo-Saxon type bore the brunt of Gilded Age nativism. After giving citizenship to African Americans with the Civil Rights Act of 1866 and the Fourteenth Amendment, in 1870 Congress refused to alter the nation's long-standing policy, dating back to George Washington's presidency, of denying it to "non-white" immigrants. This particularly affected the Chinese. Political-economist Richmond Mayo-Smith, despite his efforts to present well-founded information objectively, typified the growing nativist sentiment when he deemed migrants from "countries like Italy, Hungary, and French Canada [*sic*]" to be "at best ignorant." Francis A. Walker, respected economist and former superintendent of the census, doubted that those same immigrants had "in any high degree, the capability of responding to the opportunities and incitements of their new condition." The IRL averred that their increasing numbers signaled an overall decline in immigrant quality and a growing threat to the United States.[17]

Although plenty of Americans concurred with such bigotry toward and distrust of the immigrants themselves, larger social and economic conditions also contributed to the outbreak of late-nineteenth-century xenophobia. The rural-agrarian character of the early American republic had long since disappeared, and the dramatic rise of big business, with its attendant social disorder, engendered many of the immigrant-related concerns. "The ghost of Thomas Jefferson still walks," noted one commentator, but only among those who were ignorant of recent "facts." Rapid industrialization had created a world dominated by burgeoning cities instead of rural countrysides, seemingly disgruntled factory workers instead of contented yeoman farmers, and large monopolistic corporations instead of small businesses, changes that cumulatively produced a host of new maladies. It was these—urban squalor, social decay, and violent strikes—in association with the growing prevalence of new immigrants, that had aroused natives' ire and given the newcomers their bad reputation.[18]

Settlement patterns not only increased immigrant visibility but also invited negative scrutiny. Foreigners' settlement in urban areas and other industrial centers gave credence to the Turnerian idea of a vanished frontier and the end of an age. Moreover, many of the new arrivals came with limited funds, and others, because they were trying to send money home or to accrue a large sum in preparation for a triumphant personal return, compromised on amenities. When combined with immigrants' tendency to settle among others from their home country, these characteristics produced an image of the immigrant ghetto as an impoverished slum. In 1890 Jacob Riis poignantly and provocatively conveyed such images of New York's Five Points neighborhood to a receptive American public. The way the other half lived, he explained, was dark enough "to send a chill to any heart." It mattered little that the neighborhood's bad reputation had preceded the arrival of the recent immigrants.[19]

Indigenous American whites, or natives in the parlance of the day, particularly worried about the newcomers' antisocial tendencies. Alleged transgressions included criminal propensity, alcoholism, truancy, pauperism, and an unwillingness to pursue naturalization and the responsibilities of citizenship. While those involved in the settlement house movement that was begun in the late 1880s sought to improve these "huddled masses" by working with them within their American environment, other natives believed that the nation could not eradicate immigrant-related problems without removing the source. For these restrictionists, the elimination of future immigration was perfectly logical. The IRL used this argument, bolstered by a healthy dose of unabashed bigotry, to advance its stated cause. Had illiterates been excluded since the start of the post–Civil War rush, the League asserted, ethnic "slums would now be of insignificant proportions instead of being hotbeds of crime, disease, and pauperism,—a menace to the immigrants and to the community at large."[20]

Advocates for the working class who viewed new arrivals as a threat to high wages and "an American standard of living" supported restriction as a means of protecting labor's interests. Immigrants, they contended, in comparison to natives, would live under wretched conditions and work for pauper pay. Given this tendency, recent arrivals forced out higher-paid workers and allowed management to reduce everyone's compensation. Union leaders, fearing that employers could replace strikers with immigrant "scabs," argued that an unchecked stream of foreign-born workers would cripple the efforts of organized labor. The IRL contended that "the Union workingman has only to fear the competition of degraded and low immigrants," and even socialists including Eugene Debs at times expressed similar views, although Debs ultimately came to reject the calls for restriction. The padrone system, in which one individual would control and often exploit the employment of others from the home country, also troubled many Americans, who viewed the practice as incompatible with their notions of free labor.[21]

Those concerned with social control mistrusted immigrants also because they perceived them to be associated with imported radicalism. This perception could take two forms. One variation held that the purveyors of radical doctrines, exemplified by the likes of "Red Emma" Goldman and Alexander Berkman, came from foreign countries. Historian John P. Diggins has demonstrated that twentieth-century manifestations of an American left were largely of native origin, but his assertions would have found few believers among restrictionists. They, along with many other Americans, found it inconceivable that the native-born could possibly embrace subversive leftist ideas. Radical outbursts could be blamed instead on incorrigible aliens, who therefore must be excluded. The nation already had as many "communists, anarchists, nihilists, bombthrowers . . . as we can digest at present," the impassioned Massachusetts Republican Elijah A. Morse told the House of Representatives in 1896.[22]

Antiradicals' fear of pliable masses produced a second reason for distrusting recent arrivals. Incidents of class violence, such as the great railroad strike in 1877 and the Haymarket Square bombing in 1886, heightened concerns about fanatical provocateurs. Natives, envisioning these agitators as participants in an imported conspiracy who were bent on destroying the nation, displayed what has been called a "convulsion of deep-rooted and violent prejudice." A simple provision worded so as to exclude radicals of virtually every stripe could have barred admissions and permitted deportations, but that would not have been enough to satisfy most natives. Far more menacing, in the minds of many, was the threat posed by the masses of ordinary immigrants. They were perceived as being ignorant of the dangers and liable to fall victim to agitators' spells and to become unwitting tools in their nefarious schemes. Eliminating this scenario would require more extensive types of restriction than the simple exclusion of foreign-born radical leaders.[23]

Changing ideas about governance also influenced how Americans responded to immigration. During the early republic, states' rights ideology held great sway, and with the exception of passage of the 1798 Alien Act, most of the efforts to formulate immigration policy took place at the state level. Reaction to the arrival of almost two million Irish between 1820 and 1860 provides a salient example. Primarily Catholic, the Irish often found themselves to be targets of the nativist bigotry manifested in what has been called the Protestant crusade or the Know-Nothing movement. However, this movement failed to produce any national restrictions. Members of the Thirty-Fourth Congress concluded that they lacked the power to exclude particular types of immigrants, no matter what their character or quality. During the 1850s, those associated with the nativist Know-Nothing party did secure passage of several state laws addressing education, militia service, naturalization in state courts, and lay control of church property, but that was the extent of their success.[24]

The antebellum Supreme Court did provide the first step toward the creation of a truly national immigration policy. New York and Massachusetts, along with other states and port cities, had passed laws assessing a head tax on arriving immigrants. The measures were opposed by steamship companies, which had to bear the added cost, and the matter eventually reached the Supreme Court. In the 1849 passenger cases, a 5–4 majority ruled that the assessments violated the national government's exclusive power to regulate interstate and international commerce. The Court's decision would seem to have indicated the need for national legislation, but the notion of states' rights, articulated in Chief Justice Roger B. Taney's dissent, remained strong. Localities would continue to administer the processing of arriving immigrants until the 1880s.[25]

By then, the situation had changed considerably. Reconstruction, with its attendant constitutional amendments, had solidified the predominance of Washington, D.C., over the states. In addition, the rise of powerful interstate businesses prodded Congress and the courts to increase the national government's regulatory powers. These included the control of immigration. The growing anti-Chinese movement led to passage in 1875 of the Page Act, which excluded Asian contract laborers and prostitutes and anyone "undergoing a sentence" as a result of a criminal conviction. Congress then passed the 1882 Chinese Exclusion Act, which prohibited the immigration of Chinese laborers, or coolies, for the next ten years. A harbinger of the extreme quotas of the 1920s, this legislation was extended in 1892 for another decade and was made permanent in 1902. Congress also enacted more general exclusion in the Immigration Act of 1882, which prohibited the admission of "lunatics," "idiots," and any person "likely to become a public charge."[26]

Rather than bringing closure, the enactment of the 1882 laws signaled the onset of a protracted and contentious debate. By 1890, armed with the belief that existing statutes had failed to protect the nation from immigrant-related dangers, restrictionists called for more rigorous limitations on all new arrivals. "The general belief," asserted the *New York Times,* "is that the time has come when we should begin to put up bars." In his pathbreaking *Emigration and Immigration,* economist Richmond Mayo-Smith argued that it was "desirable to correct certain evils which flow from the perfect freedom of immigration." *The Nation* contended that employers lowered the wages of native workers every time they hired "a fresh lot of hands from the Old World." New England blue blood Henry Cabot Lodge, who subsequently would figure prominently in congressional debate on immigration and in the work of the Dillingham Commission, claimed that the 1890 census showed that a disproportionate number of immigrants were criminals, paupers, and juvenile delinquents. Americans had recently taken more note of such matters, he concluded, and it was time for Congress to act.[27]

Conversely, those who could loosely be called antirestrictionists argued that the United States should continue its traditional policy of excluding only those who posed a specific and well-defined danger, such as criminals or persons afflicted with contagious diseases. Austrian-born U.S. Immigration Superintendent Joseph H. Senner, who would later help to organize an Immigration Protection League and whose work with the Bureau of Immigration drew restrictionists' ire, disagreed with those who, like Lodge, foresaw "'a perilous change in the very fabric of our race'" due to increased immigration. When in 1893 Senner did voice support for moderate new exclusions, he nonetheless believed that an immigrant clearing house to direct new arrivals to places where they were most desired would be superior to any new eligibility test. He thereafter came to oppose what he considered to be the more "injurious" and "cruel" restrictions. Similarly, *The Nation,* which seemed to vacillate on the issue, asked how immigrants could be held responsible for such national maladies as the tariff, disorderly currency, a passion for foreign aggression, and (except in New York City) the numerous problems in municipal government.[28]

Growing concern, coupled with a lack of consensus, highlighted the need for accurate information. "The discussion of the subject of immigration has now reached such a stage," declared Gustav H. Schwab, American agent for the North German Lloyd Steamship Company, "when the calm consideration of rational and practical measures for the protection of this country must take the place of wholesale denunciation, wild theories, and impractical propositions." Schwab's proposal was short on specifics, but it clearly reflected his professional interest in perpetuating immigration. For example, he contended that steamship companies should be allowed to police themselves in excluding those already in prohibited classes. Still, regardless of his motives, Schwab's suggestion drew favor, and shortly thereafter others did pursue his idea of collecting more detailed information about immigration matters.[29]

One such effort involved editor Henry Rood of New York's *Mail and Express*. After studying Pennsylvania's immigrant coal miners, he concluded that southeastern Europeans did not have the necessary attributes for citizenship. They came only for monetary gain, lived crowded together in unsanitary dwellings, sent large amounts of cash back to Europe, and kept their children out of school. Rood professed "profound pity" for those who could not hope to improve their lot except by coming to the United States, but he also wondered what would happen to the nation "if the gates are left open." Believing that Congress lacked the requisite information with which to answer such questions, he proposed creating a permanent immigration commission. It would be appointed by the president and would consist of three members serving ten-year terms. Given the scope of their task, these must be "the best men to be obtained," without regard to party affiliation. The commissioners would "personally study the immigrants in every section of the United States" and extend their inquiry abroad, "so that we might know positively just what to expect from Europe." The commission would make annual reports to Congress on the basis of these investigations.[30]

Although such a far-reaching effort would not materialize until 1907, when the Dillingham Commission was established, several groups did attempt to glean more insight into immigration matters. Congress initiated one of the first such investigations in July 1888, when Michigan Democrat Melbourne H. Ford called on the House to study the workings and shortcomings of U.S. immigration laws, as well as attempts to evade them. The resultant Select Committee on Immigration, a five-man panel chaired by Ford, reported to the House on 19 January 1889. The panel's majority, Ford explained, agreed that "the time has come to draw the line, to select the good from the bad, and sift the wheat from the chaff." Although past immigrants had aided greatly in the Republic's development, the same could not be said about current arrivals. Coal miners drew particular scorn. Echoing Henry Rood's description, the committee contended that the miners had low intelligence and little interest in citizenship and that they were willing to live in horrid conditions.[31]

Two committeemen disagreed with the calls for new restrictions. Prussian-born Richard Guenther, a Wisconsin Republican, concurred with the majority's opinion that certain aliens were unlikely to benefit the nation, but he could not support any measure that would punish desirable immigrants. Democrat Francis B. Spinola, representing immigrant-rich New York, also objected to any new law that would interfere with the migration of honest men and women. These, and not the various types of undesirables, Guenther and Spinola believed, made up the bulk of present immigrants. Since the House took no further action on immigration during that session, the committee's differences of opinion went no further legislatively, but they did foreshadow sharper disagreements to come.[32]

Congress undertook a more intensive inquiry during the next session. In January 1890, Senator William E. Chandler, a New Hampshire Republican, called for the Senate Immigration Committee and the House Select Committee on Immigration and Naturalization to work together on an investigation into the effectiveness of existing legislation. To ensure the fullest possible inquiry, Chandler wrote to prospective witnesses, explaining the committee's work and requesting that those with similar interests or expertise in the field appear at one of the hearings and present their views. The *New York Times* would later praise Chandler for his investigatory efforts, saying that his "penetrating mind" had been "well and profitably employed in directing this inquiry into a vast evil and in guiding the search for a remedy."[33]

The Chandler Committee held hearings in St. Louis, Chicago, Cincinnati, and Washington, D.C., during the summer of 1890. Responding to the lawmakers' invitation, a variety of immigrant leaders, English and foreign-language editors, government officials, and union spokesmen offered their views on current immigration and on the possible benefits or consequences of several proposed policy changes. The various testimony offered a wide range of opinions. *Cincinnati Free Press* editor M. A. Jacobi advocated the taking of some action to exclude undesirable immigrants but acknowledged the difficulty of determining the proper method. Immigration inspector Robert D. Layton also supported greater restriction. Others disagreed. For example, *Chicago Daily Scandinavian* editor John Anderson testified that he "would not like a law that would exclude any poor boy or girl from this country."[34]

Not surprisingly, given these divergent opinions, committee members came away from the hearings with mixed ideas about how best to answer the "restriction question." According to Chairman Chandler, no member thought the time had come to deny the right of immigration to persons who would make good and valuable additions to American society. A minority did favor expanding the list of those excluded, but most of the lawmakers concluded that proper administration of existing laws had more public support than any new legislation. As a result, the committee recommended adherence to the traditional policy of excluding only those whose presence constituted a specific danger. Accordingly, anyone who suffered from a loathsome disease or practiced polygamy should be excluded, and newcomers traveling on prepaid tickets should bear the burden of proving that they did not belong to one of the proscribed classes.[35]

Nonetheless, restrictionists continued to press their cause. Some believed that the United States should establish a system of consular certification, whereby government agents would inquire into the background, physical condition, and character of emigrants prior to their embarkation, and those who could not pass muster would not be allowed to board the ship. Such a system had been used in China to deter the emigration of prostitutes, but some authorities questioned its practicality for screening Europeans: since people from many different countries flocked into the port cities, it would be all but impossible to check into their backgrounds. Other authorities thought that a high entrance fee, or head tax, would effectively winnow good from bad migrants. Most significantly, there was support for a literacy test, or educational qualification, as first proposed by economist Edward W. Bemis in 1888. The test would limit immigration of people over fourteen years of age to those who could read and write some language, with exemptions for certain family members.[36]

By the mid-1890s, the literacy test had become the restriction of choice among members of Congress. It allegedly would "shut off that element of immigration which is economically the least beneficial and socially and politically the most injurious." Henry Cabot Lodge, one of the test's principal champions, believed that its passage would be one of his crowning legislative achievements: "I am vain enough to think that if I succeed in getting that bill, I shall have rendered one great public service." *The Nation*, however, observed that although Lodge had the advantages of the best available education, "a very large proportion of the thinking men of the country look on him as a citizen who does more damage to the nation than a hundred thousand, or we might say, a half-million, ignorant Europeans."

Unabashed nativism certainly contributed to the literacy provision's appeal. IRL spokesman Robert Ward labeled southern and eastern Europeans the continent's "most depraved and illiterate people" and stressed that the educational test would go a long way toward ensuring their exclusion. For example, his figures indicated that, if the test had been in operation in April 1896, it would have barred 67 percent of Italians who arrived that month at New York City. Other statistics indicated that there would be comparable results among Poles and Russians, but not among Germans, Scandinavians, and British. South Carolina Democratic representative Stanyarne Wilson also endorsed the test's anticipated exclusion of members of undesirable groups, "miserable specimens of humanity" including Italians, Poles, Jews, and Austrians. Lodge contended that it would primarily affect "races" far removed from those that had made the United States a great nation. Chastising his unconvinced congressional colleagues, who he believed did not appreciate the magnitude of the "danger which threatens us is this matter," he urged them to shake off their "indifference and timidity" and enact the literacy requirement.[37]

By Lodge's standards, Congress proceeded cautiously. Following the Chandler Committee's recommendations, the Immigration Act of 1891 added polygamists, paupers or others likely to become public charges, and persons suffering from contagious diseases to the list of those excluded and required those traveling on prepaid tickets to prove that they did not belong to any of the excluded classes. Another new provision required that any steamship company that transported a barred person return that individual to the port of embarkation at no additional cost. A separate section created a new office, that of the Superintendent of Immigration. The act did not, however, contain provisions for a literacy test or any other means of general exclusion.[38] Unlike provisions designed to exclude a specific group due to its perceived danger, these types of measures, which would become the focus of the era's immigration policy debates, were instead intended to reduce the overall number of immigrants.

Shortly after the passage of the 1891 law, the Treasury Department, which at the time administered the various immigration policies, sought to make "a careful examination of the immigration question on the other side of the water." The department particularly wanted information about voluntary and induced emigration of criminals. Rumors abounded, especially among restrictionists, that other nations were violating the Page Act by sending their unwanted convicts and other undesirable types to the United States. In May 1891, Treasury Secretary Charles Foster appointed an investigatory committee comprising Minnesota attorney Judson N. Cross, Wisconsin insane asylum director Walter Kempster, Pennsylvania labor leader Joseph Powderly, and U.S. Immigration officials Herman J. Schulties and John B. Weber; the latter acted as chairman.[39]

Secretary Foster instructed his Special Immigration Commission to look into the effectiveness of relevant U.S. statutes, especially those that prohibited certain types of assisted, or stimulated, immigration. In addition to legislation addressing concerns about the immigration of convicts, there were the Contract Labor Law of 1885, which prohibited third parties from paying for aliens' tickets in exchange for those persons' future service, and the Immigrant Act of 1891, which excluded immigrants who had been induced by employers' advertisements. The commissioners were charged with ascertaining, as far as possible, "the principal causes which operate in the several countries of Europe to incite emigration to the United States"; the extent to which immigration was "promoted or stimulated by steamship or other carrying companies through their agents"; the extent to which agents engaged contract laborers for export to the United States; the degree to which relatives, communities, and governmental authorities aided members of excluded classes; and the manner in which steamship companies conducted background checks of their passengers. Foster also charged the commissioners with reporting on the practicality and cost of having American consuls examine emigrants in foreign countries.[40]

After observing the emigration process and interviewing pertinent offi-cials, the commissioners filed four separate reports. As suggested in their in-structions, they had worked largely independently of one another, with each investigating a different part of Europe. Cross found some evidence of systematic emigration of convicts from Liverpool, England, and he later ex-pressed concern over assisted immigration in general. He did not, however, believe that the United States should exclude poor or illiterate immigrants, many of whom made themselves "worthy as true American citizens." Com-bining tolerance and bigotry, he expressed hope that "we can and will be liberal in our welcome to White Christian people from Europe; we will I fear, turn the cold shoulder to others." Powderly concluded that the gov-ernment should take steps to deter habitual seasonal migration—the mi-grants were popularly referred to as "birds of passage"—and the immigra-tion of prostitutes. Weber and Kempster, who had observed few immigrants who were poor or of doubtful quality, jointly ridiculed consular inspection as a "panacea for what our investigations show to be largely imaginary evils." Weber then reiterated these views in the popular press.[41]

Only Schulties, who in the mid-1890s would serve as commissioner-general of immigration while concurrently having close ties to the IRL, suggested sweeping new policies. Believing that numerous parties were engaged in the recruitment of Europe's "diseased, decrepit, and criminal population" with the intent of sending them to the United States, he proposed remedial policies including a system of inspection in Europe, im-proved scrutiny at U.S. ports, the imposition of a head tax, better steerage conditions, and a prohibition on the use of prepaid tickets. It is not clear whether Schulties intended the prohibition to include tickets purchased for family members, a seemingly unfair proscription, or just those purchased for workers, the target of the existing exclusion of laborers already under contract to or induced by U.S. companies. He did make it clear that the na-tion must exclude European radicals who sought "to bury popular sover-eignty beneath a mass of un-American jargon and bomb-throwing anar-chy." Schulties also wanted to give the president the power to suspend immigration in times of war or pestilence or in the case of other exigencies. He subsequently recommended enacting "an educational qualification cov-ering native language, for persons over 14 years of age."[42]

The Treasury Department's investigation, like its predecessors, failed to spur Congress to enact any sort of general restriction. Instead, Senator Chandler secured passage of the Immigration Act of 1893, a limited meas-ure that dealt primarily with the preparation of passenger lists by ship cap-tains. Writing in the *North American Review* thereafter, Chandler surpris-ingly called for stricter control of immigration from Europe. His suggestions included a one-year moratorium on new arrivals to counteract the threat of cholera during the coming summer's Columbian Exposition. Such a hiatus would allow Congress time to debate and formulate a comprehensive im-migration policy. Chandler also called for a literacy restriction, and before the House had even finished its work on the Immigration Act of 1893, he had introduced a bill to that effect. Although the new bill passed out of committee, the Senate took no further action on it. A majority likely believed that existing laws would suffice to address the nation's most pressing immigration-related evils.[43]

To achieve the passage of more restrictive provisions, Lodge believed, there would have to be more strident public clamor, and this was steadily materializing. "To get an efficient legislation to cure this evil," he wrote in 1891, "the movement must come from outside and be much more concentrated and of much greater strength than has thus far been the case." By 1895 hundreds of newspapers, including the New Orleans *Times Democrat,* the St. Paul *Pioneer Press,* and the Philadelphia *Telegraph,* had endorsed more stringent exclusion, and the IRL had grown to 531 members in fourteen states and had branch chapters in several major cities. It had published five pamphlets, of which over thirty-eight thousand copies were circulated, and had sent memoranda to every member of Congress. The League also conducted its own observations at Ellis Island and predictably concluded that "an education test is absolutely practical and applicable without any considerable change in the present machinery and methods employed under present law."[44]

From 1895–1897 Congress gave the matter more serious consideration, and if it had not been for a presidential veto, restrictionists would have gained approval of the literacy test requirement. During the course of earlier debates, Lodge attempted to bolster support on the basis of specious argument: "It is also proved the classes now excluded by law, the criminals, the diseased, the paupers, and the contract laborers, are furnished chiefly by the same races as those most affected by the literacy test." While there was no firm evidence to corroborate such contentions, Cabot's statement promoted the subjective belief that the test would bar those whom "no thoughtful or patriotic man can wish to see multiplied among the people of the United States." These and similar arguments convinced enough members of Congress, and the test provision was passed in February 1897 and sent to President Grover Cleveland.[45]

Letters to the president showed the "thoughtful" public to be sharply divided. Nativist groups (often called patriotic societies in restrictionist circles), such as the Junior Order United American Mechanics, and a variety of labor unions, including the Knights of Labor and the United Brotherhood of Carpenters and Joiners, supported the bill. W. H. Allen, a representative of the Protective Labor Union of New York, combined antiradicalism and appeals to class interest, telling Cleveland that "the only persons who have openly opposed the measure are foreign born Socialist labor agitators and the agents of foreign steamship companies." Several people, especially owners of businesses near the Canadian border, did object to a provision barring "birds of passage," migrants who habitually entered and exited the United States, and others found fault with the bill's basic premise. One writer told the president that "no man ought to be excluded from God's Foot Stool, as long as he behaves himself, and especially from a country who has boasted of its being a place of refuge for the oppressed of all nations."[46]

President Cleveland's 4 March veto, which came on his last day in office, highlighted the subjectivity of the restrictionists' primary arguments. On the matter of imported radicalism, the president doubted that the literacy test would provide the sought-after protection. "I do not believe," he told Congress, "that we would be protected against these evils by limiting immigration to those who can read and write in any language twenty-five words of our Constitution." Violence did not originate with illiterates; rather, illiterates fell victim to literate rabble rousers. Ignoring the antiradical belief that it was necessary to deprive the provocateurs of their pliable masses, Cleveland averred that it would be much safer to admit one hundred thousand illiterates than one unruly, literate agitator who delighted in arousing discontent and tumult among those of peaceful inclination. Therefore, Cleveland concluded, the literacy test would do little to safeguard American citizenship or quality of life.

As to economic concerns, though Cleveland agreed that the nation's current failure to provide employment to all who wished to work was an unfortunate state of affairs, he did not believe that his fellow citizens should blame immigrants for the overcrowded state of the labor market. A phenomenal business depression had stagnated all types of production, but the president trusted that appropriate fiscal policies and the consequent resurgence of capital and industry would remedy the misfortunes of unemployed workers. Should existing conditions continue, the influx of foreign laborers naturally would slow and some people already present would travel elsewhere in search of work. Until the situation did improve, Cleveland believed, those best suited would be able to obtain employment.[47]

After the veto, which Congress failed to override, advocates of each side pondered their next move. Restrictionists, led by Senators Lodge and Chandler, prepared to send the same bill to the new president, William McKinley, who had indicated a willingness to sign such a measure. The Spanish American War then intervened, and immigrant exclusion quickly diminished in importance. In the meantime, antirestrictionist Richard Bartholdt, a Republican representative from Missouri, offered a resolution calling for an alternative approach: the creation of a commission to investigate immigration. His proposal never got beyond the immigration committee, but it did signal the growing belief that thorough investigation would aid, if not ensure, the implementation of enlightened public policy. Even diehard restrictionists, discouraged by congressional failure, seemed to realize that they would need to present more compelling arguments based on some convincing body of evidence.[48]

Yet investigation ensured neither thoroughness nor objectivity. The previous inquiries, with the exception of the narrowly focused Treasury Department study, had done nothing more than chronicle pundits' opinions, and one inquiry had endorsed particularly biased bigotry. An 1876 congressional committee chaired by Indiana Senator Oliver P. Morton had examined "the character, extent, and effects of Chinese immigration." Relying wholly on the testimony of pro- and anti-Chinese witnesses, the committee's report condemned the immigrants as wholly unsuitable for assimilation. The report even connected its economic criticisms, mainly that the Chinese would undermine Americans' earning power by working for low wages, to the immigrants' innate Asian characteristics. In his minority report Senator Morton accused his colleagues of assailing Asians because they differed from white Americans, but the majority's opinion held sway and contributed to the passage of the 1882 Chinese Exclusion Act.[49]

The Industrial Commission of 1898 afforded the opportunity for a broader inquiry. Ten congressmen, drawn equally from the House and Senate, joined nine presidential appointees in a two-year investigation of "questions pertaining to immigration, to labor, to agriculture, to manufacturing, and to business." Once again, testimony of key witnesses, including IRL representative Prescott Hall, Italian Immigration Bureau chief Egisto Rossi, and U.S. Commissioner-General of Immigration Terence V. Powderly, made up the bulk of the 1901 report dealing with immigration. Several interviewees criticized immigrants from southern and eastern Europe, noting their high rates of illiteracy, tendency toward urban living, and general failure to pursue citizenship, but others tried to downplay such characteristics. Economist John R. Commons examined the disputed connection between immigration and U.S. wages, specifically whether the newcomers adversely affected the earnings of natives, but he failed to determine the exact relationship. Witnesses also disagreed on the propriety of existing laws. Given this ambivalence, the 1901 report did little more than reiterate common arguments, and it certainly did not direct authorities toward closure on the issue.[50]

The Industrial Commission's work did signal the transition to a more progressive approach to social problems. The investigation, which came after years of wrangling about its necessity, was a manifestation of the gradual shift away from decision making based primarily on emotion and toward that predicated on accurate information. The resulting report made at least an implicit connection between the so-called immigration problem and the larger problems of the nation's new industrial milieu.

Gilded Age nativism had not disappeared—perhaps it had not even abated—but it alone had not been enough to prompt the passage of a general restriction law. Even passionate xenophobes were coming to realize that they needed more convincing ways to make their arguments. As President Cleveland had said of change to the nation's policy of welcoming all but the morally and physically unfit, "its disadvantages should be plainly apparent," and any substitute to the present policy must be "free from uncertainties."[51] Such thinking would characterize the emerging Progressive Era and set the stage for the creation of the Dillingham Immigration Commission.

CHAPTER ONE

"An Exhaustive Investigation"

Theodore Roosevelt and Creation of the Immigration Commission

"THE FEELING ABOUT IMMIGRATION is again rising very strongly," Senator Lodge wrote to his close friend President Theodore Roosevelt in September 1905, "and I think a word from you would help us powerfully in getting some action at this Congress."[1] Lodge had in mind an endorsement of the literacy test, the most preferred potential new restriction. Roosevelt would indeed play a pivotal part in the passage of an immigration act, but it would not be of the restrictionist type Lodge had in mind. Instead, the legislation Roosevelt eventually backed would exemplify progressivism's reliance on expert investigation and recommendation as the basis for reform.

Roosevelt's 1901 ascendance to the presidency following the assassination of William McKinley traditionally marks the beginning of the Progressive Era, a period when a wide variety of Americans sought pragmatic—fair, equitable, and workable—solutions to the myriad problems that plagued their now mature industrial society. The rise of big business and the growth of large urban centers testified to America's laudable turn-of-the-century emergence as a great and powerful nation, but along with these had come periodic depression, the growing threat of commercial monopolization, and all-too-frequent violent labor disputes. Moreover, the emergence of even a peaceful working class troubled those who saw the United States as a land of unparalleled social mobility where there was no fixed stratification. In the shadows of the monuments to material success in the nation's great cities lurked poverty on a scale unthinkable to previous generations. Progressives, armed with the conviction that they could eliminate these and other maladies, responded in almost formulaic fashion: they sought to identify each problem, subject it to expert inquiry, then decide on the best remedial course of action.[2]

Immigrants figured prominently in many of the perceived socioeconomic blights, but not everyone agreed about how best to respond. For restrictionists, the progressive approach seemed redundant. As they had tried to explain for more than ten years, immigrants were a serious problem, the reasons were readily apparent, and the best remedial action was clear. America already had too many immigrants, and of the wrong types, and now it had to exclude considerably more of them. An appropriate means, the literacy test, was ready and waiting. Yet this impressionistic rationale had not convinced skeptics, such as German-born Missouri senator Carl Schurz, who continued to doubt that the situation demanded the closing of America's traditional open door.[3] Some saw no need for any type of general restriction, and others wanted more concrete evidence that restriction was necessary. Now, front and center, stood the new president, and many, including his longtime confidant Lodge, realized that Roosevelt, the era's emerging "Rex," would have great sway in determining the future course of events.

Roosevelt's inconsistent and at times contradictory views on immigration were indicative of the nation's ambivalence. At times he came across as a committed antirestrictionist who placed great faith in America's ability to assimilate all but the most incorrigible foreigners, even those who could not be counted among the ranks of "whites." When he was a nascent author and public servant during the late 1880s, he had worried that too many immigrants were of an undesirable type, but he nonetheless had criticized those who exhibited excessive hostility toward the foreign-born. Speaking to a group of Republicans in 1893, Roosevelt had figuratively extended America's hand to all hard-working, healthy, honest, "manly" immigrants. Presumably, this would also include their virtuous wives and children. Protestant and Catholic alike, they had helped to make the United States a place wonderfully unique in all the world: in 1907, at the Jamestown site of England's first permanent American settlement, Roosevelt described the United States as the product of unparalleled ethnic mixing. Indeed, three years later Henry Bowers, leader of the anti-Catholic American Protective Association, accused the ex-president of "doing more to flood our country with undesirables than any other element."[4]

Yet Roosevelt repeatedly expressed restrictionist sentiments. In 1888 he wrote that the United States soon might have to enact more stringent laws to protect its own workers "from the stress of undue rivalry," and in an 1893 Appomattox Day speech, he excoriated the "scores of thousands" who were as "emphatically a curse to us as their fellows are a blessing." The incorrigibles included immigrants with radical tendencies or immoral character and those, especially the Chinese, whose standard of living allowed them to underbid and impoverish American workers. The worst were those who were unwilling to assimilate. "We are not Englishmen or Irishmen, Germans, or Frenchmen or Italians," declared the future president, "and those of foreign origin who come here must become American; they must become like us and not seek to make us like them."

These sentiments led Roosevelt periodically to endorse restrictionist proposals. He "heartily" approved of Lodge's 1896 literacy-test bill and, as a Republican, took "a kind of grim satisfaction" in Democratic President Cleveland's eventual veto because that "last stroke was given to injure the country as much as he possibly could." Almost twenty years later, avowed racist Madison Grant contended that Roosevelt's "only objection to the literacy test was that it did not keep them [the Jews] out." This statement may have been more indicative of Grant's feelings than of Roosevelt's position, especially given Roosevelt's reaction to Russian anti-Semitism between 1903 and 1906; still, Grant was unequivocal about Roosevelt's support for restriction. In 1920, after World War I had aroused his xenophobia, Roosevelt himself wrote that he felt "very much the same" about immigration as Grant did.[5]

President Roosevelt did not act on these beliefs when he was president. At a time when his endorsement could well have ensured the literacy test's passage, which would have established in law the idea that the United States needed to reduce its overall immigration, he chose a more progressive approach. Test supporters would claim that as president he consistently called for the literacy test's passage, but that was not the case. In his 1901 annual message, Roosevelt did endorse a "careful and not merely perfunctory educational test," along with the exclusion of anarchists or others hostile to all governments, asserting that such a measure would decrease the numbers of the ignorant masses upon whom radical agitators preyed. He also argued that Congress should act to secure proof of an immigrant's ability to earn a living, so as "to dry up the spring of the pestilential social conditions." However, in spite of strong urging by his friend Lodge, he did not repeat this literacy-test endorsement in 1903; nor did he do so in any subsequent message. Some restrictionists nonetheless continued to believe that Roosevelt would have signed literacy-test legislation if only Congress had sent it to him.[6]

Perhaps Roosevelt would have signed such legislation, but by most indications the president had begun to moderate the opinions he had held in 1901, for a time moving away from his support of general restriction. Proper immigrant character and distribution to desirous destinations within the United States, not restriction, became his primary concern. He also worried about restriction's partisan ramifications. "If we say anything on the subject at all," he wrote of the 1904 Republican Party platform, "I think it might be limited to a very brief amplification of the statement that we can not have too many immigrants of the right kind, and should not have any at all of the wrong kind." By the time of the 1906 elections, Roosevelt and other Republicans, including eventually even Lodge, thought that avoiding the issue altogether would best serve their interests. President William McKinley and Ohio senator Marcus Hanna had brought ethnic voters, especially those in the Midwest, into the party by emphasizing harmony and by downplaying cultural divisions. Those voters would resent any endorsement of more stringent restriction. If the matter was broached at all, Roosevelt thought, it would be best raised in a presidential address.[7]

Violent anti-Semitic events in Russia also may have influenced the president. Jews had been slaughtered in Kishinev and Bessarabia, and similar outbreaks had followed in other cities. Such pogroms troubled Roosevelt, who received a delegation of Jewish leaders at the White House and pondered how best to respond to the despicable situation. One of the visitors, Leo Levi, urged a strong response so as to "stem" the Russian Jews' "rush to this country," but Roosevelt lauded American Jews, including those with whom he had served in the Rough Riders. Ultimately he backed a condemnatory petition to the tsar, sent as a nongovernmental epistle. He considered his handling of the affair to be one of his administrative achievements. Anti-immigrant concerns along the lines put forth by Levi may have been what spurred Roosevelt's involvement, but his overall reaction indicates sincere sympathy for Russian Jews, who composed a growing proportion of American immigrants. The Kishinev affair may have softened some of his nativist and restrictionist feelings.[8]

In any case, Roosevelt made no mention of the literacy test in his annual message of 1906; instead, he emphasized his newfound commitment to America's traditional policies. "All we have a right to question," he said, "is the man's conduct." He initially supported the literacy-test bill that then was pending in Congress, but only to the extent that its enactment would at least assist in keeping out undesirables if no other immigration legislation were passed. Yet he preferred alternatives, such as some form of consular inspection prior to emigrants' departure from a European port. By August 1906, to the displeasure of his friend Lodge, Roosevelt had decided not to press for the bill's passage. In 1915, again according to Madison Grant, Roosevelt indicated that he would have signed a literacy-test bill if one had been sent to him, even though he had not been "particularly enthusiastic" about that means of restriction. Such might have been the case up to midsummer 1906, but thereafter even this expression of indifference likely overstates the level of his support.[9]

For reasons that went beyond mere political concerns, Roosevelt clearly had started to question the wisdom of enacting a literacy qualification. "You stated to me in October," immigration advisor James B. Reynolds wrote to the president in reference to a 1906 conversation, "that you had doubts regarding the expediency of the literacy test." Although Reynolds was one of the Immigration Restriction League's vice presidents, he made clear that he and the president shared common concerns. Another League official, Joseph Lee, similarly recognized Roosevelt's growing opposition to restriction, saying that the president tended to take the attitude of "the more the merrier." Since Lee regarded the subject very differently, he declined even to discuss the matter with Roosevelt. Other restrictionists also doubted Roosevelt's commitment to the literacy test; even Lodge acknowledged in August 1906 that he and the president disagreed on the matter of restriction.[10]

Roosevelt had embraced the idea of conducting "an exhaustive investigation into immigration matters." This would allow him to put before Congress "a definitive solution to the immigration business." Even if a restriction bill passed during the 1906 session, it would not alleviate the need for more study, and numerous problems would persist. Roosevelt raised the need for an inquiry at a June 1906 meeting, and he subsequently suggested that it be undertaken by the executive branch as opposed to the legislature, whose work might be tainted by constituent or party obligations. These concerns about outside influences conflicted with his own plans to have Commissioner-General of Immigration Frank P. Sargent, a former labor leader with strongly restrictionist beliefs, oversee the investigation, but Sargent would work with the more objective labor commissioner, Charles P. Neill, who had been part of a successful investigation of the Chicago stockyards and would later sit on the Dillingham Commission. Roosevelt had discussed the matter with Sargent and Neill, and they had agreed that such an inquiry would be better than one done by a congressional committee.[11]

Roosevelt's actions coincided with the culmination of a string of events stretching back to the aftermath of Cleveland's veto. Restrictionist agitation after the veto had declined precipitously, and while hardliners such as Senator Lodge continued to advocate for the literacy test, other pressing issues—the disposition of new territories acquired as a result of the Spanish-American War, finances and revenue, and military appropriations—dominated congressional debate. The United States also was experiencing the return of prosperity, which alleviated some concerns about immigration's negative economic effects. Finally, many politicians were worried about losing ethnic votes, especially from German Americans. Believing that continued lobbying would come to naught, the Immigration Restriction League (IRL) curtailed its efforts in Washington. Not even the assassination of President McKinley by Leon Czolgosz, an American-born anarchist with a foreign-sounding surname, could produce high levels of xenophobia. Authorities did conduct a frantic hunt for Russian-born Emma Goldman, believing that she was somehow connected to Czolgosz's plot, and Congress did pass the Immigration Act of 1903, which barred anarchists. Still, despite Lodge's efforts, the new law did not impose any general restriction, and neither did the 1904 legislation, which moved jurisdiction over immigration from the Treasury Department to the newly created Department of Commerce and Labor.[12]

Several developments then contributed to a mid-decade resurgence of restriction sentiment. After 1897, the annual number of new immigrants began to rise steadily, building toward a record high of 1.2 million in 1907, and the immigrants' tendency to settle in urban areas also had become increasingly apparent. This unleashed a new wave of nativist vitriol. Samuel Gompers, on behalf of the American Federation of Labor (AFL), petitioned Congress for relief from the growing evil of induced and unrestricted immigration, which threatened the standard of living not only of laborers,

Gompers argued, but of all Americans. Restriction League leader Joseph Lee feared that unchecked immigration would soon leave the nation with a ruling majority of "the Slavic and Mediterranean races in place of the highly selective English stock" that had so far been dominant. Lee seriously doubted that these "new races" could contribute to America's democratic experiment; the hoped-for passage of a literacy test would, to a great extent, proscribe their entrance.[13]

A new influx of Asians, this time Japanese, also contributed to the growing anti-immigrant sentiment. "Japanophobia" had risen only slowly before the late 1890s because the number of Japanese immigrants was small, but once unleashed as their numbers rose in the 1900s, it took on even more racist overtones than had been evident in the earlier anti-Chinese movement. "Japanese coolie immigration is the worst undesirable class possible," wrote *Fresno Republican* editor Chester Harvey Rowell in 1900, "and we are quite right in objecting to it and demanding that something be done about it." When the exclusion of Chinese laborers became permanent in 1902, many hoped that it would be the first step toward a prohibition against all immigration from Asia. This sentiment was especially strong in California, where Japanese immigrants were most prevalent.[14]

Immigration restriction also had a progressive appeal, which contributed to the movement's revival as much as the various negative perceptions, developments that historians have come to describe collectively as "the loss of confidence." Many of the restriction movement's leaders came from the ranks of reformers. The xenophobic Joseph Lee, after graduating from Harvard Law School, distinguished himself as a social worker and philanthropist. He founded and served as president of the Massachusetts Civic League, promoted the playground movement, and sat on the Boston School Committee. Writing in 1905, Lee's IRL compatriot Prescott Hall joined academics Henry P. Fairchild and John R. Commons in tying immigration restriction to the amelioration of social ills—low standards of living, sloth, poverty, and various moral maladies—and to the very success of the American republic. Nativism never died, but its adherents increasingly realized that they would need to use more progressive approaches, not just emphasize immigrants' alleged differences from natives.[15]

In February 1906, Congress inadvertently moved toward the archetypical progressive approach, expert investigation, when Senator William P. Dillingham of Vermont, at best a moderate restrictionist, introduced a bill that eventually would result in the creation of the immigration commission. Dillingham's sweeping proposal contained provisions for raising the head tax, or immigrant entrance fee, from two to five dollars and for adding new classes, such as women imported for immoral purposes, to the list of those who should be excluded. Another section of the proposal called for the creation of a division of information within the Bureau of Immigration, which would promote beneficial geographical distribution of newly arrived foreigners within the United States. Ironically, Dillingham did not call for the creation of the commission to which others would later attach his name. The bill passed the Senate on 23 May 1906, but not before Lodge and other ardent restrictionists had convinced their colleagues to add a literacy test.[16]

The Senate's deliberation aroused dormant public interest. Junior Order United American Mechanics leaders urged the members to press senators and representatives to vote for restrictionist provisions. Similar messages went out to the ranks of labor. As the letters and telegrams began to arrive at the Capitol, expectations rose. Reports coming out of Washington indicated that one-third of the incoming mail concerned the Dillingham bill. Senator Lodge happily noted that the Samuel Gompers–led Federation of Labor had "at last awakened" to the importance of proper immigration control. "The outlook for legislation," wrote IRL lobbyist James Patten, "is very bright indeed." The bill would next go to the House, where the lobbyist prophetically anticipated Speaker Joseph Cannon's opposition but was not overly worried. Patten mistakenly thought that mounting public pressure would ensure passage of the Senate's restriction provisions.[17]

Instead, an unlikely group comprising mainly tradition-oriented Republicans with little personal connection to immigration or any particular ethnic group maneuvered the House into accepting the idea of an investigatory commission. One might have expected German-born Richard Barthold, a Missouri Republican and long time antirestrictionist, or Illinois Democrat Adolph Sabath, a Bohemian Jewish immigrant, to have led the charge, but that distinction went to Republicans Joseph Cannon of Illinois, Charles Grosvenor of Ohio, and James E. Watson of Indiana, all of whom had multigenerational American roots.[18] Together, using a combination of House rules, guile, and determination, they engineered the defeat of the literacy test and ensured the creation of the immigration commission.

As the congressional session drew to a close, Republican John Dalzell of Pennsylvania, upon whom restrictionists were counting for help, presented a special resolution for consideration of the Dillingham bill. The committee on Immigration had substituted its own literacy-test provision, written by Augustus P. Gardner, a Massachusetts Republican and Lodge's son-in-law, but had failed to give it unanimous recommendation. A minority report by Republican William S. Bennet of New York, criticized the provisions for both the literacy test and the increased head tax. Dalzell proposed to have a discussion in the committee of the whole that would be limited to the two sections containing the literacy test and the increased head tax, on which the immigration committee had disagreed. During the three hours of debate any representative would be able to offer amendments to or substitutions within those two sections. Afterward the full House would reconvene and vote aye or nay on the bill, however it was revised, and at that point no representative would be allowed to offer further amendment. These special rules set the stage for an all-or-nothing showdown. If the literacy-test opponents could expunge that proposal or substitute for it during committee discussion, it could not be reintroduced thereafter.[19]

House Speaker Joseph Cannon was the force behind this ploy. "Czar Joe" Cannon's actions related to immigration legislation have generally been described as either the machinations of a tyrant or the manifestation of a deep-seated opposition to organized labor, especially the Samuel Gompers–led American Federation of Labor, which now supported the literacy test. Both of these interpretations have some validity, but Cannon's heritage provides a far better basis for understanding his role in defeating the literacy test and creating an investigatory commission. Cannon was a self-described "homespun product" of the Illinois plains who came to political maturity while the forces of modernization wrought by industrialization were engendering myriad calls for reform. Paradise could be at hand, the faithful cried, if only Congress would "enact some new fangled law or impose some new prohibition." Cannon disagreed. Although he prided himself on having contributed to the unparalleled social advancement of the day, he rued the accompanying loss of traditional practices and proprieties. He especially distrusted the swell of reformist agitation, which threatened to sweep the nation from its tried and true moorings. Ironically, in the case of immigration Cannon chose the typically progressive weapon of an investigatory commission to fight against demands for deviation from America's traditional open-door policy.[20]

Cannon reconciled his seemingly contradictory beliefs in both progress and tradition by exploring alternatives while maintaining the status quo. If the nation did need a new policy, he and other Midwestern Republicans wanted proof that it would work as well as, if not better than, the status quo and other proposed alternatives. He now applied this approach to the matter of immigration.[21]

During his congressional tenure, Cannon had developed a particular disdain for the literacy-test proposal. He had voted for restrictions on Chinese and contract laborers, and in 1896, during preparation of the bill that would go to President Cleveland, he had seen fit to give the test a limited endorsement. Citing the premium Americans placed on education, he had said that he was willing to agree to the literacy test if the test was not intended to discriminate against any particular group. He wanted a simple test which would allow the immigrant to use any language. Over the next several years, however, he came to reject even that type of measure. "A so-called educational test," he wrote in 1906, "is not conclusive of the fitness of the immigrant on the one hand or of his unfitness on the other." The test would exclude neither anarchists nor adventurers who sought to profit from the efforts of others, but it would block the entrance of decent people who would work hard and make upstanding citizens. If the provision had been in effect a century before, Cannon contended, "multiplied thousands of the sons, grandsons, and great-grandsons of men who came over then, including myself, would not now be citizens of the United States."[22]

On 25 June, during the final minutes of discussion of the immigration bill in the committee of the whole, Cannon lieutenant Charles Grosvenor offered a key amendment. Grosvenor's roots reached deep into America's Yankee past, to the same colonial and Revolutionary soil as those of the restrictionist Henry Cabot Lodge, but for many of the same reasons as Speaker Cannon, Grosvenor disliked the literacy test. Given that radicals and other malcontents could usually read and write, he believed that the test would be of minimal value, more injurious than beneficial. Illiterates had bravely served the nation, defending it in war; educated people had been "Tories and delegates to the 1814 Hartford Convention." Grosvenor, whose grandfather Thomas had served on General George Washington's staff, likely intended the latter barb for Senator Lodge's ears, as Lodge's grandfather had played a key role at the ill-fated Hartford meeting.[23]

Now the Ohio congressman intended to strike a major blow against those who sought to curtail the arrival of new immigrants. Grosvenor's amendment called for eliminating the provision for a literacy requirement and replacing it with one calling for the establishment of an fact-finding commission. Approval of the Grosvenor amendment not only would block the current attempt to enact a literacy test; it would also almost certainly postpone the consideration of a test, or of any other new restriction, until the commission had finished its work. Fitting with the speaker's general strategy, a commission investigation would show the need for any new policy before it would be implemented. Cannon had endorsed the initial plans for the Treasury Department's 1892 commission and had briefly agreed to serve as chairman. He eventually declined the appointment, probably because he was reelected to Congress that fall, but his initial willingness to serve indicates a long-standing interest in examining pertinent aspects of American immigration.[24]

Literacy-test supporters tried to no avail to defeat Grosvenor's motion. They asked the chair, James E. Watson, to rule that it was not germane to the bill under consideration, but he refused and called for a vote. Test proponents seemed to have defeated the commission proposal, 136 nays to 123 ayes, but William Bennet called for a roll-call vote, or "the tellers" in the day's congressional parlance. Watson concurred, and near chaos ensued. Cannon, who was working the floor, swiftly sprang into action, first casting his own vote and then turning his attention to his colleagues. When he spied many fellow Republicans patiently awaiting the call for the negative side, he briskly walked from desk to desk, compelling congressmen to vote for the Grosvenor substitute and venting his wrath upon those who refused to take heed of his wishes. "In two instances," noted one report, "Speaker Cannon was seen to grab members by the coat collars and jerk them from their seats in his efforts to force them to pass between the tellers and defeat the educational test, and in many instances, after the members had refused to arise and obey his order the Speaker viciously shook his fist in the faces of the members." His histrionics did the trick; five additional congressmen voted for the commission, and twenty fewer voted against it. The final total was 128 ayes and only 116 nays.[25]

Forty years later, William Bennet, who had opposed the literacy test, had supported the commission, and had later served on it, made a startling revelation. He professed that Chairman Watson had erred in ruling that Grosvenor's commission amendment was germane and in letting it come up for a vote. If Watson had ruled otherwise, the literacy-test provision almost certainly would have passed, and any notion of conducting an extensive study of immigration would have ended, at least for a time. It would have made for an interesting situation when the literacy-test bill reached President Roosevelt, who at the time was leaning toward some type of investigation. Unfortunately, there is no record to show whether some cloakroom order from the speaker precipitated Watson's ruling, but other evidence suggests that something of this nature took place.[26]

Watson's actions in the committee of the whole did not conform to his earlier beliefs. He had previously supported the literacy test, saying that it would shut out large numbers of Russian Jews, Poles, Hungarians, and Italians. These groups, he had argued, furnished the population of "our jails, our eleemosynary, our benevolent and our penal institutions all over this country." His remarks had earned high praise from hard-line restrictionists: one group called him "a true patriot, a true American, and a right seeing legislator." A Watson constituent anticipated a positive response when he pleaded with Watson to "Close our gates, close our gates," but by accepting the Grosvenor amendment as germane, Watson acted against the literacy test and contrary to the wishes of restrictionists.[27]

Evidence suggests two possible motives for Watson's behavior. IRL lobbyists had predicted that he would avoid any "conflict with the machine" led by Cannon, and his actions certainly seemed to validate that deduction. Yet Watson may also have been influenced by the same partisan considerations that concerned Theodore Roosevelt. Later that summer, the president would write Watson a lengthy letter regarding political issues facing Republican candidates in the upcoming fall elections. In that letter Roosevelt did not mention immigration, and when Senator Lodge reviewed a draft, he encouraged the president to make some such reference. Roosevelt declined, believing that highlighting such a controversial subject would "probably be a disadvantage" to the party's candidates. "It is not the time," he wrote to Cannon of the upcoming campaign, "for academic discussion." In private, Roosevelt agreed with Lodge's contention that the literacy test would benefit the nation—a position about which he would shortly come to have doubts—but he worried that a public endorsement would prove to be detrimental to Republicans in the fall elections. Lodge did not think support for the test would endanger Republican hegemony because the electorate was evenly split on the issue, but he grudgingly accepted that Roosevelt's prudence was "very likely right."[28] Perhaps Watson felt similarly and wanted to minimize the potential damage of associating Republicans with the passage of a restriction bill.

Whatever his motives, Watson's procedural decision and the subsequent vote assured commission supporters of a partial victory, but conferees now had to try to resolve the differences between the House and Senate bills. Cannon, who, as speaker, named the House conferees, chose men he knew would not waver in their support for the House version. He selected William Bennet; New York Democrat Jacob Ruppert Jr., who had joined with Bennet in the immigration committee's minority report, which objected to the literacy test; and New Jersey Republican Benjamin F. Howell, who as chair of the immigration committee was duty bound to support the House's action. The Senate chose Lodge, Dillingham, and Democrat Anselm J. McLaurin of Mississippi as its conferees. Because Lodge intended to oppose any bill that did not contain a literacy test and Cannon's emissaries would contest any legislation that included one, impasse was likely.[29]

As restrictionists fumed about the House's removal of the literacy test and the subsequent standoff in the House-Senate conference, Cannon emerged as their principal villain. AFL leader Samuel Gompers urged the speaker to accept the Senate's version of the bill. The Patriotic Order Sons of America also criticized the House bill, claiming that the absence of a literacy test made the measure little more than administrative. The Sons hoped that the House (their thinly veiled euphemism for Cannon) would see its way clear to supporting the Senate version. Similarly, the Ohio Council of the Junior Order United American Mechanics warned Cannon that at their recent convention, "a resolution was unanimously adopted protesting against your action in securing the defeat of the Immigration Bill through your personal solicitations." Unless Cannon assumed a different attitude toward immigration legislation, the Order warned, Ohio Juniors would stand in the way of his future political career, notably his rumored bid for the 1908 Republican presidential nomination.[30]

Jesse Taylor, the Juniors' national legislative lobbyist, especially found Cannon's actions appalling, and he did not mince words when he expressed his anger. "And it is my opinion, YES DAMN IT, I have it in black and white," Taylor wrote, "that the majority of Republicans in the present House are in favor of such a bill." He went on to state that the leadership should "at least keep its hands off" and permit the bill with the educational test to become law. Trying to use the political situation to support his argument, Taylor wrote that he hoped Cannon would reconsider his position upon completion of the fall elections, after which the literacy test would not be such a sensitive issue.[31]

Other critical observers simply saw Cannon as an obstructionist. Writing three years later, lobbyist James Patten offered a testy explication of what had happened. Allegedly, congressman Howell and Joseph A. Goulden, a New York Democrat, had visited the speaker in January 1906, and when they posed the question of creating a commission, the speaker had "'damned' it out of probability and possibility": there was no need for such an investigation—too much money already had been spent on studying immigration. Then in June Cannon had defeated the literacy test by using Bennet's minority report and "substituting an expensive immigration commission, . . . breaking his word" to fellow congressmen. His motives, according to Patten, had been simple; he did not want Congress to pass "a damn bit of legislation on immigration."[32] This last basically was true in terms of restrictive measures, but although Cannon did not support the literacy test and may at one point have "damned" the commission idea, there is ample evidence that by the time of the measure's passage the speaker did support creating an investigatory commission.

Immigration bill conferees, meeting during the summer and fall of 1906, failed to reach an agreement, and in early 1907 the bill became entangled in another controversy. The San Francisco Board of Education, in a demonstration of the Pacific Coast's growing anti-Asian nativism, had excluded Japanese students from "white" schools, infuriating the Tokyo government and placing President Roosevelt in a difficult situation. The president harbored some agreement with those who saw exclusion of the Japanese, like that of the Chinese, as the ultimate solution to the California controversy, but he also wished to avoid offending the Tokyo government, which after the Russo-Japanese War represented a legitimate world power. Even the xenophobic Lodge recognized his friend's dilemma, finding the San Franciscans' behavior to be "incomprehensible at this time from every point of view." The senator was "heartily in favor of barring out coolie labor whether Chinese or Japanese, but it must be done discretely and reasonably—in fact there is no other way."[33]

Roosevelt struggled to find a acceptable way to resolve the situation. Wishing to avoid an international conflict, he used his annual message of 1906 to urge Congress to allow opportunity for naturalization to those Japanese wanting to become citizens. Statutory change was necessary because current laws limited the privilege of naturalization to "white persons." Efforts to overturn that discriminatory policy had failed in 1870, and now, when Roosevelt and Commerce and Labor Secretary Oscar Straus, himself a Bavarian Jewish immigrant, similarly could make no headway on Japanese naturalization, the president turned to restriction as an alternative resolution to the pending conflict with Japan. Here he encountered the congressional logjam on the pending Dillingham-Gardner bill, to which he wanted a Japanese exclusion provision added. Matters of Asian and European immigration were suddenly commingled.[34]

According to a common misconception, Roosevelt feared that "agitation on the general question of immigration" might delay or even scuttle negotiations between the United States and Japan. Quite to the contrary, the president realized that Congress had to resolve the disagreements impeding the disposition of the Dillingham-Gardner bill before taking up the question of Japanese exclusion. Roosevelt, Secretary of State Elihu Root, and pro-immigrant and Japanese-friendly Secretary of Commerce and Labor Oscar S. Straus had drafted a Gentlemen's Agreement that did not mention

Japan by name but would exclude from the United States all members of Japan's laboring classes, conditions that were acceptable to the Tokyo government. Roosevelt and Root believed that Japan would take offense and perhaps resort to military confrontation in response to any other course of U.S. action, especially some sort of by-name Japanese exclusion, which would be seen as a national insult; therefore, the American leaders sought to orchestrate a resolution of the congressional immigration deadlock and have the Gentlemen's Agreement written into law.[35]

Roosevelt and Joe Cannon also moved toward resolving the congressional deadlock. "I have to say," the speaker wrote in response to a union representative in mid-1906, "that on a careful reading of the President's annual message to the late session of Congress I have been unable to find anywhere a recommendation that immigration be restricted by an educational test. I do heartily agree with the recommendations that the President did make in the premise." Having found common ground on that matter, Cannon and Roosevelt soon would agree on the desirability of creating an investigatory commission. The two men discussed the project during the summer of 1906, and although the president expressed his wish to have the investigation done by the executive branch, the two leaders reached a consensus on the basic premise. Their shared support eventually made the investigation the key part of the 1907 Immigration Act, and Roosevelt had already embarked on his plan for an investigation by Commerce and Labor.[36]

Desiring the fullest possible immigration study, Roosevelt told Commissioner Charles Neill to make it as "thorough and as comprehensive as you can," with both domestic and foreign investigation. Roosevelt also wanted the study to be confidential. During the summer of 1906, Neill took preliminary steps in that direction when he assigned Commerce and Labor Department statistician Frederick C. Croxton to conduct a study of immigration to the South. Neill apparently decided to concentrate on that region because of recent efforts, especially in South Carolina, to recruit immigrant laborers to work in cotton mills, resulting in a marked divergence from immigrants' usual tendency to settle in the East or Midwest. It is not fully clear whether Croxton's trip to the South was part of the investigation for which Roosevelt had called, but the timing and focus suggest a connection.[37]

As Croxton canvassed the southern states, he looked for areas with large numbers of immigrants; then he and his associate L. D. Clark visited several of these enclaves. Their destinations included Polish and Russian settlements in Virginia, Italian communities in Georgia and North Carolina, and a Japanese agricultural colony near Miami. The investigators also gathered information about how employees, employers, and the general public felt about the coming of foreigners. In his unpublished memoirs, Croxton recalled that current workers often questioned whether the arrival of immigrants would keep wages low and reported that some people worried about "interracial" marriages. Little else is known of this investigation because creation of the Dillingham Commission ended its work and precluded publication of its final report. The Dillingham Commission would, however, return to the issue of immigration to the South.[38]

With Roosevelt and Cannon in general agreement, it was almost certain that the Dillingham bill would authorize some form of investigation instead of imposing significant new restrictions. All that remained was for those involved to work out the final provisions. Years later William Bennet reported that the executive branch had begun to lobby on behalf of a commission. According to Bennet, "Pres. Theodore Roosevelt and Secretary of State Elihu Root requested the omission of that particular provision [the literacy test] and the substitution of a provision for an immigration commission." Bennet also explained that his own efforts to gain a consensus in support of the House bill had Cannon's "strong support" and Roosevelt's "assistance." As the last surviving participant in the events of 1906–1907, the former congressman may have taken some of the license that is afforded those who outlive their contemporaries, but his scenario does concur with the stated views of both the president and speaker.[39]

Determining the nature of Secretary Root's role in facilitating the ultimate agreement is problematic. One might suspect that as a conservative and a former corporate lawyer, he would have supported restriction as a means of social control. When he went to the Senate in 1910, he did introduce his own particularly stringent version of the literacy test. However, Root was also a strongly partisan Republican, and coming from New York, the most polyglot state in the Union, he must have realized the importance of wooing southern and eastern European voters, if only to deny them to the Tammany Democrats. These voters would certainly look askance at the supporters of restriction. The best explanation for Root's actions in 1907, however, is his capacity as an administrator who was able to secure consensus on volatile issues. His superior, President Roosevelt, wanted certain results, and Root helped him to obtain them.[40]

During February, Root requested that the four Republican conferees—Lodge, Bennet, Dillingham, and Howell—meet in his office. The conferees there amiably "settled amongst ourselves all matters in controversy," opting for the commission instead of the literacy test and writing the Gentleman's Agreement on coolie labor into the bill's first section. These developments so pleased Democratic conferee Jacob Ruppert that he later moved to have his name added to the conference report. Lodge praised Roosevelt's and Root's management for opening "a door by which we can obtain a final settlement of this vexed question," and he took personal credit for inserting the "Japanese amendment" into the immigration bill and thereby putting the exclusion of Japanese immigrants on proper legal footing. When the bill reached the Senate, Lodge offered no opposition to the changes that had been made by the conferees, although he did note that the conferees' version differed very little from existing law.[41]

Both chambers of Congress passed the revised bill, but not without further ruckus. Some legislators tried to question the conferees' powers, and others wanted to replace the president's Gentleman's Agreement on Japanese immigration with a provision barring all Asians. One senator complained that the bill should contain a literacy test or nothing at all. It turned into quite a fight, but in the end these criticisms came to naught, with even literacy-test supporters realizing that their provision of choice was a dead issue. Representative Gardner poetically told the House that he had come "to bury Caesar, not praise him." Both houses eventually agreed to the provisions of the bill, and Roosevelt made the agreement official when he signed the act into law on 21 March 1907.[42]

Participant observers responded as one would expect. IRL leader Robert Ward's reaction epitomized restrictionist sentiments: "It is a very poor apology for an immigration bill, I must confess, but it will be better than nothing." Under the right circumstances, Ward hoped, the new commission might amount to something positive, which for him meant an endorsement of the need for more extensive immigrant exclusion. He also worried about the Restriction League's future. Until the commission finished its work, Congress would take no action on immigration, and this would leave the League with little to do. Ward could see little use in organizing. Instead, a few members could stay active in Boston, watching developments, working with congressional friends, and letting sympathizers know the restrictionist movement was not dead.[43]

Some of the restrictionist movement's adherents, however, had come to appreciate the value of collecting accurate information. Two years before the passage of the act, resigning IRL leader Curtis Guild Jr. had argued that the changing conditions of the previous ten years "required study . . . as to the best method of dealing today with this very important subject."[44] Now League vice president Joseph Lee, though disappointed with the literacy test's removal and angry at Cannon, expressed his belief, in a letter to future Dillingham commissioner Jeremiah Jenks, that more knowledge of immigrant conditions would help restrictionists make their case. The IRL had already bombarded its audience with a host of facts and figures relating to economics, crime, and pauperism, and Lee hoped that Jenks could supply additional information, broken down by race, on immigrants' political capacities. This, he believed, would provide compelling support for the restrictionist argument.

Lee anticipated that the findings would validate his fear that the more newly arriving ethnic groups would have problems participating in self-government. The combination of rising immigration and a declining native birthrate, if continued, would make the Anglo-Saxon United States a predominately Slavic and Mediterranean nation. Lee proposed studying the effects of this substitution, particularly its political ramifications, paying special attention to Slavs and Jews. Investigation of them in their "native habitat" would show whether these newly arrived groups were superior or inferior to Anglo-Saxons. If the study showed that the immigrants were less successful than people of the "American race," then they were almost certain to fail in matters of self government, and "such immigration must be considered the greatest misfortune that the world has ever suffered." Lee did not specifically call for the creation of a commission, but his desire for more thorough knowledge suggested the value of the very type of investigation the Dillingham Commission would pursue.[45]

Developments leading to the establishment of the Dillingham Commission could hardly have been more pleasing to antirestrictionists such as Congressman William Bennet, who saw its creation as a restrictionist defeat. He made this clear in a speech to the Liberal Immigration League of New York City. "I cannot speak too highly of the work of your league during this past Congress," he told the audience, "without which it is quite certain there would have been an educational test upon the statute books today, thereby excluding yearly about 200,000 deserving immigrants." Given the number of actual denials for illiteracy after a test was enacted in 1917, it is questionable whether such a measure would have barred anywhere near that number, but at the time the test's defeat and the substitution of an investigatory commission were reason for antirestrictionist celebration.[46]

The effort to answer the immigration question had taken a progressive turn, and the fate of any future policies now rested with the soon-to-be-organized commission. No one could say what course its investigation would follow or even how long the project would take. Notwithstanding these uncertainties, however, both restrictionists and open-door advocates realized its report would hold considerable sway in Congress, likely determining the nature and extent of any new legislation. Restrictionists hoped that they would have a strong contingent on the commission, one that could at least make a forceful minority report and possibly do considerably more. Those on the other side obviously wanted findings supportive of immigration's attributes. Only time would tell what the results would be. The first step was selection of the participants.[47]

CHAPTER TWO

"No Man Afraid of the Facts"

NINE IDEOLOGICALLY AND EXPERIENTIALLY diverse men, three selected by the Senate, three by the House, and three by the president, made up the U.S. Immigration Commission. Two of the presidential appointees, Jeremiah Jenks and Charles P. Neill, were the quintessential experts, with considerable investigatory experience. The third, William Wheeler, came from the ranks of business. Senator William P. Dillingham and Representative Benjamin F. Howell fit the mold of the patrician public servant. So too did Senator Henry Cabot Lodge, but more important in this instance, he and Representative John Burnett were unequivocal restrictionists, albeit of very different stripes. Representative William S. Bennet, an avowed antirestrictionist, provided the most humanitarian and egalitarian presence. Finally, untimely deaths kept the identity and predisposition of the last commissioner from the Senate in flux throughout the investigation. Key staffers for the commission were from the Department of Commerce and Labor, and from the private sector Jeremiah Jenks recruited what one manager called "very good people," some of whom had taken part in previous government investigations.[1]

Their diversity of the commission's makeup reveals a key aspect of progressivism. Those who joined in the broad-based effort, or movement, to engender reform did not always share common beliefs; quite the contrary, they often had divergent opinions even when they agreed on the need to study a particular issue.[2] Up to the time the commission was established the nine commissioners had expressed widely different views on immigration, from passionate advocacy of the open door to equally strong support for stringent restriction. Most, however, had displayed decidedly moderate attitudes. The public and private comments of Lodge and Burnett made clear the roots of their nativist beliefs, but determining the positions of the others is more a matter of deduction.[3] The commissioners also represented various regions and those regions' propensities; they ranged from

New England Yankee to southern racist, to West Coast "Asiaphobe." These differences helped to ensure that theirs would be a thorough and far-ranging investigation.

President Theodore Roosevelt, at the bottom of a letter thanking Jeremiah Jenks for accepting a commission appointment, admonished the new commissioner, "Don't trust in too many professors." This may have been no more than a tongue-in-cheek aside to the "professor," whom Roosevelt elsewhere called an "excellent man." Jenks himself embodied the Progressive Era's academically trained and highly trusted expert. After graduating from the University of Michigan in 1878, he taught languages at Mount Morris College in Illinois while simultaneously preparing himself for a legal career. The latter proved to be a short-lived aspiration. Jenks passed the Michigan bar in 1881, but by then he had developed an interest in the new field of political economy. He completed a Ph.D. in the field at Halle, Germany, in 1885. Thereafter he taught social and political science at Knox College in Ohio, Indiana University, and Cornell University, but he did not confine his work to the academic milieu. A true progressive in his devotion to finding practical solutions to social and political problems, Jenks gained national prominence by serving as the advisor on trusts to the U.S. Industrial Commission, and he came away from that task with a deep appreciation for proper investigation. Jenks prepared the report on industrial combinations in the United States and Europe and then summarized its findings in his book *The Trust Problem*, in which he stressed the need to gather as many facts as possible and then study them in a careful and deliberate manner.[4]

In his work for the immigration commission, Jenks tried "officially at any rate, to be as open-minded as I can be on the subject of immigration, and devote myself to asking questions." This did not mean that he lacked a predisposition. Jenks readily admitted that, like most Americans, he had a certain "racial prejudice," which manifested itself in pride at being an old-stock white American. Yet so far as such emotions evoked bigotry toward those who were different, he attributed those situations to "simply an unconscious feeling which we have never reasoned out." It was "foolish" to yield to such feelings instead of acting on the basis of accurate information. Jenks believed that the commission's investigation could provide that knowledge about immigrants' standards of living, criminality, fecundity, and assimilation. Then when the facts had been firmly established, he and his colleagues, and indeed the nation, could reach learned conclusions and properly answer questions about restriction.[5]

Jenks's service on the commission, along with a book based on its findings that he wrote with staffer W. Jett Lauck, would establish Jenks as an immigration authority and provide him opportunities to clarify his views. He portrayed himself as a moderate, arguing that he had consistently favored both "reasonable restriction" and proper distribution of immigrants. Denying accusations about his belief in "racial superiority," Jenks con-

tended that he had "always endeavored to get away from such a narrow interpretation of our immigration policy." Hungarians, Italians, Chinese, and
Japanese deserved credit for their "wonderful achievements, . . . often
above those of Americans." Still, Jenks did not believe "that it would be
wise" to let unlimited numbers of immigrants from such groups into the
United States. "Differences of language, of race, of political upbringing, of
illiteracy and of customs" he concluded, "may, however, be raised as an argument against an immigrant when these very differences make fusion and
assimilation difficult."[6]

The second presidential appointee, political economist Charles P. Neill,
had also pursued an academic career that spilled over into public administration. After first working as a laborer, Neill attended the University of
Notre Dame, the University of Texas, and Georgetown University, then
completed a Ph.D. at Johns Hopkins University. After teaching briefly at
Notre Dame he joined the newly created lay School of Social Sciences at
Catholic University of America. He held that position from 1896 to 1905,
when he went into government service. Even before Neill made this career
change, President Theodore Roosevelt appointed him to the 1902 An-
thracite Coal Commission. In 1904 he helped to mediate the dispute in a
threatened coal strike in Alabama, drawing praise for brokering a unanimously accepted settlement. His demonstration of this pragmatic ability fa-
cilitated his career change. In 1905 the president selected Neill to be commissioner of labor in the Department of Commerce and Labor, and he
thereafter designated him to run the department during the secretary's absence. William Howard Taft would reappoint Neill in 1909, and as testament to the high quality of his work, as opposed to mere partisanship, Democrat Woodrow Wilson made Neill commissioner of labor statistics in the
newly formed Department of Labor in 1913.[7]

Like Jenks, Neill came to the immigration commission with significant
investigatory experience. His Department of Commerce and Labor duties
included mediation of railroad disputes under the auspices of the 1898 Erd-
man Act, tasks that necessitated full knowledge of the contentious situations involved. Following the publication of Upton Sinclair's The Jungle,
Roosevelt asked Neill and Immigration Restriction League (IRL) leader
James B. Reynolds to investigate conditions in Chicago's meatpacking
plants. Their 1906 inquiry and report substantiated Sinclair's lurid descriptions and helped Roosevelt to attain passage of the Meat Inspection and
Pure Food and Drug laws. In 1907 Neill made a similar investigation of
women's and children's labor conditions in the South and also took preliminary steps to study that region's immigration.[8]

Neill's article "Anarchism," written in the aftermath of President
William McKinley's assassination, showed its author's typically progressive
penchant for perceiving issues or problems as concrete rather than abstract. Among his fellow academics, there existed "a tendency to minimize
the character of the problem that Anarchism presents, and to mistake the

nature of Anarchism itself." To Neill, the doctrine of anarchism rested upon the twin demons of atheism and evolution. It forsook such sacred institutions as marriage and family for the pursuit of "free love" and advocated assassination and other violent acts, defining them as "'sanguinary advertisements'" intended to attract converts from among the masses. Yet intellectuals, in their myopic fascination with radicalism's theoretical aspects, failed to realize its more nefarious features and generally to understand that the problems of the day necessitated study "in the practical sense."[9]

Still, other than deducing that Neill wanted to have adequate information before making policy decisions, it is difficult to assess his precommission disposition toward immigration. His negative assessment of anarchism, which was generally viewed as a foreign doctrine, may have indicated negative feelings toward immigrants, but this would not answer the question of whether he thought all immigrants were bad, or just a few radicals. Neill's friendship with University of Wisconsin professor Richard T. Ely, considered a supporter of the IRL, and his professional association with James Reynolds also may indicate that Neill had an anti-immigrant bent. Unfortunately, Neill did not explore this issue in his writing, and a lack of evidence precludes any definitive judgment. It therefore is best to appraise Neill on the basis of his well-documented record of conducting thorough and informative investigations and to assume that he tried to do the same on the commission.[10]

William Wheeler, the last presidential appointee, came to the commission with a business background. Many forward-looking businesspeople supported the Progressive Era's quest for reform, especially when it came to efficient government service. Born and raised in California, Wheeler had become general manager and one of the directors of Holbrook, Merrill & Stetson, San Francisco importers and merchandisers, where he specialized in transportation. Later he would manage the traffic bureau of the San Francisco Merchants Exchange. Prior to his joining the commission, his commercial experience had made him keenly aware of the Pacific Coast's need for representation in official Washington. Seeking to remind the president that Californians were "in the field," he spearheaded a 1905 effort to have a westerner appointed to the Interstate Commerce Commission. This, plus the fact that he was an active Republican, most likely led to his selection as an immigration commissioner.[11]

President Roosevelt "much desired" to have California represented on the commission and used his bully pulpit to secure Wheeler's acceptance. Not only did the president desire regional balance on the commission for its own sake, but the recent San Francisco controversy involving Japanese schoolchildren had demonstrated that immigration questions were not geographically confined to the East and industrial Midwest. Realizing that Wheeler would have to spend at least a year away from home, the president appealed to the spirit of service. "I am dependent for accomplishing good work upon the readiness of men like yourself to help me," said Roosevelt, "and I very much appreciate it." Although Wheeler officially resigned from his position as acting assistant secretary of commerce and labor and returned to his business affairs in San Francisco before the commission finished its work, he returned to Washington to help with the final report.[12]

Wheeler's West Coast connection raises the question of a possible anti-Asian bias that easily could be extended to southern and eastern Europeans. A paucity of records leaves only the possibility of conjecture as to his precommission views, but by the end of his commission tenure, Wheeler did have a relatively enlightened belief that the immigration service should be run in a professional and efficient manner. He demonstrated this at the time of the anticipated appointment of a new commissioner of immigration. Drawing on his observations as a Dillingham investigator, Wheeler lauded Acting Commissioner Luther C. Steward for his record of proficient administration and urged his promotion. Especially important was the experience Steward had gained during his many years of service. If the precedent of hiring outside candidates as commissioners prevented Steward's promotion, Wheeler then preferred the candidacy of a longtime public servant, one who had always "acquitted himself with efficiency and honor."[13]

Senator William P. Dillingham, who as its chair would give the commission it popular appellation, combined a patrician's pedigree with devotion to public service. He was born on 12 December 1843 at the family home in Waterbury, Vermont, and his ancestry dated back to the Puritan colony at Massachusetts Bay led by John Winthrop. His forefathers had fought in the French and Indian War and with the Continental Army during the American Revolution. Dillingham initially practiced law but then moved to politics. He had held a number of state offices, including a customary single term as governor. The legislature acknowledged his accomplishments by appointing him in 1900 to finish out the unexpired U.S. Senate term of recently deceased Justin S. Morrill, and Dillingham thereafter won successive reelections and served until his death in 1923. A "regular" Republican, he consistently opposed progressive reforms, such as woman's suffrage and direct election of senators, and otherwise seemed to be committed to preserving the remaining vestiges of an older America.[14]

This would seem to make Dillingham a prime candidate for classification as a xenophobe and restrictionist, but his precommission career provides an ambiguous record on immigration and ethnic matters. Proud of his peerage, he devoted considerable time and energy to historical and genealogical research and served as president of the Vermont Society of the Sons of the American Revolution. He once described the Civil War as a contest between two sections of a "great people of Anglo-Saxon blood, of rare intelligence and magnificent courage." As governor Dillingham both praised the state's deeply ingrained cultural values and homogeneous population and authorized the study of immigrant recruitment as a solution to Vermont's pressing depopulation problem. Election to the Senate allowed him to influence national policy, and Dillingham primarily pushed for better means of immigrant distribution. His namesake bill, which created the commission, had not included a literacy test but had called instead only for an increased head tax and the addition of prostitutes to the excluded list. Such behavior certainly did not make him "a spokesman for the Immigration Restriction League," as some have asserted, or even much of a restrictionist.[15]

New Jersey Republican Benjamin F. Howell similarly came from a family with deep American roots dating to the colonial period and a long history of public service. Perpetuating this tradition during the Civil War, Howell enlisted in Company K of the 12th New Jersey Volunteers and took part in the battles of Chancellorsville and Gettysburg. Thereafter he held numerous local offices—township committeeman, county surrogate, member of the Board of Freeholders—and was elected to Congress in 1894. A joiner, he belonged to the Knights of Pythias, the Sons of the American Revolution, the Society of Colonial Wars, and the Grand Army of the Republic. Like Dillingham's, his membership in hereditary societies suggests that he had an affinity for a specious Anglo-Saxon national past, but as a congressman, Howell too had demonstrated little animosity toward immigrants.[16]

Howell chaired the House Committee on Immigration and Naturalization, but prior to his commission service, he had not addressed the House on a substantive immigration matter. He had, however, presented petitions in favor of greater restriction, secured appropriations for printing committee reports and hearings, and introduced several nationalization bills. Under rules dating back to the Jeffersonian period, various state courts had granted citizenship in a haphazard manner, most notoriously on the eves of important elections, with no oversight. In 1906 a bill Howell had introduced established uniform naturalization procedures and created a supervisory Division of Naturalization. While Howell may have been motivated by xenophobia, his bill also fits with the progressive desire to check the power of corrupt political machines that exploited immigrant voters and to replace them with responsible and democratic governance. Neither in this case nor in any other did Howell reveal strongly restrictionist views, but some in the restrictionist camp did consider him to be an ally.[17]

There was no such ambiguity about Henry Cabot Lodge, who saw immigration as both a racial and a socioeconomic threat. "Personally," he wrote in 1897, "I should like to see all immigration stopped until our people were again employed, but in this view I am in a small minority." Growing numbers of newly arrived foreigners, he believed, threatened the high quality of American wages and citizenship, but by framing laws "in such a way as to affect most strongly those elements of immigration which furnished the low, unskilled, and ignorant foreign labor," that is, the southern and eastern Europeans, the nation could avert disaster. Although Lodge declined an invitation to join the IRL, he maintained close ties with its leaders and became their principal congressional advocate. He served for many years on the House and Senate immigration committees, writing and speaking on behalf of numerous bills and otherwise mounting an unremitting campaign for more stringent restrictions. The literacy test became his preferred method of exclusion.[18]

Lodge, like Dillingham, came from a well-established New England family. He was born in 1850 into Boston's Brahman society, and his middle and surnames bear witness to his New England ancestry, which dated from the 1770s on his father's side and from the Bay Colony's inception on his mother's side. Lodge received a Ph.D. in history from Harvard College, where for three years he also taught colonial and early American history. Perhaps because of his interest in history, Lodge realized that his world—his Boston and his America—was not that of his ancestors: it was losing its long-standing homogeneity. In his autobiographical *Early Memories,* he described his formative years in terms almost metaphorical of his attitude toward newly arrived foreigners. He and his chums, boys of the "same race tradition," "waged Homeric combats with snowballs against the boys from South Cove and the North End, in which we made gallant fights, but were in the end, as a rule, outnumbered and driven back." Eventually, and more seriously, the increasing number of their opponents drove them "from the Common hills and the Frog Pond to seek coasting and skating in the country." Further on, Lodge warned his readers that a "flood of immigration" might similarly overwhelm and negatively alter the character of American civilization.[19]

A prolific writer, Lodge penned numerous other works on the dangers of mass immigration. In 1891, he analyzed the "distribution of ability in the United States," using those whose names appeared in Appleton's *Encyclopedia of American Biography* as his sample. He particularly wanted to indicate the abilities of each race, or nationality, that had settled in the United States. His well-received findings, which were of questionable value in the light of modern scrutiny, showed that the English, Scotch-Irish, and Germans had made the greatest contribution to American ability, while the Italians, Swiss, Greeks, Russians, and Poles had made the least. In terms of what had been added by immigrants, whom he defined as those who had come after the ratification of the Constitution in 1789, he ranked those from Great Britain first as contributors, those from Germany second, and those from southern and eastern Europe third. "This is a moral of wide application," he warned, one that "carries a lesson which should never be forgotten."[20]

In subsequent articles, including another brief analysis of his distribution-of-abilities study, he intensified his criticism of current immigrants, especially those from nontraditional sources, and focused his call for greater restriction. As a rule, he argued, eastern and southern Europeans lacked ambition, followed the dangerous creeds of anarchism and socialism, and soon became a burden to the American people. After an angry New Orleans mob lynched eleven Italian immigrants, alleged members of the "Black Hand," or Mafia, after they were acquitted of the murder of Chief of Police

David C. Hennessy in March 1891, Lodge contended that illiterate immigrants formed the root of the problems facing urban America. "The underlying cause," he said of the New Orleans violence, "and the one which alone the people of the United States can deal, is to be found in the utter carelessness with which we treat immigration."[21]

Lodge's restrictionist convictions never wavered, but he did not simply use his commission tenure to advance that agenda. Although his initial proposals did call for a limited focus on the shortcomings of exiting statutes, he thereafter enthusiastically contributed to a broader investigation. Even some restrictionists would start to doubt that Commissioner Lodge was being as aggressive as possible in the pursuit of what they assumed was their common agenda: securing evidence that would show the need for more stringent immigrant exclusion and a literacy test. Some would come to wonder whether they and Lodge still shared the same views. They did, but as his friend and fellow Republican Curtis Guild contended, the senator's record—which Guild laid out in detail—showed that he also was very much a part of the progressive movement. In this case being a progressive meant making a thorough investigation of the pressing problem of immigration and writing an accurate report.[22]

Congressman John Burnett of Alabama shared Lodge's restrictionist convictions, but while the senator's grew out of his Yankee New England milieu, Burnett's antithetically represented those of the Jim Crow South. Having received his early education in the state's common schools, he studied law at Vanderbilt University. In 1899 he won election to the U.S. House for the first of ten times, representing a state that had demonstrated mixed feelings about immigration. Many southerners considered immigration a way to increase the white population, which thereafter would "constitute the only guarantee of safety and tranquility." During Reconstruction, the Alabama legislature had created a commission to recruit immigrants but had failed to provide funding. Attitudes started to change in the 1880s when Bourbon Democrats began to oppose immigration, equating it with radicalism and preferring the labor and proximity of increasingly obsequious blacks to that of foreigners. Some Alabamians continued to harbor pro-immigrant sentiments and were ready to take anyone "willing to work," but others did not accept the newcomers as "white," construing them instead as threats to the white race's hegemony.[23]

Burnett's racially explicit 1906 House speech placed him clearly in the restrictionist camp. Speaking to what he called a "white congress," Burnett began by saying that he had nothing personal against foreigners, but then he went on to lambaste newcomers from southern and eastern Europe, describing them as lazy slum dwellers who were incapable of assimilation. The South, he continued, did not want the likes of a "dirty Bohemian who vends bananas." In asking his colleagues to support the literacy test, he referred to restriction as a necessary step in the "struggle for our white civilization." The South partially had settled its existing race problem by segregating African

Americans, but hordes of "Italians, Austrians, Hungarians, Syrians, Bohemians, and others of that class" threatened to create an even "greater race problem." Burnett beseeched his colleagues not to let that happen.[24]

Yet southern idiosyncrasies did place limits on the preventative methods Burnett could recommend. When the conference committee reported back the commission bill, Burnett took charge of the opposition. He reiterated his desire to have the bill include a provision for a restrictive literacy test but objected to a section that would allow the president to exclude an entire nationality if some members surreptitiously used passports intended for entry into third countries or U.S. insular possessions to gain admission to the United States. Since the United States did not require passports for admission, this provision would seem to have been of limited value and importance, but Burnett believed that it gave the president too much power at the expense of states' rights. This thinking clouded how he might react to possible commission recommendations, especially specific provisions that would enhance executive-branch power.[25]

The presence of other southern commissioners with conflicting views further complicates the making of any overall assessment of how their regional association may have influenced their commission service. Asbury Latimer, a South Carolina Democrat, replaced originally appointed Anselm J. McLaurin at the latter's request in March 1907. Born and raised in rural South Carolina, Latimer received his only formal education in common schools near Lowndesville, but this did not impede him from becoming one of the wealthiest planters in western South Carolina. His other interests included banking, fertilizer production, and cotton manufacturing. Latimer climbed the political ladder, held various Democratic party offices, served ten years in the House of Representatives, and then moved to the Senate in 1902. His behavior there suggests that he was a political conservative who was concerned with serving his electorate. He associated himself with "Pitchfork" Ben Tillman's often racist agrarian reform movement, but historians have dubbed him "an inoffensive Tillmanite." During his congressional tenure, his claim to fame was his advocacy for more federal aid for public roads, efforts that gained him the sobriquet "Good Roads Latimer." He also championed free rural mail delivery and took up other progressive causes, such as increasing the Department of Agriculture's experimental work, which he believed would benefit his primarily agrarian constituents.[26]

Nothing in Latimer's public record suggests that he felt the same sense of mandate when it came to restricting immigration. Although he remained largely an invisible member of the Senate immigration committee, his few remarks, linked with other evidence, indicate that he held moderate views. In 1904, as part of an effort to attract textile workers, South Carolina had established a Department of Agriculture, Commerce, and Immigration. Growing opposition resulted in the dropping of *Immigration* from the title and in the curtailment of immigrant recruitment. These conditions could have induced a constituent-oriented legislator like Latimer to adopt similar anti-immigrant views, but during debate of the 1906 Dillingham bill, Latimer worried that its restrictive provisions might interfere with a state's ability to recruit immigrants. He concurrently supported the construction of an immigration station at Charleston, South Carolina, saying that it would enhance immigrant distribution to the Southeast. These concerns indicate attitudes far different from those of Ben Tillman, Latimer's ideological mentor, and of John Burnett, both of whom condemned the conference committee for its removal of the literacy test from the 1907 Immigration Act.[27]

Latimer directed most of his discontent about immigration at steamship companies, not at the aliens themselves. He blamed the companies for indiscriminately canvassing Europe in their search for customers and then transporting large numbers of undesirable immigrants. Rather than calling for new or more stringent restriction, Latimer wanted to increase the penalty for any company that transported an immigrant with a detectable disease and allow such immigrants to collect damages from the company. This hopefully would result in greater self-restraint on the part of ticket agents and thereby alleviate concerns about poor-quality immigrants. He also supported a Lodge proposal, eventually voted down, to put an American medical examiner on board every immigrant steamer, but he said nothing about the restrictionist parts of the Lodge-Dillingham bill. Latimer's premature death cut short his commission tenure and limited his influence, but his colleagues recognized his "zealous service" in getting the investigation under way.[28]

Anselm McLaurin, the man Latimer had replaced, subsequently returned to the commission in February 1908. A Mississippi Democrat, he had earned his fame, and infamy, in local machine politics. He won election to the state's House of Representatives in 1879, cast one of the state's electoral votes for the victorious Grover Cleveland presidential ticket in 1888, and filled a vacant U.S. Senate seat from February 1894 to March 1895. Between 1896 and 1900, McLaurin was the last in a long line of Confederate military veterans to serve as governor, and in that role he developed a reputation for being a bastion against "Negro rule." His need to placate white southerners sent an ambiguous message as to how he might feel about immigrants: he could equally well view them as "white reinforcements" or as yet more of the "racially impure." He did little to clarify his feelings when he returned to the Senate in 1900, where, like Latimer, he served without distinction on the immigration committee.[29]

In February 1910, Democrat LeRoy Percy replaced the deceased McLaurin, his old adversary, in the Senate and on the commission. He was the third southerner to hold the latter position, and his appointment suggests a desire to give that region some representation. A wealthy railroad attorney and Delta planter from the Greenville, Mississippi, area, Percy had never before held public office, although he had long been active in state politics. As a traditional southern Democrat, he adhered to the twin notions of white supremacy and "colored" disenfranchisement, but he also enjoyed a reputation for being a relative moderate on racial matters and was often described as a paternalist.[30]

From 1905 to 1907, Percy was involved in a scheme to secure an adequate labor supply for the Mississippi Delta, one that involved an intriguing immigration-related twist. He had helped to recruit northern Italian farmers in an effort to reduce the region's dependence on black laborers. During debate on the commission bill, antirestrictionist William Bennet had coincidentally made reference to Percy's praise for the Italians. A letter from the future senator claimed that they raised 30 percent more cotton than blacks. Bennet, who had gotten the letter from House colleague John S. Williams, Percy's fellow Mississippi Democrat, intended for it to show the positive attitudes southerners had toward immigrant laborers and their desire to receive still more immigrants. Elsewhere, however, Percy criticized the recruited immigrants as "no more honest than the Negro," a statement that was reported in one account as "those Italians stole worse than niggers." Finally, as the commission was preparing to make its recommendations, the same observer claimed that Percy regretted his earlier remarks lauding the recruited Italians and now agreed completely with fellow southerner Burnett on the need for restriction. How he contributed to the recommendations would be the true test.[31]

The final commissioner, New York Republican William Bennet, who had been instrumental in having the commission substituted for the literacy test, displayed progressivism's humanitarian and egalitarian impulses, especially when it came to immigration. A former lawyer, state legislator, and municipal judge who now represented immigrant-rich New York City, Bennet attributed the calls for greater restriction, including the literacy test, to "bigotry and intolerance" largely emanating from rural areas and primarily directed toward Jews and Catholics from Italy, Austria, and Russia. Disapproving of this prejudgment on the basis of nationality, he would devote his congressional career, and thereafter much of his life, to securing fair treatment for all immigrants. Bennet deemed anyone who came with a family and intended to make a home in America to be a "most desirable kind of immigrant." In an attempt to ensure their entrance, he opposed not only the literacy qualification but any provision that would penalize good men and women.[32]

This does not imply that Bennet's commission service involved little more that advocacy of his predisposed beliefs. He pursued his assigned task with vigor, and even his ideological opponents would attest to his objectivity. In 1908, when Prescott Hall accused the investigators, especially Bennet, of malfeasance, restrictionist Henry Cabot Lodge jumped to the representative's defense. Although Bennet opposed restriction, he was equally committed to getting "all of the facts," and he had done nothing to impede the investigation or to suppress any of its findings. "On the contrary," Lodge concluded, "he has brought out much, he has suggested more lines of inquiry than any one and has been one of the most valuable members of the Commission." In the end, even Bennet would agree with the premise that under certain conditions, the United States could legitimately impose stricter restriction, but he would refuse to endorse immediate implementation of any one means.[33]

Along with the commissioners' varied and conflicting views about immigration, other personnel decisions also dispel notions that any particular predisposition dominated or drove the investigation. Two cases show how those who would have sought to advance a specific agenda, either pro- or anti-immigrant, were not selected for commission service, and while in each instance the commissioner who principally opposed the appointment likely did so to preclude the hiring of an ideological antagonist, these actions helped to ensure that those who took part would conduct a more objective inquiry. Other examples show a pattern of employing well-qualified men with notable investigatory experience, including cases of close personal friendship. Even President Roosevelt's intervention on behalf of an old friend got the support of both Lodge and Bennet.

When it became clear that Congress would create a commission rather than passing a literacy test provision, restrictionists were led to believe that they would have a voice in naming one of the commissioners. A consensus formed for the appointment of IRL lobbyist James H. Patten. League leader Prescott Hall went so far as to urge Patten to take the position, where he would be able to keep his eyes open and do much valuable work. There is no evidence to suggest that the rumor of Patten's appointment ever reflected anything more than restrictionists' longing, but Patten had assisted James Reynolds, Commissioner Charles Neill's Department of Commerce and Labor partner in the stockyard inquiry, with investigations at Ellis Island and in the South in 1906. Patten later indicated that he had not sought the appointment but had lobbied for Reynolds. It would be interesting to know whether Roosevelt seriously considered appointing either IRL leader, and if so, why he rejected them both. In the absence of evidence, all that can be said is that restrictionists wanted Patten or someone of his stripe on the commission, but no one of that type got an appointment. Patten did apply to work on the commission's staff, but because of his IRL connection, William Bennet nixed his application.[34]

On the opposite end of the spectrum, Lodge wanted to squelch the possible appointment of South Carolina governor Earl Hayward. Hayward was leading his state's effort to solicit immigrants and had devised a plan for using industrialist-provided funds. This aroused Lodge's ire because it clearly would violate contract labor laws, and Lodge wanted the governor to know that existing statutes would be strictly enforced. After finding out from Senator Latimer that Hayward wanted a presidential appointment to the commission, Lodge moved quickly to dissuade Roosevelt, arguing that the governor was about the "last man to go on the Commission, and the last man I fancy that you would think of." Like Patten, Hayward failed to receive an appointment. Later, when it came to securing competent staffers, Lodge criticized the southern commissioners for their "invincible determination . . . to appoint family members and others with no especial fitness to make inquiries as to immigration."[35]

The makeup of the commission's support staff provides an additional indicator of the group's ideological bent. Morton E. Crane; C. S. Atkinson, who requested a furlough in 1908; and William W. Husband were the chief administrative officers. Crane's appointment came at the behest of Senator Lodge, who considered his "old and attached friend" to be "absolutely safe and loyal" to both the president and himself. Roosevelt, for his part, considered Crane to be "a very excellent man." Lodge's support has convinced some historians that Crane's nomination was nothing more than an effort to place a restrictionist in "a crucial post," but such a conclusion does not hold up under scrutiny. Crane's duties as disbursing officer "were solely financial." Further, when the IRL called some of the commission's activities into question, Lodge suggested Crane as someone who could impartially refute the charges. This could have been an elaborate ploy on the part of the commissioners to create the impression that they were impartial while they sought to promote restriction behind the scenes, but Lodge gave every indication that he wanted to avoid any appearance of impropriety.[36]

William W. Husband held the pivotal position of executive secretary, which made him, in effect, the commission's chief administrative officer. Born and raised near St. Johnsbury, Vermont, and educated at local academies, he thereafter clerked at a general store and a shoe company. He gained civil service experience when he worked for two years as an assistant postmaster, and between 1898 and 1902 he was a reporter for the *St. Johnsbury Caledonian* and edited the *Montpelier Journal.* In 1903, Husband became secretary to Senator Dillingham, thus beginning a lifelong association with the formation and implementation of immigration policy. He clerked for the Senate immigration committee during Dillingham's chairmanship, then joined the senator in working on the commission, where he oversaw daily operations, kept official records, and supervised much of the fieldwork. Husband would be instrumental in the commission's recommendation of and Congress's eventual enactment of the immigrant quota system.[37]

Economist W. Jett Lauck directed the far-reaching "Immigrants in Industry" study. Born in West Virginia and educated at Washington and Lee University and the University of Chicago, he returned to his alma mater in 1905 as professor of economics and politics. He simultaneously worked as a consultant in these fields, especially on matters of labor relations. Initially appointed to the commission as a special agent for the Committee on Statistics, he spent the majority of his time with the commission coordinating the study of immigrants in selected key industries. He edited fourteen volumes of the final *Reports* and thereafter worked with Jeremiah Jenks to coauthor a one-volume compilation of the commission's findings. It appears that Lauck supported the literacy test during the 1910s and the imposition of quotas during the 1920s, but he did so because he wanted immigration to be handled in a fair and effective manner.[38]

Frederick C. Croxton served as chief statistician. A close associate of Charles Neill's in the Department of Commerce and Labor's Bureau of Labor Statistics, he too had considerable investigatory experience, including a precommission, department-sponsored study of immigration to the South. The study was never published, but Croxton's comments do not indicate that he came away from the task with any negative predisposition with which to start his work on the Dillingham Commission. He assisted in planning the various lines of commission inquiry and stressed a need for close scrutiny. He also prepared the commission's standard forms, or schedules, supervised tabulation, and wrote and edited some of the final reports.[39]

In some cases, such as those of Husband and Morton Crane, familiarity or favoritism did enter into staff selection, but an effort to advance a particular ideology evidently did not. The story of a former Rough Rider named Murphy, whose employment was endorsed by both Lodge and Bennet, provides an amusing example of the roll of ideology in staff selection. When Bennet wanted Murphy to have a position, President Roosevelt supported his candidacy, cryptically noting his alleged "right views on immigration." Lodge immediately gave his approval, agreeing that Murphy's Rough Rider service made superfluous any additional discussion. "I understand," explained the senator, "that that demonstrates at once his character and fitness, and possibly, that he has been in jail, but nevertheless he shall have my support when Bennet brings him up." How his service as a Rough Rider qualified him for investigative work and what his "right views" were remain a mystery, but perhaps Murphy was the kind of man President Roosevelt had in mind when he made his quip about not having too many professorial types. In any case, if Murphy had some bias for or against immigrants, it was not enough for either Bennet or Lodge, who had blocked other appointments, to oppose him.[40]

Overall, investigators showed that they could put aside their predispositions. "We went into this in the spirit of investigation," said Bennet of their approach to commission work, "dropped politics and our personal views, and took as our motto that there was no man on the commission that was afraid of a fact."[41] The pursuit of information would take them first to the lands whence the immigrants came, then to virtually all parts of the United States, and even into the arcane anthropological world of craniometry. Ultimately, forty-one volumes of reports would attest to the breadth and depth of their inquiry.

CHAPTER THREE

"Every Part of Europe"

WHEN THE SS *CANOPIC* DOCKED at Naples, Italy, on 30 May 1907, an unusual group of observers joined the regular assortment of returning migrants. Immigration commissioners William Dillingham, William Bennet, John Burnett, Benjamin Howell, Asbury Latimer, and William Wheeler—along with two secretaries, an official reporter, a medical expert, an Immigration Service inspector, and two stenographers—had come to investigate the sources of European emigration. Even Senator Henry Cabot Lodge, who wanted the commission to focus on domestic affairs, considered making the trip, though he eventually declined because of his wife's failing health. Secretary Morton Crane described his shipboard duties as those of "social secretary," evoking images of pampered plutocrats on a pleasure cruise, but by the time the investigators finished their work abroad, at least one commissioner had "visited practically every part of Europe from which immigrants come to the United States." Before they even disembarked the *Canopic* in Europe, investigators had interviewed 108 immigrants who were returning to their home countries; they sought to learn why these "birds of passage" had left the United States.[1]

The European inquiry, one of the few parts of the commission investigation for which there is ample evidence as to how participants conducted their work, exhibited several significant characteristics. First, the trip indicated the commissioners' commitment to thoroughness. Second, it offered investigators a chance to confront at their sources the negative mythologies surrounding the various new immigrant groups. Third, officials could test allegations that steamship companies and local officials conspired to evade U.S. laws by transporting obviously inadmissible immigrants. If the investigators reported negatively on the sources and character of those leaving Europe, it could lead to hasty closure of the overall investigation and almost certainly to a negative report, one that would provide powerful ammunition for those calling for more stringent restrictions. If, however, the commissioners found favorable conditions in Europe, of both people and departure procedures, it would serve well the interests of immigrants and their supporters. By studying prospective migrants in their native environs, the commissioners could determine whether the "immigration problem," if indeed it existed at all, was imported or caused by conditions in the United States.

The commission, officially designated the U.S. Immigration Commission, began work on 22 April 1907 and quickly agreed to conduct a broadly based inquiry. After unanimously naming Dillingham chair, authorizing subcommittees, and empowering members to take testimony, in contradiction of their later emphasis on gathering objective evidence, the investigators turned to the substance of their work. While Lodge wanted the inquiry to focus on the workings of existing statutes, likely with the aim of showing their shortcomings, Bennet wanted to undertake a wider-ranging study, one which would look extensively at all aspects of immigration, including conditions in the European homelands. The commissioners tried to accommodate both agendas, but by approving a trip to Europe, they ensured that the investigation would progress more along the lines envisioned by the antirestrictionist Bennet than along those envisioned by the ardently restrictionist Lodge.[2]

The plan for the European investigation initially called for a rather narrow study of national emigration laws and their enforcement, but the commissioners subsequently broadened the plan, deciding also to study "the economic conditions of the different peoples, their manner of living, and the causes that induce them to leave their native lands." Realizing their time constraints, but still wanting to be as thorough as possible, the investigators prepared a questionnaire for distribution to U.S. consuls. It requested information about local crop production, farming techniques, land prices, nonagricultural employment opportunities, wages, bank savings, and family size. The investigators later divided themselves into three subcommittees so as to cover more territory.[3]

The commissioners also drew on the findings of other investigators, whose predispositions may have prejudiced their reports. Those consulted included Robert Watchorn, commissioner of immigration of New York City; Dr. George W. Stoner, surgeon in charge at Ellis Island; and Terence V. Powderly, director of the Bureau of Immigration's Division of Information. Both Watchorn and Powderly, a longtime Knights of Labor leader, had expressed moderately restrictionist views, but Powderly's subsequent pro-immigrant sentiments and bureau appointment had drawn the Knights' wrath. Secretary of Commerce and Labor Oscar S. Straus, from whom Commissioner Bennet acquired pertinent information, also had positive attitudes toward immigrants, including the much-maligned Japanese. Finally, the Bureau of Immigration had sent its own investigators over to Europe, and the Dillingham commissioners selectively incorporated some of that group's findings into its report titled *Emigration Conditions in Europe*.[4]

The commissioners' investigatory strategy incorporated the popular old immigrant–new immigrant dichotomy: for the purposes of its report, it divided European emigrants "into two classes, which for convenience may be designated as the old and the new immigration." Although careful to avoid the appearance of an a priori acceptance of the underlying contention that southern and eastern Europeans were somehow of lesser quality, investigators predicated their decision to divide old from new on "the fact that the widespread apprehension in the United States relative to immigration" was due chiefly to the recent predominance of the new groups. The commissioners similarly decided to spend most, but not all, of their time in the new peoples' homelands. The report *Emigration Conditions* reflected these decisions. It provided in-depth analysis and description of the major new-immigrant nationalities—Austro-Hungarian, Italian, Russian, and Greek—but practically none for those whose members primarily had arrived earlier.[5]

Italy was an appropriate place for the commissioners to start their study of the new groups. Roughly three million Italians had emigrated to the United States since 1820, with over two million having gone there since 1900. During the latter period, they had made up approximately one-quarter of all American immigrants, and their numbers remained high. They also had a decidedly negative reputation. In 1896 Immigration Commissioner Herman J. Schulties described illiterate Italians as "Sicilian chimpanzees." Such disparagement resulted in part from Italians' tendency to settle in America's crowded cities. In order to study the situation in Italy more fully, Dillingham, Wheeler, and Howell decided to meet with government officials in Rome, while Bennet, Burnett, and Latimer traveled through southern Italy. Burnett and Latimer thereafter visited several northern cities.[6]

In Rome the Dillingham party met with Royal Italian Commissioner of Emigration Egisto Rossi. Rossi explained that while his government did not encourage emigration, many Italians exercised this protected right as a matter of necessity. Most went to the United States seeking economic improvement. The government in Rome did try to control ticket agents, and all emigration centers had to have a committee composed of public administrators to provide for travelers' needs. Officials also attempted to winnow out those who could not pass the immigration laws of their intended destination. This pleased the commissioners, who let stand without comment Rossi's contention that it would be redundant to have American Bureau of Immigration agents conduct nonmedical examinations in Italy.[7]

The Bennet group's trip to southern Italy touched on a contentious ethnic-identification issue. The U.S. Bureau of Immigration, employing a prevalent distinction, classified Italians as either northern or southern. Even though there were significant regional and local distinctions in Italy, as opposed to a single Italian national identity, pernicious stereotyping, not efforts to provide accurate ethnological divisions, often motivated the American bifurcation. Southern Italians, who made up the majority of Italian immigrants, had a reputation for being ignorant and inherently criminal and for having a generally low standard of living. One contemporary described them as being "shorter in stature and more swarthy, and on the whole much inferior in intelligence to their northern counterparts." These derogatory characterizations tended to cause Americans to think of southern Italians as difficult to assimilate.[8]

As they toured the southern Italian countryside, the commissioners gathered a good deal of useful information, but they found little evidence to support the prevailing American xenophobia. They observed that southern Italians were industrious people who had the misfortune of inhabiting a particularly poor region. Agriculture provided their only employment, and primitive farming methods predominated. Facing the prospects of continued poor remuneration, many peasants opted for emigration. The first migrants, in the words of locals, went "to get bread"; those who followed, having learned of their predecessors' American success, went "to make and save money." The commissioners noted high illiteracy rates in the southern *compartimenti,* but they concluded that "backwardness along educational lines" was not inherent in the residents. The illiteracy rates simply conveyed the region's inability to provide adequate public instruction.[9]

Burnett and Latimer found far different conditions during their visit to northern Italy but came away with similarly favorable opinions. Stopping in Florence, Venice, and Milan, areas that had sent few immigrants to the United States, the commissioners found what they described as Italy's finest farmers. Their careful cultivation of fields and their thrift—they even collected "fertilizer" along the highways—produced high yields from less-than-ideal soil, and they exhibited exemplary sanitary habits about their persons and homes. Local women drew particular praise for being fully as capable as males when it came to fieldwork. As a whole, the region had very law-abiding citizens, who committed almost no "foul crimes" and had no problems with epidemic disease. The commissioners thought it unfortunate that relatively few northern Italians had emigrated to the United States. Prosperous local economies fueled by good agricultural production and new opportunities for work in manufacturing absorbed surplus labor and gave the citizens few reasons to leave. Going to America seemed to have little attraction.

U.S. Consul James E. Dunning, with whom the commissioners met in Milan, did stress the potential for more emigration to America by northern Italian farmers. The region currently was sending some nine hundred thousand agriculture laborers to various parts of Europe during harvest times. Dunning encouraged the commissioners to take steps to promote an organized emigration of northern Italians to the United States, where they could "open up new lands or cultivate the old." Already many high-quality men and women had left from Lombardy, and others could be induced to follow their lead. However, those who did would likely choose alternative destinations, such as Argentina, if the United States did not formulate a plan for their recruitment. Representatives of American states that desired the immigration could invite specific farming families, taking care to match them to regions most suited to their particular expertise and making careful preparation for their arrival and settlement.[10]

Overall, conditions throughout Italy impressed the commissioners, and little in this section of *Emigration Conditions in Europe* supported negative American stereotypes. Although the investigators based their findings on the perceived ethnological distinction between northerners and southerners, they concluded that Italians of both types were naturally "strong, vigorous, and capable of great physical endurance." Specific characterizations bore this out. Since 1900, over 75 percent of Italian emigrants had been males between the ages of fourteen and forty-four. "It is the strongest arms that are leaving us," was the lament in one Sicilian newspaper. Northern Italy supplied more skilled laborers than southern Italy, but the commissioners concluded that this said more about the region's development than about the character of its people. As to vices, neither northerners nor southerners showed a propensity for debilitating practices, such as drinking too much.

Italian criminality did elicit the commission's concern, as it long had in the United States, but the commission reports presented contradictory findings. Citing statistics for personal violence, robbery, blackmail, and extortion in Italy, to support notions of Italian criminal propensity, the commissioners reported that "it cannot be denied that the number of such offenses committed among Italians in this country warrants the prevalence of such a belief." Yet, the commission's own tables show relatively few crimes in the "Robbery, extortion, and blackmail" category as compared to the number of "Offenses against the public faith and credit." *Emigration Conditions* makes no comparison between Italians and other ethnic groups; in fact, the sections covering the other nationalities do not even include crime statistics. Hence, the commissioners did not provide adequate support for their concerns about Italian criminal proclivity.

Equally suspect was the commission's assertion that several sources believed that Italian crime had diminished because those with a criminal tendency, especially members of the "Black Hand" Mafia, a generally misunderstood but allegedly large and well-organized Italian criminal syndicate, had gone to America. In 1891, Congressman Lodge had made this an issue after the lynching of nine Italian Americans who were allegedly Black Hand members. Before the lynching, these nine had been tried for the murder of New Orleans Police Superintendent David Hennessy; six had had been acquitted, and the trials of the others had resulted in hung juries. The commission's report minimized the alleged Mafia danger, demonstrating that through the issuance of passports the Italian government was making a concerted effort to proscribe criminal emigration to the United States.[11]

At Italian ports U.S. medical authorities enjoyed a special, but not always congenial, relationship with their local counterparts. The Italians wanted to safeguard the welfare of their citizens, and therefore the government sought to ensure that steamship companies did not knowingly transport men and women who could not meet their destination's entrance requirements. This concern had moved the Italians to enter into a unique agreement with the United States, under which the U.S. Public Health and Marine Hospital Service paid for and supervised emigrant medical inspections at Naples, Palermo, and Messina that helped to ensure compliance with U.S. laws. Because they did not want to pay fines or penalties, officials of the steamship lines always accepted the Americans' rulings. The commissioners found the inspections at Italian ports to be very thorough but wondered whether the added American expense produced any benefits beyond those derived from the procedures at other European ports.[12]

One final problem with Italian immigration troubled William Bennet. At some point during his European travels, he started to worry about "undesirables" who legally could not obtain passports, such as known Black Hand members, masquerading as sailors and then jumping ship at an American port. Because the ersatz seamen were not considered immigrants, inspectors paid them scant attention, and they therefore had easy access to American soil. Bennet suggested that the Bureau of Immigration examine all arriving sailors. Commissioner-General of Immigration Frank P. Sargent agreed to implement corrective measures; as a labor leader and strong restrictionist on whose opinions the Immigration Restriction League looked with favor, Sargent no doubt would have been pleased to implement any and all means of barring immigrants. More notable, the move to keep out fraudulent sailors reveals that even the antirestrictionist Bennet could see the value of excluding some foreigners.[13]

Commissioners Latimer, Burnett, and, later, Howell next visited France and Switzerland, where what they found did support prejudices based on distinctions between old and new immigrants. These old-immigrant nationalities drew praise, but few from either country migrated to the United States. Swiss officials reported that not more than five to six thousand people left the country each year, with about 70 percent going to the United States. Most were young, male peasants from large families that did not require their assistance and who wanted to improve their economic condition. Because the French enjoyed national prosperity, an agreeable climate, satisfactory living conditions, and readily available public education, not many of them were likely to emigrate either. Native conditions in France had produced happy, contented people who would have made good immigrants. This portrayal contrasted starkly with that of transients passing through these nations from other lands.[14]

The commissioners found an especially disturbing situation in Marseille, France, which served as a way station—"practically a detention camp"—for people traveling between the eastern Mediterranean–Black Sea region and the United States. The commissioners encountered large numbers of Syrians from Beyrouth, Greek Smyrnaand, whom they characterized as "extremely dirty, and not especially intelligent . . . living like cattle." Carrying no baggage, the Syrians had "evidently no intention of changing their apparel until they reached their destination." They and all other emigrants did have to pass a medical inspection before they could continue their journey, and if officials decided that they did not meet U.S. entry standards, they were returned to their homes. Still, the whole scene troubled the investigators, and what they heard from an American official reinforced their negativity.

Robert P. Skinner, U.S. council-general at Marseilles, lambasted Mediterranean steamship companies for their practices in transporting the Levantine emigrants. Company agents would sell tickets to those clearly unable to meet American entrance requirements and then transport them as far as Marseilles. Intercontinental lines would not accept such passengers because the company would have to pay the cost of their return transportation, as required by U.S. law, if the immigrants were excluded, but this did not dissuade the ticket sellers. Rather than abandon their lucrative business, the agents used claims of marriage fraudulently to establish American citizenship. Also, unscrupulous ticket agents routed many Syrians through Mexico, an unnecessary distance for those who could meet U.S. entry standards and a way to evade the law for those likely to be excluded. Skinner believed that existing U.S. laws could not stop the influx of undesirable immigrants.[15]

Despite Skinner's derogatory comments and their poor impressions of vagabond Syrians, the visits to Marseille and other French ports convinced the commissioners, including the previously skeptical Latimer, that local authorities were making a concerted effort to see that all emigrants would be able to meet U.S. entrance requirements. American consuls monitored the process. Emigrants in transit through Marseille were inspected before they were allowed to proceed, and no one could leave for the United States until they had been cleared by the medical staff. Everyone received vaccinations and a physical examination. Those showing signs of disease underwent a second examination, and if they were unlikely to pass American scrutiny they were not allowed to board the ship. The commissioners also witnessed good inspections at Le Havre and Cherbourg, France, and good ticketing procedures in Switzerland.[16] These observations spoke well of the selection process for both old and new types of immigrants and cast doubt on charges of systematic circumvention of U.S. laws.

Thirteen control stations maintained by steamship companies along the German-Russian frontier provided the next venue at which investigators observed new immigrants and processing procedures. The majority of those passing through the stations came from Austria, mainly Slavs, and a few migrants were from Russia. The latter were mostly Jews. Overall these transients appeared to be in good physical condition. Records show that significant numbers were rejected because they would not have been able to meet U.S. requirements forbidding the entrance of those suffering from contagious disease. Ninety percent of those rejected had trachoma, or "granular eyelids," which caused corneal inflammation and could result in partial or total blindness. Others suffered from such maladies as favus, or ringworm infected scalp; syphilis; and tuberculosis. Those denied permission to proceed further were returned to their homes.

At the Myslowitz station the commissioners had an opportunity to watch the screening of emigrants on their way to various embarkation ports. Physicians first examined the emigrants for contagious diseases, particularly trachoma. Anyone who appeared to be in poor health received a more thorough inspection. Next, the gendarme reviewed each emigrant's passport and other papers, and agents arranged for the traveler to purchase a transatlantic ticket. Like U.S. law, German law held steamship companies that had sold tickets to subsequently excluded immigrants responsible for their return. Therefore, officials took great care in screening the emigrants, who received yet another inspection at their embarkation ports.

Sanitary conditions at both the stations and at German embarkation ports also received high marks. Each control station set aside special rooms for detainees, and another part of the compound served as a steam "disinfecting plant." If the examining physician deemed such action necessary, the emigrant was required to strip naked and take a thorough shower. The traveler's clothes and luggage were concurrently passed through the disinfector. Officials provided towels for drying and a "cheap and coarse" bathrobe to be worn until the garments had completed the decontamination process. The visiting commissioners praised this system, noting that, when ready to leave, each emigrant had "clean clothes and . . . a very clean person indeed." At the Port of Hamburg inspectors separated males and females in an effort to protect the females' modesty and virtue. The report did not specify whether this segregation applied to people traveling with their families or just to single people. Special care was taken to preserve decorum at the disinfecting plant: the door to the men's chamber closed automatically when that to the women's chamber opened.

Officials at the Hamburg *Auswandererhallen,* run by the Hamburg Amerika steamship line and called the "most complete station in Europe," divided the emigrants by nationality. Each group had its own dormitory, and modern brick chapels catered to the divers needs of Jews, Catholics, and Protestants. While the facilities for the various Christian groups shared the same structure, those for Jews occupied a separate building. Food prepared in a special kitchen according to kosher practices was served in a special dining room. Officials in Bremen also separated Christians and Jews, taking care to provide for the latter's dietary needs. The commissioners found all food to be "of good quality and quite appetizing."[17]

From the emigrants' perspective, conditions at the stations may not have been as positive as the commissioners perceived. Anna Herkner, an agent hired by the commission to investigate steerage accommodations, disguised herself as an Austrian emigrant and passed through the same Myslowitz station that the Burnett-Latimer-Howell group had visited. She found the state of affairs atrocious. The attendants were drunk, and "the walls . . . were alive with vermin." It is interesting that her observations were put in a separate volume of the reports, which raises the question of whether there was some effort to hide them. Differences in focus—the commissioners' on administration and Herkner's on the treatment of emigrants— provides one plausible explanation. The separation of the reports may also testify to the breadth of the investigation, which produced more information than could be carefully organized. In any case, the separation of Herkner's findings allowed the commissioners to maintain their overall positive summary of the emigration situation in Europe, and Herkner's report would help secure passage of new laws to improve steerage conditions.[18]

While Burnett, Howell, and Latimer examined the conditions of Austrian emigrants in transit, Dillingham and Wheeler visited Austria. The Austro-Hungarian Empire, a duel monarchy since 1867, trailed only Great Britain and Germany as an overall provider of American immigrants. Most of the 3.2 million arrivals who had given Austria-Hungary as their home country had come after 1900. Their numbers included Croations, Slovenians, Germans, Hebrews, Magyars, Bohemians, Poles, Slovaks, and a smattering of less represented groups. With the exception of the ethnic Germans, these again were the stereotypical new immigrants as defined by both geographic origin and date of arrival.

As a technically sovereign entity, each of the namesake countries of the empire had its own emigration policy. Austria nominally required passports but did virtually nothing in the way of enforcement. Persons could cross its borders at will. Conversely, Hungary imposed stringent prohibitions and procedures. A 1903 statute forbade the emigration of draft-eligible men, anyone under criminal investigation, and anyone who could not meet the entrance requirements of the intended destination. The law also regulated steamship lines and other agents for emigrants. After reviewing the situation, the U.S. commissioners concluded that the Hungarian government wished "to exercise complete control over emigration" and made every effort to see that its laws were being strictly enforced.

The investigators paid special attention to allegations of steamship-agent malfeasance. Austrian sources reported that some companies were using secret agents to induce emigration to the United States, in violation of American law. A member of the Krakow Chamber of Commerce said that two of the leading transatlantic carriers, North German Lloyd and Hamburg Amerika, had between five and six thousand agents selling tickets in Galicia. Dillingham discussed the matter with a government minister, who said that company agents had little effect on emigrant numbers. In Hungary the commissioners also heard charges of agent misconduct and obtained evidence of the government's efforts to eliminate the problem. While both the Austrian and Hungarian accusations likely had some merit, the commissioners believed that economics, more than sales tactics, convinced most emigrants to leave their homes.

Hungarian officials made a point of showing their distaste for the nation's mass emigration, but within a year of establishing its strict standards, the government had contracted with the Cunard Line for direct service between Fiume and the United States. The port handled only a small percentage of all Austro-Hungarian emigrants because most traveled overland to Atlantic ports. The commissioners found Fiume to have a model station, one of the best in Europe. Officials inspected the emigrants upon their arrival and, if necessary, told them to bathe. The travelers then could enter the station's "clean" section. Prior to the emigrants' embarkation, local inspectors and officials of the U.S. consulate conducted medical examinations and disinfected baggáge. Commissioners found the procedure to be "strict in the highest degree."

The investigators likewise came away with favorable impressions after their visit to Trieste, Austria's only transatlantic port. A considerable number of Austrians, Hungarians, Russians, and members of Balkan peoples departed the from the port on either the Cunard or Austro-Americano Line. The U.S. consul reported that during the initial years of service, 1903–1906, passenger examination had been superficial, at best. As a result, in April 1906 one-third of the emigrants who had departed from Trieste were turned back at New York. The Austrian government then implemented more rigorous examinations, dramatically reducing the number of rejections. The system at Trieste involved the local U.S. consul to a greater extent than the system at any other embarkation port.

The commission's reports offer a mixed assessment of Austro-Hungarian emigration. For example, they favorably note Hungary's efforts to curtail its "enormous exodus of the masses," but criticize the lack of medical inspections at the control stations along the Austrian frontier. Authorities did, however, warn "doubtful cases" that they likely would be rejected somewhere along the line. As to the emigrants themselves, those who most closely fit the American description of the new immigrant fared least favorably. Literacy rates offer a case in point. Most emigrants from provinces near the German and Swiss borders could read and write, but the percentage of emigrants from areas close to the Adriatic Sea who were literate was lower. The commissioners' derogatory explanation was that illiteracy existed "to a much greater degree in those Provinces most removed from the influences of western Europe." They did note that economic and cultural considerations, such as which language was used in schools, likely affected regional literacy rates.[19]

Dillingham and Wheeler next visited imperial Russia, where they encountered several unique situations. First, Russia did not recognize the right of emigration. Thousands did leave every year, using loopholes that allowed Jews to emigrate and others to take temporary trips abroad. The laws covering the latter sojourns lacked uniformity. The government recognized that citizens might want to relocate, especially peasants trying to escape increasingly oppressive conditions, but officials encouraged them to migrate eastward, to sparsely inhabited Russian lands such as Siberia. A quasigovernment publication reprinted in the commission's report painted a pitiful picture of those who opted to cross the Atlantic. Preyed upon by corrupt agents and buffeted by terrible conditions, the publication claimed, "many of them perish before ever reaching the distant shores of their destination," and "many among them would have gladly abandoned the intention to emigrate had they known the conditions of the journey."

Investigators observing at the German control stations learned that the Russians used drastic measures to prevent illegal emigration. Armed guards patrolled the entire length of the frontier, on orders to shoot people who tried to pass at locations other than the regular checkpoints, but the guards had a reputation of being notoriously easy to bribe. The guards also tended to impose hardships on rejected emigrants, but steamship agents tried to mitigate such treatment by escorting those rejected all the way to their villages instead of leaving them at the stations. Standing on a bridge between the two countries, the commissioners watched guards hiding in the tall grass and saw two people arrested for carrying improperly prepared passports. The guards refused those investigators entrance into Russian territory.[20]

Although the Russian government aimed to keep Russian people at home, it could not counteract the abhorrent conditions that motivated emigrants. The commission found that Russians peasants, 83 percent of the population, led impoverished lives. Emancipated from serfdom in 1861, they struggled to eke out a meager existence. Unequal land distribution, overpopulation in many areas, poor educational facilities, primitive farming methods, and the scarcity of nonagrarian employment opportunities minimized their prospects. The American visitors saw little hope that the situation would improve. "The peasants are poor," the commissioners concluded, "and are becoming poorer every year." Seeking escape, more than two million had emigrated to the United States since 1880. Here, indeed, were "huddled masses yearning to breathe free."

Jews, who had made up 44 percent of Russian immigrants to the United States since 1900, faced even harsher conditions than other Russians. Their migration pattern resembled that of other emigrants, who went to America primarily for economic reasons, but the commission concluded that due to virulent anti-Semitism the Jews' situation was unique. One observer concluded that because of the Jews' tenacity in earning a living and their involvement in revolutionary activities, Russian resentment toward them was as bitter as that directed at "the Negro" in the American South. Jews could not own land and could only live within the legally defined Pale of Settlement. This tyranny not withstanding, the worst oppression came in the form of pogroms, mob violence directed against Jewish people and their property. From October 1905 to the end of 1906, pogroms had devastated 661 towns, killed 985 people, widowed 387 women, and orphaned 177 children. According to reports, officials had done little to alleviate the situation, and soldiers sent to maintain order often joined in the carnage. The commission cited officials of the Baron de Hirsch Fund, or Jewish Colonization Society, who asserted that Russian Jews emigrated primarily because of these horrible conditions.[21] If the Jews and other peasants had undesirable qualities because of their poverty, the commission made clear the external causes.

One of the commissioners, likely Wheeler, embarked from Libau, Russia, which gave him a chance to observe emigration procedures at the port. The procedures lacked the rigor found elsewhere. Those buying tickets from "sub-agents" had to undergo a medical exam, followed by a second exam at the port, but the investigator described these as "cursory," with no U.S. consular participation. Officials seemed to be more concerned about maintaining an orderly exodus. Because the Russian government considered many of the emigrants to be revolutionaries, large numbers of police monitored departures to keep the radicals from displaying their freedom "by singing Marseillaise and waving red flags."[22]

William Bennet extended the commission's investigation to Greece and the Middle East. Staying in Athens for "about a fortnight" in early July, he met with American and Greek officials, including the minister of foreign affairs, and visited the main embarkation station at Patras. He also spent time in Beirut, Syria, then part of the Ottoman Empire, and traveled through other areas of Asia Minor. The volume of emigration to the United States from the region had been relatively small, but it was growing, and the migrants constituted the newest of the new. Of the approximately 186,000 Greeks who had arrived in the United States since 1819, 90 percent had come after 1900. They accounted for only about 2 percent of all American immigrants, but the commissioners believed that they warranted more than cursory mention because of their rapidly increasing numbers. Most Greeks went to the United States for economic reasons. Although investigators found little abject poverty in their homeland, there were few indicators that the natives were experiencing significant financial gain. Therefore, more and more Greeks sought to better their fortunes across the Atlantic.

The Greek government looked favorably on emigration, believing that those who left would maintain close ties to their homes and eventually return to their native land. They also sent back large amounts of money, despite myriad problems with the Greek postal system. The commission acknowledged the substantial amount of these remunerations, which benefited the local society, but it could not substantiate the assertions about Greeks' transitory migration. Quite the contrary, commission statistics showed a higher percentage of Greeks staying in the United States, as compared with other groups. These differ notably from those compiled by historian Thomas Archdeacon (see table 1).

These discrepancies between the commission's statistics and those compiled by Archdeacon, although noteworthy, are not necessarily problematic in terms of assessing the commission's work. One explanation may be that the commission's study covers only the three fiscal years ending 30 June

Table 1

Nationality or Ethnic Group	U.S. Immigration Commission Rate for Remigration (in %)	Archdeacon Rate for Remigration (in %)
Greeks	25	53.7
Croatians/Slovenians	56	36.3
Magyars	64	46.5
Poles	30	33.0
Slovaks	59	36.5

1910, while Archdeacon's covers a longer period, from the 1890s to the 1920s. Or if researchers used bad or incomplete data, one or both sets of statistics could be wrong. In the case of the commission this cannot be proven because we do not know how or where it collected its data. The differences do show the difficulties in statistically analyzing social phenomena about which it is hard to gather accurate information, and this should provoke some caution in accepting the commission's counts and percentages. However, even if Archdeacon is right and the commission was wrong, and even if that shows definitively the latter's sloppy methodology, it is significant that the commission erred in favor of Greek immigrants by minimizing a negative perception.[23]

Greeks could travel directly to the United States from the ports of Patras and Piraeus aboard the Austro-Americano Line, whose inspection procedures received mixed reviews. The Greek government did not require medical inspections, but the company had implemented its own system to ensure that its passengers could get into the United States. Each emigrant had to undergo a preliminary examination when he—over 95 percent of Greek emigrants were male—purchased the ticket, and he had to pass another one on the day of embarkation. At that time every emigrant accepted for passage received a wrist stamp intended to deter the substitution of a less fit individual. The commission found this system to be "both theoretically and practically, a most excellent one," but Bennet had concerns about fraudulent examinations. Doctors on ships carrying Greek migrants allegedly "fixed" trachoma by removing the granulations in such a way as temporarily to mask the other symptoms, thereby enabling the migrants to pass through Ellis Island. In their advertisements, ticket agents promised afflicted persons that the procedure would enable them to land. Believing that the advent of direct steamship connections from Patras would only exacerbate the situation, Bennet wanted to put U.S. authorities on the lookout for the "masking" practice. The U.S. officials he contacted agreed that the situation warranted close scrutiny on the part of Immigration Service medical inspectors.[24]

Bennet made a second "most interesting" trip to Europe in November 1907, but others would come to doubt its value. Three years later Representative Robert B. Macon, an Arkansas Democrat who had grown tired of waiting for the commission to report, lashed out against what he called Bennet's "junket" to Bucharest, Romania, where Bennet and his wife had an audience with King Carol I and Queen Elizabeth. The commissioner issued a terse response. Since 1899, over 55,000 Rumanian immigrants had arrived in the United States. Most were Jews who had come to escape anti-Semitic persecution. The pogroms had reached such levels that Secretary of State John Hay had sent an official memorandum of concern to various European heads of state. Bennet believed that the emigration aspects warranted firsthand observation, and since no commission official had as yet visited Romania, he had taken it upon himself to add information on its conditions to "an exhaustive investigation."[25]

Bennet also went back to Greece and Italy. After the commission's earlier visit, the Italian government had appointed its own fact-finding group. It too traveled through southern Italy, asking the same questions as those asked by the Americans. Bennet's second trip allowed him to get copies of the Italians' findings, which were subsequently incorporated into the commission report. He then went back to Greece and reported that he had lived "amongst the kind of Greeks that come to this country." One may well question the extent to which a U.S. congressman, who had dined with the king of a neighboring nation, truly lived amongst the predominantly lower-class men who came to the United States, but as a sincere advocate for immigrants and their interests, he no doubt put himself in situations that would allow him to gain knowledge or experience that would help him defend the incoming masses. In response to later criticism, Bennet argued that this subsequent trip allowed him to acquire pertinent information that had been missed on the earlier journey and that was then added to the data previously collected at the Greek ports.[26]

Northern European ports received far less scrutiny, in large part because of the commissioners' decision to focus their attention on places associated with the more numerous new immigrants. After the other members departed for the United States, William Wheeler remained in Europe to visit Finland, Sweden, Denmark, and various Atlantic ports. Officials at Christiana, Norway, and Copenhagen, Denmark, performed limited medical examinations, but immigrants who departed from those points had the lowest rejection rates at U.S. ports. At Antwerp, Belgium, the few men and women carried by the Red Star Line underwent thorough medical examinations, but American officials had no part in the process. Steamship companies did do inspections at British ports, largely because they did not want to bear the burden of returning rejected passengers, but Commissioner John Burnett was not impressed with what he observed at the Port of Queenstown, perhaps because he disapproved of the Irish emigrants it served.[27]

Burnett found that when the third-class passengers prepared to board, the attending physician merely stood on the gangway and watched them pass; "not a single eye or head was examined, nor any other examination made." The gatekeeper confirmed that this was the norm. When queried by Burnett, the U.S. consul attested to the procedure's rigidity, and the limited number of rejections at U.S. ports supported this contention. Unfortunately, however, figures do not indicate the ratio of rejections to overall departures. The best explanation for the contradiction between Burnett's observations and those of others is a double bias. The xenophobic Burnett, perhaps because he had concerns about the large number of Irish emigrants, wanted "rigid" examinations, while the other commissioners, in *Emigration Conditions in Europe,* noted that "the necessity of a thorough medical examination is not so great there as at ports where southern and eastern Europeans embark."[28]

Still, the European investigation produced no stinging indictments, and time after time the commission found good conditions at ports and stations which served the southern and eastern Europeans. "The present emigration," the commission reported, "whether or not desirable as a whole, nonetheless represents a stronger and better element of that particular class from which it is drawn." It took a certain wherewithal, a combination of strengths and determination, to leave one's homeland and journey to a strange new land. Further, U.S. laws culled bad would-be emigrants and dissuaded the questionable ones. Those who passed muster tended to be young males, ages fourteen to forty-four, and though they generally lacked specific skills, they came to America intending to find work and to prosper.

The commissioners showed some negativity toward new immigrants, but they tried to keep their assessments objective and fair. The assertion that Queenstown's lack of thorough medical inspection was innocuous because the port did not service southern and eastern Europeans provides an example of latent prejudice, but the discussion of European illiteracy demonstrates the commission's concern for balance. Literacy rates were lower among southern and eastern Europeans, but the investigators could not determine whether this was "due chiefly to environment or to inherent racial tendencies." Downplaying evidence of disparate rates of literacy for groups with similar living conditions, the commission decided that poverty was "probably" the chief cause of illiteracy. If a literacy test went into effect, it would disproportionately affect certain groups, such as southern Italians, but the commissioners doubted "whether such a test would very greatly reduce the coming of the morally undesirable."

Other conclusions showed a similar ambiguity. Figures for adults who showed their money to U.S. entry point inspectors indicated that newer immigrants brought in less money and that, except in the case of Jews, they tended to be less permanent. Yet among these more transient groups the commission found little evidence to support the commonly held belief about habitual migration. Most of those who left the United States for their home country did not come back. Not surprisingly, conditions in the United States played a big part in migration patterns. Good economic times, such as those of 1907, produced record immigration, but depression, such as that of 1908, induced many to leave. Those who had least established themselves would logically be the most likely to go back to Europe. Yet the commission also found that returned emigrants "frequently elevated" the character of their native communities.[29]

The commissioners also gleaned considerable information and reached generally positive conclusions about the operation and evasion in Europe of local rules and U.S. immigration laws. Steamship companies, the commissioners concluded, took primary responsible for conducting the medical examinations, largely because they did not want to be responsible for transporting someone whose affliction could have been detected prior to departure. Without this U.S. law, there would not have been any examinations "worthy of the name." However, company examinations varied in thoroughness. Using admittedly incomplete data despite what they described as their best collection efforts, the commissioners estimated that authorities had refused transportation to fifty thousand intending emigrants between 1 December 1906 and 31 December 1907. Trachoma and other eye diseases were the most common causes of rejection. These were impressive numbers, but the commission also reported that European inspections offered little protection against the emigration of those excluded on nonmedical grounds.[30]

Frequent allegations of induced or supported emigration (transportation costs being paid by a third party) also came under commission scrutiny. Beginning with the Immigration Act of 1885, the United States had prohibited the entrance of contract laborers and had placed restrictions on the use of prepaid tickets. Laws did exempt individuals who were helped by relatives and personal friends, and the commission found that almost all of those traveling on prepaid tickets, who accounted for about 25 percent of all immigrants, had received the aid from friends and relatives. Certain groups, such as the Jewish Baron de Hirsch Fund, had a reputation for sponsoring emigrants, but the commissioners could not substantiate the allegations. Congressman Bennet visited a sweatshop in Bucharest, Romania, and learned that Hirsch Fund representatives did council prospective emigrants, but did not buy them tickets. Overall, the investigators found that contract laborers did not make up "any considerable portion" of emigrants to the United States. Many travelers did, however, have word-of-mouth information about where to find jobs.

The commission similarly found little evidence of governmental assistance for emigrants. The number receiving such assistance, in violation of American law, was "so small as to be of little or no importance." The investigators found no evidence to support claims that certain governments were promoting the emigration of criminals. Although Americans had exaggerated this notion, U.S. inspectors did have to be on the lookout for convicts and outlaws. Toward this end, European governments could provide assistance by running background checks and requiring passports of all emigrants. Local officials did reign in steamship agents who promoted emigration, in violation of American law, but that had not eliminated their illicit conduct.[31]

These conditions likely influenced the commission's decision not to recommend the implementation of official U.S. inspections on foreign soil prior to embarkation. Commissioner-General of Immigration Frank P. Sargent, a known restrictionist, advised placing Immigration Service agents at European ports and hoped that the commissioners would study the possibility as part of their European investigation. The Dillingham group did look into the matter, but in *Emigration Conditions in Europe* they failed to endorse any extension of the U.S. presence abroad. The American government already supplied U.S. Public Health and Marine Hospital Service officers at Italian ports and derived little benefit there beyond that provided by the examination systems at other embarkation points. Comparisons between the large number of immigrants arriving in the United States and the small number who were excluded at its ports must have provided support for the favorable assessment of European examinations.[32]

Historical analysis of the commissioners' European trip poses additional questions. The investigators wanted to gather information about causes of emigration, classes of emigrants, various national emigration policies, and the effects of U.S. laws on emigrant departure. They intended to make personal observations, consult with American and foreign officials, and collect large numbers of pertinent documents.[33] As government officials, they could find ways to communicate with their foreign counterparts and thereby acquire materials, but did they have the language skills or proper interpreters to talk to others, including those who worked with emigrants, in all of the various nations and regions they visited? Could they collect all of the information they wanted? Finally, as the case of Bennet's second trip to Greece prompts us to ask, could these American elites relate to the decidedly lower-class subjects of their investigation?

These questions may be answered two ways. First, it is very possible that better-trained observers with better linguistic skills could have gathered better, or at least more complete, information. This would be especially important for those who would like to use the report's historical information. The discrepancy between the commission's figures for Greek return migration and those of historian Thomas Archdeacon demonstrates this problem. Still, although the report for the European trip is one of the least statistical and most impressionistic, there is nothing to suggest that the overall findings cannot be trusted. A second answer comes from the report's contemporary use. Overall, the volume covering conditions in Europe was positive about immigrants, and most notably about the new ethnic groups. Therefore, even if most of its information was incomplete or even wrong—and again, this is debatable—the commission did not use the report to pillory immigrants. The findings, regardless of their accuracy, did not suggest such a need.

This was the European investigation's most salient result: if there was an immigration problem, the commission did not find the roots of it in Europe. Quite the contrary, much of what the investigators found actually challenged prevalent nativist assertions, such as the persistent claims that foreign governments induced the emigration of criminals and deliberately attempted to evade U.S. laws. Most stations adequately screened departing passengers, and steamship companies took their responsibilities seriously. Therefore, if indeed there was a compelling reason to impose new or more exclusive entry requirements or restrictions, the evidence would have to be found within the United States. That search would be the commission's next step.

CHAPTER FOUR

"Observations at Home"

IN THE MIDST OF THE EUROPEAN investigation, Commissioner-General of Immigration Frank Sargent lauded the commission for diligently fulfilling its "arduous duty." He hoped that the investigators would be "taking wise measures to furnish the United States the most intelligent observations on the entire subject, not only from the foreign standpoint, but also from observations here at home." Commencement of the domestic investigation awaited completion of the European phase, but once it was begun, it too demonstrated the investigators' commitment to thoroughness. Despite Senator Henry Cabot Lodge's initial wish that it conduct a limited investigation, largely a study of the weaknesses and failures of present laws, the commission decided to collect new data on virtually all pertinent topics. Eventually, even its most committed restrictionists came to endorse and then contribute to this type of innovative and exhaustive inquiry.[1]

The progressive pursuit of so-called hard evidence dominated the domestic investigation. Early on, members determined that any study that confined its fact-finding to "expressions of opinion from persons interested in various phases of the subject under consideration . . . would yield very little new information that would be of value to Congress in a serious consideration of the Government's immigration policy." Hence, investigators conducted relatively few hearings or forums, which would tend to yield nothing more than a rehashing of familiar arguments. They instead tried to collect facts and figures about topics that theretofore had received only superficial examination. As historian Charlotte Erickson aptly notes: "The Dillingham Commission showed great respect for pragmatic fact, even though the commissioners did not ask all or just the same questions today's historians want to put."[2]

The commission's working papers and internal correspondence were destroyed, and review and analysis highlights the problems posed by this destruction. Except in a small number of relevant manuscripts and in a few cases in which the reports narrate the course of inquiry, there are scant clues as to exactly what the field agents did and how they collected the vast amount of data. The commission reported that it had secured "original information" about 3.2 million people, and the reports include seventy-six pages of "Schedule Forms," the blanks used to record responses. The accompanying instructions tell how to fill the forms out but say almost nothing about actual filling-out process. There is not even an indication of how many agents worked on any particular part of the inquiry, other than mention that it was a "large number"; nor is it known which agents and with what training went to any particular place. In most cases the reports tell only what the agents found.[3]

W. Jett Lauck, who took charge of studying "Immigrants in Industries," briefly explained the investigatory procedures, highlighting the difficulties in obtaining the desired information. In select communities, data collectors distributed questionnaires, visited homes, and acquired corporation-conducted censuses of workers. To secure "other facts not susceptible of statistical presentation," investigators deviated from their quest for objectivity and used "direct observation and interviews with responsible persons among the native American and alien population." Special agents also gathered historical and economic information about each industry. When congressionally mandated due dates curtailed the collection of new information, agents obtained additional, superficial data, usually from a census or some similar inquiry, about more people and places.[4] This raises several questions about the extent of each activity and the precise nature of the data collection.

Knowledge about the process of data collection would be invaluable for assessment of the validity and value of the reports and would provide a better context for interpreting their conclusions; the loss of these key documents necessitates the use of more sketchy sources, particularly the commission's surviving minutes and those of its executive committee that detail how the leaders organized the study and how they sought to meet their statutory mandate. What stands out in these accounts are the commissioners' commitment to thoroughness and the absence of evidence that they merely sought facts and figures that would support preconceived notions. No less a force than the Immigration Restriction League (IRL) eventually would worry that its longtime confidant Henry Cabot Lodge would not do enough to create a restrictionist-friendly report.

Lodge immediately showed his expected predisposition by requesting the collection of information about the effectiveness of Section 1 of the Immigration Act of 1891, which called for the exclusion of any immigrant who was deemed "likely to become a public charge." This vague provision came the closest to providing some sort of general exclusion. For the years 1903 to 1907, Lodge wanted to know how many immigrants had been excluded under the public-charge clause, the number of cases that had then been appealed to the secretary of labor and commerce, and the number of cases that had been reversed on appeal. Lodge also wondered how the Department of Commerce and Labor, which was in charge of immigrant inspection, interpreted the statute. Would, for example, an immigrant be considered a public charge if he or she had received free treatment at a dispensary or government-supported institution, and would an alien "'likely to become a public charge' at some time in the indefinite future" be considered admissible? Clearly the Massachusetts senator wanted to demonstrate the statute's failings.

Lodge also sought clarification of the Department of Commerce and Labor's handling of "bonded immigrants." Under the Immigration Act of 1903, a person who was deemed likely to become a public charge and was therefore subject to exclusion could enter the United States by posting a bond. No person, organization, or company could post such a bond on behalf of a potentially indigent alien except on the authority of the commissioner-general of immigration, "with the written approval of the Secretary of Commerce." These seemingly rigorous requirements should have deterred fraud or misuse, but evidently Lodge was not so certain. In addition to ascertaining the number of immigrants bonded during the preceding two years, he wanted to know about the bonding procedure, the amount of money required for each person thus landed, and rules governing the bondsmen.[5]

Meeting again the day after Lodge made these requests, the commission created several additional committees, including one assigned the general task of amassing statistics. Headed by Charles Neill and Jeremiah Jenks, its ambitious task was to collect all government immigration statistics, as well as all publicly and privately amassed information about immigrant distribution and regional demands for labor. The committee also would investigate immigrant congestion in large cities by determining the number and percentage of foreign-born residents, native-born residents of foreign parentage, and foreign-born people and first-generation natives in penal and charitable institutions. Eventually, this quantitative approach would dominate the domestic investigation. Information in the reports indicates that only occasionally would agents take testimony or interview pertinent parties. Most of the time they collected statistics.[6]

Jenks, likely because of his academic background and investigatory expertise, eventually came to lead or cochair several key endeavors. He and Neill received authorization to continue studies that Neill had previously undertaken as commissioner of labor. Commission associate Frederick C. Croxton had helped with several of these projects. William Wheeler suggested that Jenks also head an investigation to determine the extent of illegal immigration by members of excluded classes. On the basis of this "evasion" study, Jenks was to report on any defects in existing laws. Jenks initially confined his efforts to the Mexican and Canadian borders with the United States and had a preliminary report ready by January 1908.[7]

These endeavors were the extent of the domestic inquiry until December 1907, when the commission established permanent quarters in Washington, D.C., and approved bylaws. The latter, prepared by Lodge, spelled out a number of operating procedures, including the creation of a powerful five-member executive committee. Having representation from each appointment group, it initially was to consider and make recommendations to the full commission on all requested expenditures of over five hundred dollars and could, by unanimous vote, approve those for under five hundred dollars. (The full commission subsequently authorized individual members to spend up to that amount on personal investigations.) The committee also approved the creation of new committees, such as those to investigate "Chinese and Japanese" and "Congestion in Cities." In April 1908, at the suggestion of Charles P. Neill, the commission gave the executive committee plenary power to direct the commission's work, including the making of all other committee appointments, for the remainder of the year. Lodge, Neill, William Dillingham, Benjamin Howell, and William Bennet made up the original executive committee, and Lodge served as its first chair.[8]

Two of the new committees focused on regional studies. In an effort to discern the extent of and sentiment toward Pacific Coast immigration, Jeremiah Jenks devised an extensive investigatory strategy. His agenda called for studying the opportunities for and obstacles faced by recently arrived immigrants, their geographic and industrial distribution, and their social condition. Jenks also intended to survey regional agencies that promoted immigration to determine whether and how they contributed to immigrant settlement. The focus area would stretch from the coast through the states of the intermountain West. The commission eventually opened an office in San Francisco, and to oversee the investigation they hired University of California economist Wesley C. Mitchell, whose interest in money and banking included related labor issues. Mitchell also had worked briefly for the Census Bureau.[9]

Senator Asbury Latimer, along with Representative Bennet and Charles Neill, took charge of a similar examination of southern views on immigration. This had become a particularly contentious issue. Much of the South needed workers, but this did not necessarily mean that the inhabitants wanted any and all types of labor. After conducting its own investigation shortly before, the IRL characterized southerners as having a "deep rooted hostility to the illiterate classes from Southern Europe and a decided preference for Northern Europeans." Native whites did not want the South to become an immigrant dumping ground and did not want another "Negro problem." A resolution by a 1908 immigration convention held at Tampa, Florida, with delegates representing labor, business, and railroads, expressed a desire for white natives above all others and called on Congress to reduce the number of undesirable immigrants. The Virginia legislature expressed concern for the fate of "Anglo-Saxon supremacy" in the face of protracted immigration.[10]

The goals and objectives for the commission's southern investigation paralleled those for the Western study, with a few notable distinctions. In ascertaining regional sentiment for and against new immigrants, including opinions about their regulation or restriction, investigators were to compare past and present arrivals and determine the attitudes of employers and "competing wage workers." "The necessity for more labor and the class of labor that will meet the demands" were considered to be particularly pressing questions, as were those pertaining to social and civic assimilation. The investigation eventually encompassed sixteen states, stretching from Maryland to Texas and reaching as far north as Missouri and Tennessee. When Latimer died, Anselm J. McLaurin took over as committee chair, and the commission hired L. Martin Heard of Elberton, Georgia, to supervise the project. William Bennet believed that it would take six men over a year to gather all of the pertinent information.[11]

The commission granted Lodge permission to hold a hearing on Section 42 of the 1907 Immigration Act, which dealt with steerage accommodations. Amending a similar act of 1882, it specified how space on various decks must be allocated for each passenger, and it set standards for light and ventilation. Certain ambiguities, such as what constituted the main deck, had engendered numerous questions as to the law's effectiveness. On 18 January 1908, the commission heard testimony from P. A. S. Franklin and S. C. Neal, vice president and the legal counsel, respectively, for the International Mercantile Marine Company; Thorndike Spalding, representative of the White Star Line; and U.S. Commissioner of Navigation Eugene T. Chamberlain. These hearings propelled the commission to take a number of additional actions.[12]

In the spring of 1908, Bennet took charge of a full-scale investigation of steerage quarters and treatment of passengers, which was later enlarged to cover all aspects of the immigrant steamship trade. He assigned agents to make several transatlantic trips in the guise of immigrants in order to gain firsthand knowledge. The investigators found that like the immigrants themselves, steerage accommodations could be divided into old and new types. Companies that used the old-style service followed the letter of the law but treated their passengers "as so much freight." Sleeping compartments held up to three hundred people in one large room, with each passenger assigned to a small berth that doubled as a sleeping compartment and a place to store hand baggage. Ships of this sort lacked separate dining facilities, and most immigrants ended up eating in their berths. New steerage resembled second-class accommodations. Passengers enjoyed larger berths in enclosed, cabin-type compartments; designated dining areas; and better washrooms. Equally important, women enjoyed the privacy and security of segregated sleeping accommodations.[13]

Anna Herkner, a clandestine agent who later took charge of compiling the report on steerage conditions, disguised herself as a Bohemian immigrant aboard an old-style vessel. The conditions appalled her; they defied comparison to anything to be found on land. Females suffered particular indignities: "I can not say that any woman lost her virtue on this passage," she reported, "but in making free with the women the men of the crew went as far as possible with out exposing themselves to the danger of punishment." Complaints, she discovered, brought less than satisfactory results. Additionally, the quality and preparation of food was poor. When the bell rang announcing meal time, each passenger rushed to grab a share; tardiness could result in a missed meal. "If steerage passengers act like cattle at meal times," she reported, "it is undoubtedly because they are treated as such." Add to this the filthy toilets and the cold-saltwater washrooms used concurrently by men and women, and the conditions made for a horrible voyage.[14]

This state of affairs did not have to exist. When Herkner traveled on a ship providing new steerage accommodations, she encountered a "plain and simple" version of the facilities and considerations given to cabin passengers. The company divided the steerage deck into staterooms, each with two to four berths, along with hooks for clothes and storage for hand baggage. Men and women were provided with separate quarters, and stewards kept the entire ship clean and neat. Herkner did report that certain Jewish passengers, whose compartment was "distantly removed" from those of the others, complained of anti-Semitism on the crew's part, but the company was the only one that provided a Rabbi-approved special steward to care for the needs of its Jewish passengers.[15]

The commission's investigation had an immediate effect on steerage laws. Following his hearings on Section 42, Lodge introduced a bill to amend the law by adopting more appropriately descriptive language, borrowed in part from British statutes. When the bill reached the House, Bennet drew on his commission research to defend the changes. Ironically, John Burnett also made references to the commission's work when he argued that the Lodge hearings had been nothing more than a ploy to placate steamship company wishes. Breaking with the commission's other pronounced restrictionist, Burnett hoped that the representatives would defeat the proposed changes. Lodge and Bennet persisted, and in the end Congress passed a new steerage bill that provided for more passenger air space than did any previous legislation.[16]

Not all of Bennet's efforts demonstrated his overtly liberal attitude toward immigrants. It was he who reported on alien criminality and suggested a related amendment to the act of 1907. Section 21 allowed for deportation, within three years of their arrival in the United States, of immigrants who were found to be in violation of the law's entry provisions. Bennet wanted the law also to allow for the expulsion of alien convicts, including those presently incarcerated, after they had completed their sentences. The commission postponed consideration of the provision until it had completed more of the overall investigation, but the proposition of such a measure by an avowed antirestrictionist shows the extent to which all members were willing to put aside their predispositions when making policy recommendations.

The response to Bennet's proposal set a precedent for how the commission would deal with the matter of recommendations. Although it was willing to discuss preliminary findings about the workings of existing statutes, such as those governing steerage, the commission generally hesitated when it came to suggesting statutory changes. These would wait until the end of the overall investigation. In the case of Bennet's plan for revising deportation standards, however, it did authorize the creation of a committee to study immigrant criminality. Thus it was left undetermined exactly how the commission would comply with its charge to make pertinent recommendations—whether it would address specific statutes, such as those dealing with steerage, or deal only with broad generalizations.[17]

The commission's recommendations for capital expenditures at various immigration stations, along with the steerage changes, provide an interesting comparison with the commission's reluctance to give premature consideration to exclusionary statutes. William Bennet secured authorization for individual commissioners to examine conditions at stations on the East Coast, and at the same January 1908 meeting at which they declined to take action on Bennet's deportation recommendations, the commissioners did discuss the need for new immigration stations at Baltimore, Boston, and Philadelphia. Lodge had promised customs agent Jeremiah McCarthy that the commission would study the conditions at the Boston facilities, and McCarthy had sent Lodge some related information. The commission then recommended the construction of new buildings at Philadelphia and Boston and ordered an inspection of those at Baltimore. Policy recommendations would have to wait if they dealt with new limitations or restrictions, but they did not necessarily have to do so if they dealt with immigrant treatment.[18]

With most recommendations put on hold, committee work dominated the commission's 1908–1909 activities. The executive committee met for the first time in January 1908 and received Jenks's progress report on evasion and exclusion. The professor reported that he had found evidence that there were criminals among Italian immigrants and that substantial numbers of women were being imported for immoral purposes. On the basis of these preliminary results, Jenks wanted to gather more information. Groups studying prostitution in New York City had collected information on the subject, and the executive committee authorized him to purchase their materials. The committee then approved the appointment of Michael Clayton, theretofore with the Department of Commerce and Labor, to help with the investigation. It also created new committees to study "Immigrant Homes and Employment Agencies," "Chinese and Japanese Immigration," and "Alien Concentration in Cities."[19]

In hiring Clayton the commission demonstrated its commitment to impartiality as well as thoroughness. The executive committee absolved Clayton of all contact with the Department of Commerce and Labor and promised protection against any interference by his former employer. This included legal aid to defend against any charges brought or influenced by Bureau of Immigration officers. As these individuals had responsibility for executing and enforcing the nation's immigration laws, they most certainly would bear the brunt of any criticisms or accusations of dereliction that resulted from the commission's investigation. Given their vested interest, the individuals on the bureau could very well try to taint the results. The executive committee intended that its actions would safeguard Clayton and the other investigators, as well as protect the overall integrity of the commission's work. Ironically, however, the commission later fired Clayton for "not obeying the instructions of members in charge of his work."[20]

A second southern issue aroused significant controversy. In January 1908, Florida Democrat Frank Clark asked for the appointment of a special House committee to look into charges of immigrant peonage in the southern states, and Mississippi Democrat Benjamin Humphreys sought a similar inquest into the treatment of immigrants on cotton plantations in Mississippi and Arkansas. Charges of peonage had been made in the foreign-language press, especially Italian newspapers, and this had hindered legitimate efforts within the identified states to recruit immigrants. The House decided to have the Dillingham Commission look into "the treatment and conditions of work of immigrants" at cotton plantations in the Mississippi Delta; in the states of Mississippi and Arkansas; and at turpentine farms, lumber camps, and railroad camps in Florida, Mississippi, and Louisiana. In order to placate some southern members of Congress, who thought that the resolution singled out their region, the phrase "and other southern states" was changed to simply "and other states." In giving control to the commission, supporters stressed the body's impartiality, but southern critics still objected to outside scrutiny of their region. The commission conducted the investigation using on-site investigations and its subpoena power, and, in William Bennet's opinion, its work led to significant improvements.[21]

When Jenks and Neill reported to the executive committee about their work with the Committee on Statistics in February, they received authorization to have W. Jett Lauck investigate the relationship between wages and immigrant distribution. Shortly thereafter, the commission allocated $15,000 for the acquisition of related census schedules, steamship manifests, occupational information, and comparative data on wages and costs of living. Eventually the scope of Lauck's work was expanded to include investigation of the number of hospital admissions, grouped by ethnicity and reason for admission. In April, Neill requested an appropriation of up to $15,000 more for the Committee on Statistics to investigate "the effectiveness of the various systems of examinations now existing at ports of embarkation and elsewhere abroad" by studying what happened when emigrants arrived in the United States. Neill believed that a review of rejections and questionable cases at American ports would show whether those starting at particular foreign locations had a disproportionate number of entry problems, indicating laxity on the part of overseas examiners. The commission subsequently made such a study part of its comprehensive plan. In part, the plan called for statistical analysis of special appeals made by migrants who had been refused admission to the United States, broken down by port of embarkation.[22]

The comprehensive plan originated with Neill. At his private request, his former Department of Commerce and Labor colleague Frederick Croxton organized various lines of new and existing research into an overall scheme, and the commission approved the resulting proposal in April 1908. Allowing for future modification, the plan divided all of the commission's endeavors into the study of six general topics: economy, sociology, statistics, steamship transport, legislation, and future immigration. Neill believed that this configuration would allow for centralization, efficiency, and coordination between various endeavors, while preventing duplication. For example, those engaged in the regional studies would direct their own inquiries, but their findings would furnish information on immigrant occupations to the economy section and contribute information on states' attitudes toward immigrants to the legislative section.

Neill's scheme gave considerable discretion to the administrative staff, suggesting a growing trust in its ability to collect the most accurate and relevant information. It also indicates that the commissioners did not find it necessary to ensure that the work would validate any particular agenda. The executive committee still would direct the overall investigation, but the secretaries at the Washington office would manage day-to-day operations. Morton Crane took control of accounting and payroll, Croxton served as chief statistician, and William Husband handled administration. Thereafter, they would direct the various studies, receive and integrate all of the fieldwork, and compile the subsequent reports.[23]

In studying economic matters, investigators tried to determine the "effect of immigrants in selected localities," primarily in the North Atlantic states and the Midwest. This would include the effects of each ethnic group's competition with native workers. Despite later contentions to the contrary, the examination of each ethnic group's occupational tendencies did take into account the number of years members of the group had been in the United States. The commission sought answers to such far-reaching questions as whether the "establishment or expansion of industry" would have been "possible without immigrant labor" and whether immigrants had been "used as strike breakers." It also hoped to determine whether immigrants joined trade unions and how those organizations reacted to them. In terms of class interest, then, the commission cannot rightly be accused of catering to the interests of one particular group, such as businesspeople, at the expense of any other.

The commission also sought to determine how the continuing influx of new immigrants affected established workers. Did it contribute to their upward or downward socioeconomic mobility? Investigators would try to answer this question in part by examining the "wages paid new immigrants compared with the wages paid others in the same occupation." If newly arrived foreigners displaced natives, the commissioners wanted to know, what became of the natives? Did they enter more-skilled occupations? Charges had been made that immigrants lowered American standards of living, so investigators planned to compare different immigrant groups' standards of living with those of the natives in selected industries. Field-workers would also try to determine whether members of certain ethnic groups showed a greater tendency than members of other groups to lower local living standards.

The study of economics also would examine various assumptions on the part of natives. Neill thought it would be interesting to discover which immigrant groups contributed to accidents in coal mines, thereby testing the contention that members of some groups caused most of the disasters. According to critics, because members of certain ethnicities were careless and did not know English, they engaged in unsafe practices, thereby engendering unnecessary accidents. Some critics went so far as to say that members of particular groups placed relatively low value on human life. Consideration of these claims was remote from other economic research, but investigators could accomplish it fairly easily by reviewing the findings of existing state and federal agencies.[24]

Sociological study would focus on various aspects of Americanization. The commissioners wanted to know which agencies most affected Americanization and to what extent Americanization was occurring among children and adults, as broken down by ethnicity. They also hoped to determine whether churches, fraternal societies, and other nationality-based groups retarded assimilation. Adults would be polled about citizenship, "appreciation of American institutions," and adoption of American customs. Children would be queried about their ability to speak English, their allegiance to both America and the country of their parents, and intermarriage with those of other ethnic groups. Immigrant education, again on the basis of race or ethnicity, would be examined in terms of school enrollment; physical condition of the pupils; grade school, high school, and college attendance; and language used in schools. The commission hoped to determine whether there was any appreciable difference between foreign-born children and children of alien parentage who were born in the United States.

Commissioners also intended that the sociological study would bring hard evidence to bear on several of the most common allegations made about immigrants. Jeremiah Jenks would complete a study of immigrant congestion in cities. Other investigators would contribute information about immigrant education, criminal activity and incarceration, instances of insanity, and medical tendencies. For each of their statistical groupings, such as criminality or insanity, the commissioners wanted to know literacy rates, which suggests that they intended to test restrictionists' assertions about the benefits of enacting a literacy requirement. They also wanted to show the extent to which members of various ethnic groups had relied on charity within five years of their arrival.[25]

The statistics plan overlapped with the economy and sociology plans. It called for compiling an immense amount of data about virtually every imaginable characteristic of immigrants. In addition to information about ethnicity, national origin, sex, age, and occupation, the commissioners wanted to know how much money immigrants brought with them, their "pro rata distribution" by state, and the number that had been denied admission, grouped according to nationality and cause for rejection. Statistics gathered by foreign governments both would profile each country's emigration and allow for comparisons between those who still lived in the old country and those who had emigrated to the United States. For example, the commissioners wanted to know whether immigrants from each supplying nation were, as a group, more illiterate than the overall population of that nation; if they were, this would indicate that the United States was getting some of the least educated—whom some natives considered the least desirable—of a particular country's people.[26] In typical progressive, goal-oriented fashion, inquiry would supply data, and data, in turn, would influence lawmaking and thereby bring about positive results.

The investigation of steamship transport would focus on various national laws and individual company practices. U.S. Navigation Bureau and shipping company records would reveal the number of passengers carried by each line, broken down by year and by ports of embarkation and arrival. Incorporating the earlier investigation of steerage conditions, this part of the overall report would review each line's sanitation practices, food service, and passenger accommodations. It would also work with the sociological section to determine culpability on the part of any of the steamship companies for transporting aliens of the excluded classes. The commission also hoped to study the practices of ticket agents.[27]

The legislative digest work, foreseen as a relatively brief endeavor, involved the straightforward task of creating a compendium of domestic and foreign laws and reports. Materials gathered during the commission's European investigation would provide a survey of different governments' attitudes toward emigration and immigration. In addition, the legislative digest would provide a history of U.S. immigration and trace the evolution of corresponding statutes. This and some of the information from foreign reports would overlap with the reports of the statistical section.[28]

Neill included an examination of the prospects for future immigration in the plan in case the commission was asked to recommend legislative changes. If its suggestions were to be used to address coming needs, "it would be well to secure information concerning the probable and possible immigration of the future." In the absence of "obstacles not now existing," new immigrants would likely come from eastern and southern Europe, southern Asia, and perhaps India. Older sources would continue to supply some immigrants, but that migration would be "natural rather than forced as during earlier periods." The distinction between natural and forced immigration was not clarified, but natural immigration, undoubtedly the best kind, was that of migrants who had not been recruited by steamship companies or employers and who had not come as the result of foreign governments' deportation of undesirable types.[29]

Plans for compiling information with which to assess the prospects for future immigration shows the commission's acceptance of contemporary ideas about race. The study would use an elaborate forty-nationality classification system that emphasized accepted notions of innate distinctions among people. The commission went even further when it suggested separating the groups into "Racial Grand Divisions" according to the practice of the Immigration Service, which produced some dubious associations. In the Slavic category, for example, the expected Croatians, Bosnians, and Slovaks would be lumped together with Russians, Jews, and Bohemians. Spanish and Portuguese people went into the Iberic group, but so too did Syrians. The latter's close geographic neighbors, Armenians and Turks, were placed in the catch-all category "Other." Northern Italians made it into the Celtic category, but their southern countryfolk were classified as Iberic. The criteria for classification, obviously neither ethnic nor geographic, was not made clear. The commission, with its penchant for objectivity, foresaw then creating an exact immigrant classification system, an effort that resulted in the final report's volume entitled *Dictionary of Races*.[30]

Adoption of the comprehensive plan led to the creation of a host of new committees and resulted in several new hires. As called for in the sociology section of the plan, the commission prepared to study immigrants' children, both foreign-born and native-born. Agents under the direction of Commission Superintendent Roland Faulkner would spend the next year researching existing records and gathering new information at selected schools. Another committee prepared to examine medical records and charitable organizations. Upon executive committee recommendation the commission also commenced preparation of a digest of foreign laws and began collecting information about competition between immigrants and other wage earners as called for in the economics section. Eventually, at Neill's suggestion, the statistics committee took control of the competition inquiry.[31]

Seasoned investigator Jeremiah Jenks took charge of the new endeavors. Armed with a $5,000 appropriation, he, Lodge, and Bennet began a study of distributing agencies. Plans called for investigation of the padrone system, immigrant banks, and assisting organizations; this research helped to determine where immigrants went and how they reached their final destinations. The executive committee then placed the same three men in charge of the Committee on Criminality, directing them to "thoroughly study the immigration of criminals and recommend some plan for excluding criminals." The commissioners' thereafter decided to combine this effort with Jenks's earlier study of resident-alien criminals. Since he previously had found that a high number of Italian criminals were illegally entering the United States, the commissioners decided to pay special attention to that ethnic group. Jenks and William Wheeler also received authorization to investigate San Francisco officials' alleged malfeasance in the admission of Chinese immigrants, the target of general exclusion since 1882.[32]

During the summer of 1908 the executive committee notably enlarged the scope of the overall investigation. Until that time the only places or regions designated for specific inquiry were the South and the Pacific Coast. Charles Neill proposed that commission superintendents Roland Faulkner and W. Jett Lauck study the effects of immigration in all states not included in either of those two investigations, using the same criteria and methodology. The executive committee envisioned that their work, funded by the appropriation for the general investigation and operated from the Washington headquarters, would compile much of the material needed to complete the planned study of economic effects. The $50,000 allocation for this task was by far the largest approved by the commission.[33]

Lauck formulated standard procedures for combining the economic and general investigations. He and Faulkner, in consultation with the central office, would assign trained agents to selected localities, where the agents would conduct an immigrant survey. The standard data-collection method involved distributing so-called individual slips, which asked for the person's name, occupation, sex, age, marital status, country of birth, and "race." After an initial review of the summary findings that resulted, the superintendents, working with Husband and Croxton, would decide what other information should be gathered and how best to coordinate with those working on special topics. In some communities they would obtain information about immigrant unionization; other places would be better suited for the study of charitable organizations or family structure. This research would detail the social and industrial ramifications of immigration. Lauck believed that fifteen trained agents with fifteen assistants could canvas several large cities in a year, and the standardization would make it easier to organize and report the findings.[34]

By the fall of 1908 the commission had sixteen working committees costing $182,500. Jenks sought an author to write a history of immigration, clerks feverishly prepared the schedules, and recently hired examiners began the laborious task of reviewing their reports. The commission hired twenty extra tabulators for the Washington office and shortly thereafter moved all office work to that facility. Frederick Croxton and Dr. J. A. Hill were appointed official statisticians. Commission minutes report progress being made in the processing of census data, but only the processing for Rhode Island had been completed. Worried about finishing the other forty-four states, commissioners allowed Neill to explore the possibility of establishing some kind of joint effort with the Bureau of the Census. Still, despite their concerns, commissioners concluded in mid-November that "several lines of work" would be "completed in time for presentation to Congress at the next session."[35]

The commission also faced fiscal obligations. Neill and others realized that they could not spend indefinitely. In their effort to cut overall expenditures, they decided to discontinue the separate Pacific Coast and southern investigations. That work would proceed under the direction of the central office, where it would be merged with Faukner and Lauck's general investigation. The combined inquiry would pay particular attention to immigrants in industries and industrial communities. The study of certain topics, such as immigrants in agriculture, would continue to be divided by location, and senior staffers would still collect information on special regional problems, such as those in the South.[36]

Urgency did not diminish the commission's sense that its domain was exclusive. In 1908 New York governor Charles Evans Hughes appointed a state immigration commission to study immigrant welfare and employment conditions, and that commission now wanted to coordinate with the Dillingham group. Worried about duplication of effort, the New Yorkers met with Jenks and William Husband to talk about sharing the U.S. commission's information about immigrant homes in New York City. Because the commission was empowered to report to Congress, the commissioners decided that any preliminary disclosure of its findings would be inappropriate. Once Congress had received the report, suitable arrangements could be worked out with other agencies. The commissioners also decided not to share the group's "blanks and schedules" and opted not to use Harvard University students to collect data.[37]

Plans called for the commission to finish its work in March 1910, but by the spring of 1909, some in Congress were wanting an early report. Fearing an invasion by Asia's "yellowman" and the dwellers of Europe's "cesspools," South Carolina Democrat Frank Gary presented a resolution requesting a brief summary of the commission's activities and expenditures. He also wanted to know how long it would take to complete the investigation. In agreeing to Gary's request, Dillingham promised that the commission's findings, "authentic" and "scientifically secured," would address many of his concerns and help Congress to draft appropriate legislation. Jenks, Bennet, and Dillingham then prepared the requested summary.[38]

In addition to summarizing its activities and expenses, the commission asked Congress for $300,000 to complete its work. Funding originally had come from the head-tax supported Immigration Fund—a designated allotment that recently had been discontinued (but the tax itself remained in place)—at least in part because legislators wanted more control over the commission's spending. This necessitated that the commission use specifically appropriated general revenue for any additional expenses. Despite vocal opposition, such as Kentucky Democrat J. Swagar Sherley's castigation of the commission for its "extravagant expenditures," Congress approved a smaller allocation of $150,000. Along with the appropriation came the expectation that the investigators would meet their March 1910 deadline. These and other concerns about time and money would soon lead to questions about the quality of the commission's work.[39]

Although the commission later described the appropriation as "entirely inadequate," it sought to comply with the imposed limitations. On 30 June 1909 it ended all field investigations except authorized "supplementary and special work." Upon completion of their current assignments all agents were to move to Washington, where they and forty newly hired clerks would help with statistical tabulation. As soon as possible the New York City office would be consolidated with the one in Washington, D.C., and the West Coast office would conclude its operation by 15 May. Various reports, including those on peonage, steerage, and anthropology, were assigned to particular staffers for final preparation. The commissioners thought that by taking these steps they would able to finish data compilation by 1 November, which would allow them to make a final report to the next Congress during its first regular session.[40]

All of these steps toward termination, however, did not preclude the pursuit of new endeavors and the extension of old ones. The commission found plenty of opportunities for so-called special work. It granted Wheeler and Dillingham the authority to investigate immigration conditions in Hawaii and gave Wheeler and Jenks permission to conduct a similar inquiry in Canada. Until 1 September fieldwork continued on the West Coast, primarily the study of "Japanese and Hindus." The commission also approved Bennet's request for an examination of immigrants in agriculture, especially those living in "colonies," or settlements composed of a single nationality. They then authorized additional funds for wrapping up that investigation by the end of the year. The peonage investigation also received an additional allocation. By January 1910, the commission's total expenses had reached $611,000, and there were more to come.[41]

Unforeseen problems in tabulating the great amount of already collected material made it impossible to comply with the 1 March deadline. At the commission's bidding, Dillingham asked Congress for an additional $125,000. None of the new appropriation would go toward fieldwork, no commissioner would receive compensation for service rendered after 1 March, and a final report would have to be ready when Congress reconvened during the first week of December. In lobbying for both the extension and the additional funding, the commissioners argued that the public would be the great loser if a considerable amount of valuable information went unused. The original act had not placed any limits on the investigation but had allowed for a far-reaching inquiry, and the congressionally imposed time and money restrictions were "out of proportion" to the volume of data that had been collected.[42]

The most heated debate over Dillingham's request took place in the House. Speaking for those who supported an additional appropriation, Minnesota Republican James A. Tawney asserted that pervious congressional funding had allowed for the completion of "very necessary" fieldwork and that the commission now needed more money for the organization and preparation of a final report. Others were not so sure. Adolph Sabath, an Illinois Democrat and devoted antirestrictionist, worried about "malicious and cowardly" libel against Jews. Calling the entire project a "complete waste of time," Arkansas Democrat Robert B. Macon accused the investigators of fiscal malfeasance, especially in the case of their "junket" to Europe. He later introduced a resolution calling for a joint committee to review the commission's expenditures. Even Commissioner John Burnett, who had not voted when the commission decided to ask for more funds, had concerns about further delay. Although he disputed Macon's accusations, he did believe that the extension might be a political ruse to hold off passage of a restriction bill during an election year.

Commissioner Bennet stridently defended his colleagues and himself against charges of fiscal malfeasance. He acknowledged that the commission had spent $650,000, but he and the other conferees who had created the commission back in 1907 had concurrently raised the head tax specifically to cover future investigatory expenses. The increased entrance fee had added over $4 million to the Immigration Fund. After the commission's expenses were subtracted, the 1907 act had increased "the amount in the Treasury by about $3,300,000." As to the disputed European "junket," it had cost the relatively small amount of $20,000. Others joined Bennet in defending both the commission's conduct and its expenditures. Representative Tawney argued that to fail to ensure proper completion of the investigation would be to "throw away" work that had cost over $650,000. Such pleas were to no avail: the House voted against the additional appropriation for the commission.[43]

The Senate proved to be a bit more receptive after Dillingham placated critics by promising that this would be the last appropriation, but the House still refused to budge. Several representatives, including Commissioner Burnett, vented their anger about the continued delays. He argued that the work should have been concluded and added that it could be finished by the end of the session. Pennsylvania Republican Thomas S. Butler contended that the investigation had gone too far afield, exceeding its original intent. William Bennet countered that in fulfilling their charge he and the other commissioners had put aside their personal views and had sought facts wherever they might be found; the public was now entitled to a full report.

The House and Senate eventually agreed to give the commission an extension and an additional appropriation to complete its work, but not without considerable wrangling. First, a conference committee accepted Senate-imposed conditions, which were essentially submitted by Dillingham. The House twice refused to accept this arrangement and amended the conference report to provide an additional $65,000 and to set the completion date at 1 May. Thinking that the investigation had taken up enough time and had cost enough money, a majority wanted to bring it to a hasty close. Finally, after concluding that it was best to break the House-Senate stalemate, the representatives reversed themselves, allocating $125,000 for the completion of the work and setting December 1910, when Congress reconvened, as the time for the commission's termination. Dillingham and his colleagues now had just over nine months to complete their task.[44]

Despite these clashes with Congress and concerns about whether the commission would be able to finish its work in a timely fashion, the extensive domestic investigation bears witness to both the panel's integrity and its commitment to breadth and depth. The commissioners should have realized that the goal of their far-flung attempt to address any and every immigrant issue exceeded the realm of possibility, but however infeasible was compliance with wording of their charge, they literally had tried to achieve it. In three years of work the members had made a concerted effort to collect the fullest and most reliable information. They had studied virtually every type of immigrant, and their quest for relevant facts had taken them to almost every conceivable milieu, from city to country, from factory to farm, from the Atlantic to the Pacific. Their greatest fault was not myopia, but rather their inclination to try to do too much. Had they had more time and more money, they assuredly would have done even more. One investigator, reconciling himself to the fact that Congress would not pay for additional fieldwork, visited Michigan at his own expense; it was the only state to which he had not yet traveled.[45] Such was the commission's determination "to make a full inquiry."

One of the strongest testimonials in favor of the commission's work came from Representative Augustus Gardner, an avowed restrictionist who had ardently opposed the commission's creation. In February 1910, as the House argued about further funding, Gardner asserted that the investigators had "done most valuable work." "It now remains," he continued, "to put the report in shape, where legislators and the press and the public can use this vast mass of valuable facts that have been acquired." William Bennet's contribution drew special praise. Although Gardner and Bennet, who had served together on the Committee on Immigration, disagreed about the need for more restrictions, Gardner believed that his colleague had "made a profound study of immigration questions, had devoted more faithful and laborious work to it than any man on earth."[46] The opportunity to observe the ramifications of his service to the commission, and that of its other, equally committed participants, would have to wait until the investigators finished their report.

CHAPTER FIVE

"Craniometry"

Franz Boas and the Study of Immigrant Physiology

IN MARCH 1908 THE DILLINGHAM COMMISSION undertook one of its most intriguing investigations when it agreed to sponsor anthropologist Franz Boas's physiological study of immigrant assimilation. Progressive reformers frequently looked to highly trained experts, often university professors, for definitive answers. Here was a classic case of that practice.

America's premier anthropologist, Franz Boas believed that "changes in bodily form" would reveal the extent to which new immigrants had come to emulate the so-called American type, which developed "more rapidly and more favorably than the European." To prove his point, Boas wanted to take physical measurements of 120,000 immigrants and their children. He anticipated that the cumulative data would "settle once and for all the question whether the immigrants from southern Europe and from eastern Europe are and can be assimilated by our people." The issue's importance could "hardly be overstated," and the proof provided by "modern anthropological methods" would be unequivocal.[1]

Observers considered these questions to be of the utmost importance. William Williams, commissioner of immigration at New York, worried that a glut of undesirable immigrants would "dilute and debase the elements which in the past have made this country great." "It seems to me," echoed Immigration Restriction League (IRL) vice president Joseph Lee, "that the largest and far the most important as to the causes of adverse social conditions is the problem of race selection." Charities could and should keep the less fit alive, but all feeble-minded women should be "subjected to custodial restraint" to keep them from procreating. These measures offered only partial solutions, however. Something had to be done about immigration. Lee adhered to the common belief that inferior stock yielded inferior results and that assimilation would not eliminate racial traits. Still, he saw the value of a proper study that compared these immigrants with other Americans. Such research could evaluate the persistence of moral and mental heredity and determine each group's ability to serve a democratic society. The answers, Lee reasoned, would help in the protection of American citizenship and in the selection of "the wives of our grandsons and the husbands of our granddaughters."[2]

Boas agreed that such an investigation was needed, but his pioneering work dismissed many of the predominant anthropological presumptions, including ideas about racial classification and race's effect on social and political equality. Anthropologists and others often arranged the races hierarchically in a way that supported the perceived power of the dominant, or higher ranking, groups and then used this stratification to justify public policy decisions about matters such as who could enter the United States. Boas dismissed the underlying notion of static "racial types," believing instead that members of ethnic goups could change over time under the influence of both heredity and environment. The key to understanding such variances was physical measurement and documentation. Boas had already completed limited studies of school children and American Indians, and now he would now turn his attention to southern and eastern Europeans.[3] If his ideas proved to be true, they would significantly weaken restrictionist arguments for excluding certain types of immigrants.

A combination of personal and professional developments had aroused Boas's interest in studying immigration. Himself a German Jew, born at Westphalia in 1858, he had come to the United States in 1887. Difficulties in finding work as an ethnologist exposed the young man to American anti-Semitism, which had recently begun to intensify because of the influx of eastern European Jews. Boas eventually joined the staff at Clark University in Atlanta, where he saw racism being directed against African Americans and where he worked to develop anthropometric techniques—ways of measuring the human body to determine racial differences. Boas continued in these endeavors after moving to Columbia University in 1896, and by the time he sought work with the Dillingham Commission, he had merged his faith in methodological objectivity with his criticism of theories of racial inferiority.[4]

The plan Boas submitted to the commission called for physical evaluation of selected individuals to test for "assimilation of stability of type" and "changes in the characteristics of development." Determining a particular group's level of assimilation would require taking three head measurements and observing the hair and eye color of representative individuals. Any changes in their rate of development would be ascertained by noting body size, muscle strength, and signs of physiological maturity; where appropriate, this would involve recording the age of "the eruption of the teeth," the onset of puberty, and the beginning of senility. Analysis of this data would allow researchers to set development standards for different ages.

Demonstrating the progressive faith that a thorough investigation would yield the desired results, Boas initially wanted to study all of "the divergent racial types" that had migrated to the United States from Europe. He proposed dividing them into five ethnic categories: North Europeans, East Europeans, Central Europeans, South Europeans (particularly southern Italians), and Russian Jews. Each of these groups would be divided into categories determined by sex, fifteen developmental stages, and four classifications based on arrival status: currently arriving immigrants, returning immigrants, children of immigrants, and immigrant residents. Such detailed division would result in six hundred (5 x 2 x 15 x 4) classes of individuals. To measure a minimum of two hundred people in each class the investigation would require at least 120,000 subjects.

Interestingly, Boas's five categories included only European immigrants. There is no evidentiary explanation for why he left out Asians, especially in light of the recent controversy over Japanese immigrants in San Francisco, but practicality might offer the best explanation. Europeans made up the largest number of immigrants and attracted most of the current attention, especially on the East Coast where Boas lived and worked.

When complete, the study would show whether new immigrants, southern and eastern Europeans, "became subjected rapidly to the same influences which have determined the physique of the Americans." An estimated twenty observers would obtain the requisite data from returning and newly arriving immigrants, already-settled aliens, and their children. The taking of measurements at both Ellis Island and New York City schools would progress rapidly, but it would require more time and effort to amass information about adult immigrants already settled in the United States. Results would be compared with previously collected data, which had shown that Americans "developed more rapidly and more favorably" than their old-country counterparts and that, at least in the case of northern Europeans, people of the same nationality demonstrated "distinctions in type" on different sides of the Atlantic. Boas anticipated a year's work at an estimated cost of $19,500, but if "a considerable amount of explanation should be necessary to get the subjects to consent to be measured," more staff time would be required, which would up the cost.

After accessing all of the material, Boas would be able to answer five questions related to assimilation. First, did the "physical development and racial character" of immigrants differ from that of their countryfolk who remained in their native land? Second, were returning immigrants different from those who had stayed in America? Third, how much did the development of immigrant children growing up in the United States deviate from that of children in their home country (evidently assuming that the latter's development could be established with significant certainty), and how did their juvenile development compare with that of American children? Fourth, did the development of U.S.-born children of immigrant parents have a greater tendency than that of foreign-born children to approach the development of children of native parents? And last, how did "mixed marriages" affect the development of the progeny of those unions?[5]

Boas presented his idea to Jeremiah Jenks and, stressing the need for a full study, asked about the feasibility of carrying it out under the auspices of the Dillingham Commission. The two men had been discussing the possibility of some sort of collaboration, and Boas believed that the commission's investigatory powers would enhance his access to subjects. He already anticipated that New York City's Board of Education and Bureau of Municipal Research would cooperate by providing admittance to public and parochial schools with large numbers of foreign-born students, and the commission could help get observers stationed at Ellis Island. This would expedite the work, which would be most valuable only if it was complete: if the requested funds "exceed what can be undertaken by the Commission, the only way of cutting down would be to reduce the number of classes . . . but any reduction of the scheme as here presented would seriously reduce the usefulness of the investigation." Given this concern, Boas hoped that the commission would make a hasty decision, as "no time should be lost with the organization of the work."[6]

"The members of the Commission were very much interested in your proposition," Jenks wrote to Boas after presenting his plan to his colleagues in early April, "and I think it very likely that it will go thru [sic]." Yet there loomed a potential problem. One member, described only as "influential," did not believe that Boas's plan had adequate connection to the commission's other, more sociologically oriented, endeavors. The unnamed member also wondered whether Boas would properly address the effects of environment on the various immigrant groups. The mystery man most likely was William Bennet, who may have worried that Boas's study would yield anti-immigrant findings. In any case, Jenks did not believe that these objections would result in a defeat of the proposal, but he did suggest that Boas draft a rejoinder.[7]

In his rejoinder, Boas explained that the commission could make better judgments about immigrant assimilation if it had information about the physical as well as the social influences of the American environment. Previous studies had confirmed that the children of northwestern European immigrants were physically superior to the immigrants themselves, but without data such as that which Boas planned to collect, the universality of this phenomenon could not be known. "One of the important things that we also do not know," he explained, is "how far there may be an inherent tendency to slower and less perfect assimilation among the east and south European." The question of environmental determinism was open for debate. Boas believed that social surroundings influenced assimilation; his study would show whether those surroundings' ability to affect change extended to physical characteristics. It would prove conclusively whether the differences between groups were of social character or "really of racial character."[8]

The commission ultimately approved the Boas investigation, but the approval process was not without complications. On 24 April it appeared to have authorized $25,000 for the project, but the commissioners later determined that the vote had not conformed to the commission's bylaws. A subsequent vote resulted in a four-to-four tie. Representative Bennet, again showing uncertainty about the project, then requested that he be allowed to change his vote to nay, thereby defeating the proposal, but instead, the commission left the entire matter pending. Those against the proposal did not believe that the results would be conclusive enough to warrant such a large expenditure. While the measurements would no doubt be accurate, the detractors thought the analysis would be disputed to the point of having little practical value.[9]

Even Jenks, who disagreed with his more critical colleagues, had started to have doubts about the project. He had talked to anthropologists at Cornell University, and although they had given generally favorable opinions, they wondered about Boas's assertion that he could show the extent of assimilation definitively. Jenks believed that the commission would need more information on three points: Did Boas have enough material for each ethnic group to compare immigrants to their countryfolk in their native lands? To whom in the United States would Boas compare the immigrants; who were the American "home type"? And what professionals would help in the investigation? Jenks wanted Boas to prepare an immediate reply so it could be presented to the commission for final resolution. He must have still supported the idea, for he noted that he might "venture to write a brief introduction for the whole investigation."[10]

Boas's response combined the scientist's certainty with the scholar's obfuscation. Over the past twenty years, he explained, anthropologists had collected materials throughout Europe. France, Sweden, and southern Italy were particularly well represented, and the statistics included measurements of schoolchildren. This would allow comparisons with both adult and juvenile types in the United States. Dr. C. Ward Crampton, an expert in the problem of the "correlation of mental and physical development," would oversee the assessment of children. He had previously done physiological studies in New York City schools. As for the American type, Boas dodged the question by saying that his study would compare immigrants and their children with the "home type" found in their native countries. He never did say how he could prove that immigrants were becoming more like the "American type" he had mentioned in his original proposal. He did assert that America's "more favorable conditions" produced accelerated physical development.

Boas also pared down his original proposal. Time was running short, and he doubted that he could finish the full investigation by his previously suggested ten-month deadline. Noting that his original projections could be modified to fit in with the commission's other endeavors, he suggested that the commission entrust him and Dr. Crampton "with the elaboration of a detailed plan of work" that would clarify some of the points he had made in his earlier submissions. At a cost of $1,000, this preliminary report would explain more clearly the problems to be considered, detail the data-collection procedures, provide an overall synopsis of the project's methodology, and show "what incidental results the anthropometric investigation will yield."[11]

Hoping that the preliminary study would indicate the possible results of a more thorough investigation, allow time for the perfection of plans for the fuller study's implementation, and provide a better idea of the overall cost, the commission agreed to sponsor the abbreviated investigation. Boas enthusiastically went to work. Telling Jenks, to whom the commission had given oversight, that they had no time to lose, the anthropologist promptly planned a trip to Ellis Island and arranged for the services of an anthropologically trained woman physician to measure female subjects. Jenks made postage arrangements and provided a letter of introduction requesting "that every person who is asked to give assistance in this investigation will do so freely and cheerfully, feeling that he is thereby not merely assisting the Commission but also rendering a genuine service to the public."[12]

The craniological study produced impressive early results, leading Boas to conclude that "the investigation will be even more fruitful than I anticipated." This meant that it would be more pro-immigrant. In May and June 1908, Boas and Dr. Crampton assembled their researchers, standardized their recording forms, and began making examinations. They quickly collected about thirteen thousand measurements, primarily of Italians, Slavs, Scots, and eastern European Jews. Given the belief that adult development depended largely on childhood conditions, the investigators tried to ascertain whether the American milieu accelerated or retarded development as compared with the effect of the home-country milieu on the same type in Europe. Observations of fourteen-year-old eastern European Jews indicated that the American environment had a positive effect on physical development and growth. The longer immigrant parents had lived in the United States, the more advanced the educational level of their children.[13] The salient physical improvements, revealed in this phase of the study and later, may have been the result of nothing more than the effects of a better diet, but the findings spoke well of the immigrant subjects. Children of American-born parents did pass through school more rapidly, but their prowess seemed to be the result primarily of social conditions.

Preliminary results also validated the need for expanding the study. No work had yet been done among the "poorer classes of children," such as those in Children Aid Society schools and in the "retarded classes" in elementary schools—children who were more than two years behind the normal grade for their age. These investigations presumably could yield different results. The changes recorded thus far "in the direction of decided assimilation" might merely reflect the fact that individuals in the study had been able to live in "favorable surroundings" and had given their children a good education. Any definitive study must also examine children in the medium and lower social strata. Results might also vary considerably by ethnicity.

Therefore, Boas wanted to enlarge the study, incorporating the idea of class and shifting its focus to younger and underprivileged children. Venues would include public and private schools, boards of health, settlement houses, athletic clubs, reformatories, asylums, and the Ellis Island Immigration Station. Boas, who had been overseas during the summer of 1908, also had plans for collecting comparative information in Europe, using materials already amassed by the Dresden Dental Hygiene Institution and doing additional work in Galicia and Naples. Boas believed that the collection of European statistics, which would be "strictly parallel to those taken in America," would cost $5,000 to $6,000. Depending on the final scope of the overall investigation, his estimates now ranged from $25,000 to $40,000.[14]

The commission reacted favorably to Boas's preliminary findings, and it concluded at its November meeting that the investigation should go forward "on the larger scale," but it appropriated only an additional $1,000. The allocation's paucity displeased Boas, who complained about both inadequate remuneration for his time commitment and the need to fund various extraordinary expenses, such as presents brought to immigrant children. "These expenditures are necessary," Boas explained, "because without them the people would probably not submit to measurement." Jenks explained that key members of the commission, including Henry Cabot Lodge, had been absent from the meeting at which the allocation was determined, and he promised to try to get more funding. The commission eventually allocated another $5,000 and raised Boas's stipend and allowed him to hire assistants. Boas wanted more money, as he would throughout the work, but the shortfalls did not dampen his enthusiasm. Quite the contrary, his requests for funding indicate his commitment to the project and the importance he attached to it.[15]

Personnel matters did try Boas's patience. The technical nature of his enterprise necessitated the use of specially trained bilingual assistants, who were often hard to find. Obtaining the services of a competent statistician proved to be especially difficult. William Bennet recommended a woman of his acquaintance, but she did not report to work, and Boas had to recruit someone else. He eventually hired his former student Leo Frachtenberg and customs house worker Olea Franche. Having two competent aids promised to speed up the work, but Boas nonetheless worried about the detrimental effects of the three-week delay. In an effort to get better cooperation from his subjects, he also requested badges for his aids and tried to hire a suitable Italian assistant to help with measuring Italian families.[16]

The added appropriation allowed Boas to carry his investigation into grammar schools and to collect measurements from southern Italians. Continued observations suggested that "changes in the second generation are not confined to changes in the rapidity of development, but we find also a change in type indicating apparently an approach to the American type." The term *American type* still had not been officially defined, but Boas must have been referring to Americans who had northern European ancestry and who had lived in the United States since birth. European Jewish children growing up in the United States appeared to be losing their foreign physique. Observations of young children in grammar schools corroborated other evidence of this type of change. Boas's findings based on these early results offered a challenge to those who feared that the infusion of "immigrant blood" would dilute "the American type."[17]

The search for suitable subjects led Boas far and wide. In early 1909 he and Dr. Crampton approached the headmaster at the Newark Academy, the Columbia University registrar, the superintendent of New York's Ethical Cultural School, and various public school officials. To locate an appropriate sample for some ethnic groups, Boas also contemplated going to Ellis Island. Some institutions, such as the Newark Academy, had participated in similar studies, but elsewhere he had to make initial contact. Boas asked each administrator to distribute forms asking students or their parents about their ethnic background and immigration history. A second form indicated the type of measurements he wanted to take. Given his special interest in the rate of physical development, Boas took care to explain that it would be "necessary to observe the children stripped" and that this should only pose a problem in situations where the children were not "accustomed to gymnasium tests." Experience showed that three observers could measure about forty-five students per hour with "minimal disturbance."[18]

Such queries met with mixed success. F. C. Lewis of the Ethical Cultural School expressed willingness to participate and asked only for an official letter describing the investigation. Administrators at Columbia's Teachers College, conversely, declined to allow measuring at the private Horace Mann School, citing parental sensitivity. The Columbia's university registrar also declined to allow the use of his office for the recruitment of students. Although he had accommodated an earlier commission request for information, likely about immigrants in education, the registrar had no way to access students except to call them into the office on an individual basis. Perhaps, he suggested, Boas could achieve the same end by contacting every student in the university directory through the mail.[19]

As the investigation progressed, Boas struggled with the issue of whether to classify subjects by ethnicity or nationality. The commissioners intended to bifurcate their findings for both Germans and Italians throughout their report, dividing each into northern and southern subgroups, but Boas decided to use a more sophisticated system based on town, province, and nationality. He agreed to designate Scandinavians simply by country although Commission Secretary William Husband thought even that division was superfluous to anyone except to the people themselves. Poles posed a special problem given the absence of a sovereign Poland and the separation of Polish people into several states. In an effort to resolve some of these problems, the commission tried, but failed, to have race substituted for nationality as a classification in the upcoming national census.[20]

In addition to pursuing his interest in the retardation or acceleration of the development of various European types after immigrants' arrival in the United States, Boas took up the study of the physical effects of intermarriage between natives and immigrants. He hoped to show whether such unions had deleterious or favorable results. Would "the continued influence of the American environment combined with the progressive intermixture of racial types" produce greater homogeneity in areas that had received large numbers of immigrants, or would it increase "physical diversity"? When he broached the subject to Jenks, seeking to use in his research the statistical information the commission was gathering on intermarriage using census reports, Jenks encouraged him to meet with the staff in Washington.[21]

Jenks did have to clip the anthropologist's wings on one matter. In April, Boas wanted to report his findings on the head dimensions of eastern European Jews to the National Academy of Science. Boas had found that individual immigrants underwent significant physical change that became more pronounced the longer they lived in the United States. Although he was appreciative of Boas's excitement about sharing this finding with his professional colleagues, Jenks had serious reservations about premature release of the commission's conclusions. Congressmen "had expressed themselves pretty strongly several times regarding the confidential nature of our work and regarding the jealousy which Congress always has of having the results of such investigation presented to it first." Jenks suggested that Boas prepare a draft of his intended remarks and send them to William Dillingham, seeking permission to make them public. Boas thereafter abandoned his presentation plans.[22]

In early March 1909, Jenks and Boas had to temper their enthusiasm in the face of fiscal reality. Congress had cut the commission's budget and mandated that it finish its work by 1 March 1910. For Boas this meant that he would not receive any additional funding except what was needed for tabulating the results. Jenks urged him to concentrate on the groups theretofore covered so as "to get a sufficient number of measurements . . . to give reasonably trustworthy results." If they proved to be "interesting and important," more funds might be available to facilitate the study of one or two more groups. While Jenks doubted that this would happen, he nonetheless believed that even a limited anthropological study would make a valuable addition to the commission's report.[23]

Boas accepted the need to be "exceedingly economical" in the use of both time and money, but he also tried to make sure that the commission appreciated both his difficulties, especially with personnel, and the importance of his work. Boas had almost finished gathering data on eastern European Jews, which involved fourteen classes with sixteen age groups, and the work on southern Italians was progressing satisfactorily. Findings about the latter did concern him, given the poor development of southern Italians living in New York City, but he hoped to test his findings by making comparisons with people in other locations. Boas believed that by 1 July he would have enough material "to draw unassailable conclusions" about the effects of the American environment on southern Italians and eastern European Jews. He still wanted to get measurements from members of the third generation, the immigrants' grandchildren, and of other ethnic groups. The study would not be of the scale originally suggested, but "so far as to show definitively what becomes physically of the immigrants into our country," it would give more important results than the investigators "were originally justified in anticipating."[24]

Despite financial constrictions, or perhaps sensing impending closure of the project, Boas did not slacken his frenetic pace. He finished tabulation of the Russian-Jewish statistics, began working on those for Bohemians, and still hoped to collect sufficient material on northern Scots, all the while complaining that material was accumulating so quickly that he needed another clerk. He was being as economical as possible, he told Jenks, but speed, not savings, was the operative priority. Jenks also wanted the work done quickly and hoped that everything would be done by 1 July 1909. By the end of June, Boas was completing the fieldwork, laying off observers, and redistributing others to meet the most pressing needs, especially the collection of more measurements from Scots, Bohemians, and Italians.[25]

Boas did not meet the 1 July deadline, perhaps because he took a month's vacation, but his subordinates continued to collect pertinent data. He and Jenks even discussed extending the anthropological investigation to the Pacific Coast. This might have included the study of Asians, but there was no specific mention of that possibility. By the end of the summer, researchers had amassed enough information about Jews, but the accumulation of Italian, Bohemian, and Scot data would take a little longer. Arrangements went slowly, making mid-October a more realistic target for completion. Given the commission's 1 March deadline, Boas feared that he would not have his findings ready in time for meaningful inclusion in the final report. He vainly hoped that the commission would see its way clear to giving him more clerks and to paying for the assistance of his longtime personal secretary.[26]

"Tabulation of my material is going on," Boas reported to the commission, "but not as rapidly as I would like. The results, however, are very striking." As he had suspected, the physical characteristics of members of studied groups were different among children born in the United States. Cephalic ratios of cranium length to width showed that Jewish children born in the United States had longer and narrower heads than those who had been born overseas. In the case of Italians, who were "excessively long-headed," findings for children of both sexes over five years old showed that the variance was in the other direction. Combining the data on changes in both Jewish and Italian head shape, Boas concluded that immigrants' children, in only the first generation, took on characteristics more typical of those he associated with native Americans. The American environment seemed to be having a positive influence on immigrants and their children, rather than immigrant groups affecting that environment negatively.[27]

These preliminary findings, presented to the commission in December 1909, convinced Boas that his investigation would "bring about a radical change in our conception of racial stability," one that would validate belief in the powers of American assimilation. He based this conclusion on a completed analysis of his statistics for Jews and a partial analysis of those for Italians, Bohemians, and Scots. A large amount of work remained to be done, and some questions awaited future consideration. The team had to compile and put in order information gathered during the previous year, and Boas had not even begun, for example, to assess the effects of rural environments on immigrants; nor had he and his team "touched upon the all important question of race mixture." Boas also hoped to make a similar study of the same races in their native lands.[28]

The commission received the preliminary anthropological report in December 1909, and the commissioners were "very much pleased" with it, but they did not pass judgment on its "scientific value." The commission did receive approval for printing the report and distributing it to Congress. Jeremiah Jenks, who had oversight responsibility, had to put a few sentences in more proper form, but otherwise he found nothing wrong with the report. William Husband, who handled the administrative details at the commission's Washington office, pronounced it to be "intensely interesting." Given the technical nature of the report, Jenks arranged to have Boas edit it and proofread the galleys.[29] The commission hoped that he could continue his work, but at that point everyone would have to make do with the information they had already collected.

"The few data which we have observed," Boas began his report, "have shown conclusively that the change in environment from Europe to American has a decided effect on the bodily form of the immigrants, and that the same surroundings are not equally favorable to different European groups." These conclusions, "of great practical importance," "were entirely unforeseen at the time when we started the investigation." Jews, despite their less than favorable new surroundings, showed better development in the United States than in Europe, while Sicilians, already of small stature in their native land, tended to lose their "vigor" in New York City. Other physical traits for members of these two groups indicated "a decided tendency to approach an intermediate type."

These findings, to Boas's mind, supported two important conclusions. The first centered on the tendency toward "greater uniformity of type among Americans than among the European stocks from which they descended," with a "corresponding change in mental make-up." If this could be proved with more investigation of immigrants in a variety of American milieus, it would challenge the nation's fundamental attitude toward immigration: if European immigrants and their descendants became more alike regardless of ethnicity or place of origin, "all fear of an unfavorable influence of South European immigration upon the body of our people should be dismissed." The investigation had not yet progressed far enough to warrant this generalization, but all evidence pointed in that direction.

The second point, which was "of more immediate practical importance," centered on "the influences of environment upon each racial type." Here Boas was less conclusive. Living in New York City had adversely affected Sicilians, but not to a great enough extent to lead Boas to make an overall negative assessment. Instead, he stressed the need for more study. It would be interesting, he suggested, to know whether other locales had the same effects. If they did not, then this information could be given to various aid societies and to the immigrants themselves, resulting in more enlightened distribution of immigrants to more beneficial locations. Comparative study could prove the point conclusively. Boas had not been able to undertake such research, but he hoped that the commission might somehow be able to fund it, especially among immigrants living in rural areas of the United States.

Boas also presented ideas about "the problem of mixture of distinct types." Although he had thus far avoided making any connection with the "Negro question," here he argued that "the mixture of negro and white . . . should receive particular attention." The large volume of southern European immigration, he thought, soon would lead to considerable intermarriage between southern Europeans and African Americans. Many southern states had recently passed laws forbidding the practice, and Boas wondered whether this would result in the perpetuation of "an industrially and socially inferior large black population." Might it not be better to lighten this group gradually with the infusion of "white blood"? Despite the present contentious debate over whether Americans of the early 1900s considered southern Italians and other new immigrants to be white, for Boas there was no such ambiguity. They were white, but they and the African Americans with whom he envisioned them procreating had no inherent limitations based on race.[30]

It is interesting that Commissioner Lodge had expressed ideas similar to Boas's. "The negro," he confided to Charles Francis Adams, "advances only when there is an admixture of white blood or when there is the pressure of a surrounding white population." Further investigation of this topic and the extent of support it received from those who, like Lodge, disliked immigrants could have offered fascinating insights into Progressive Era relations between whites and blacks. Would the Boston Brahman have put aside his xenophobia if he believed it would improve relations between whites and blacks in the nation? Unfortunately, Boas did not get to pursue the topic more fully, and we can only speculate as to what the results and recommendations would have been and how they would have been received in America's race-conscious society.[31]

Boas hoped to pursue other new areas of study as well. Most urgently, he wanted to study additional immigrant groups and check his results against measurements taken immediately before the immigrants left for the United States. In case conditions allowed for an extended investigation, Boas suggested a wholly unrealistic appropriation of $18,000 annually for three years. The first year would be devoted to an investigation in Europe; the second year to a study of immigrants in rural areas throughout the country similar to that conducted in New York City; and the third to an analysis of "mixed types." When this was completed, "a very important step forward in our knowledge of the biological conditions of immigration will have been made." "It seems too bad," he continued, "to be interrupted right at the point when new important discoveries are in sight."[32]

As it was, Boas's preliminary report attracted considerable attention beyond what it received from the commission and Congress, and not all of the responses were positive. The *New York Times* was "tempted at once to characterize Prof. Franz Boas as a 'yellow' scientist" for his "reported discovery of an 'American physical type'" among the children of foreign-born parents. The newspaper dismissed the idea that children became more physically "American," arguing that the "types" were themselves "mixtures of blood" that explained the observed changes. Unstated, but clear, was the belief that immigrants did not become more American. The *Boston Evening Transcript,* ironically a publication from the hometown of Lodge and the IRL, found favor with Boas's report; however, it contended that schools and education were the primary reason that immigrant children were "Americans in the making."[33]

Boas found the "fuss" over the report to be "rather embarrassing," but financial constraints limited his ability to respond, particularly with new research. He planned to correct the report so there would be no misunderstanding about what he meant by the American type; thereafter, it should be printed again as soon as possible so it could be widely dispersed and easily referenced. "I think the interest taken by the public in our anthropological work," Boas wrote to Morton Crane, "is quite remarkable." Unfortunately, Crane had to temper the professor's enthusiasm. Due to congressionally imposed financial constraints, the commission could not pay for his staff after 1 January 1910, and Boas's salary would be continued only until 1 March. Crane tried to mollify the anthropologist by alluding to the seriousness of his work even though at that time there were simply no funds to continue the effort.[34]

The commission did receive an extension of the due date and an additional appropriation in February 1910, but as Jenks had predicted, it could only be used for completing the analysis of information that was already on hand. This meant that Boas would have to turn in his report by October, regardless of his lack of satisfaction with its fullness. The anthropologist grudgingly made plans to comply with this deadline, intending to finish up the material for the remaining ethnic groups and make a final analysis of the "American social and climatic environments and heredity." The commission arranged for the retention of his workforce, and though Boas continued to complain about working under such pressures, he and his staff completed their tasks, including the preparation of numerous charts and tables, by mid-November. The study had not been completed, but its findings would challenge those who disliked some immigrants on the grounds of their supposedly immutable racial characteristics.[35]

Comprising 573 pages, of which 404 were charts and graphs, *Changes in Bodily Form of Descendants of Immigrants* validated Boas's preliminary findings. The study covered five groups: Jews, southern Italians, Bohemians, Hungarians, and, to a more limited extent, Scots. Data came almost exclusively from urban immigrants and their families, who were viewed as the most problematic type. For the sake of comparison, investigators had also gathered information from members of American families that had been in the United States for several generations. Boas declared that the investigation had been only fragmentary, touching on only a small part of the question of environmental effects, but it "had shown much more than was anticipated": "The adaptability of the immigrant seems to be very much greater than we had a right to suppose before our investigations were instituted."[36]

Boas presented an array of what he considered to be mostly positive findings. Along with details about the significant changes in Jews' and Italians' cranial configurations, the report presented information about the other studied groups. Bohemians, for example, experienced a decrease in both the length and width of their heads, and their physical stature increased. The modifications occurred even among those who had arrived during childhood as opposed to having been born in the United States. These developments challenged contemporary anthropological beliefs regarding ethnically, or "racially," determined physiology. Most pertinent to the study of immigrants, Boas's results attested to the positive effects of assimilation, which seemed to assert themselves almost immediately after arrival.[37]

Boas also concluded that the observed bodily changes likely indicated corresponding mental changes. "Fundamental traits of the mind, which are closely correlated with the physical condition of the body and whose development continues over many years after physical growth has ceased, are the more subject to far-reaching changes." He acknowledged that this was a matter of conjecture, but suggested that the "burden of proof" rested with those who "continue to claim the absolute permanence of other forms and functions of the body."[38] It is uncertain whether Boas would have extended the same positivity to Asian and Latino "types"—he did not comment on those groups—but his attack on racial determinism boded well for all maligned groups.

It is difficult to say whether and to what extent the different commissioners agreed with Boas's findings. At one point Jenks said that he might pen a brief introduction for the finished report, but the introduction never materialized. This may merely reflect the hectic character of the commission's final days; however, Jenks did show consistent enthusiasm for the project. As it became apparent during the investigation that the results would challenge prevailing ideas about the inability of certain groups to mix with the American people, Jenks praised Boas's "apparent success." Still, it appears that he was more interested in securing useful information than in verifying any predisposed belief. Because none of his colleagues voiced vehement opposition or criticism, it is safe to assume that Boas's work found favor with them as well—even with the restrictionist Lodge.[39]

Boas himself viewed his commission work as only a start, and thereafter he tried diligently to secure external support. As early as March 1910, he had contacted the Smithsonian's Bureau of American Ethnology, but it had declined to take up the project, questioning its scientific value. Jenks then promised to discuss the matter with Senators Lodge and Dillingham. Clearly the commission would not support anything more than finishing up what Boas already had begun, but Lodge thought that Congress might subsidize an independent proposal, especially if it were backed by an organization such as the Smithsonian. He suggested that Boas contact Smithsonian secretary C. D. Wolcott to ask that his proposal be reconsidered. In November the anthropologist made a final, impassioned appeal to Lodge, stressing the importance of finding a way to continue the study of immigrant physiology. Issues such as the effects of intermarriage between two people of the same race but from different villages had yet to be tested. Boas had some applicable data, but he had not had time to do an appropriate analysis.[40] Boas never got any additional funding; it will never be known what more he may have been able to do.

Boas's contribution to the commission and to the general study of immigration deserves high praise. The anthropologist was, in the words of historian Daniel J. Kevles, "certain that there was no proof of hereditary, racially specific mental or behavioral traits in blacks, immigrants, or any other group," and he consistently challenged people who tried to promote such theories, including IRL member and racist author Madison Grant. Critics, such as Carl Degler, have dismissed Boas's study of immigrant head measurements as "dubious" and have suggested that his work should be banished to the realm of phrenology, but these assessments miss the essence of his work. Boas was fighting against the pseudoscientific racists who wished to condemn immigrants to a purgatory of inferiority and thereby provide the basis for their exclusion from American shores. To the extent that progressive reform may be called liberal, using a definition based on more modern standards of cultural pluralism and race relations, Boas's commission work made a significant contribution.[41] However, his findings would be only a part of the full set of commission reports, and he would not have a vote on any recommendations.

CHAPTER SIX

"Vast Mass of Valuable Facts"

"I AM NOW A MEMBER of the Immigration Commission," wrote Henry Cabot Lodge in 1910, "which has been carrying on the most exhaustive inquiry into the subject which has ever been made." The commission's reports, he told former president Theodore Roosevelt, would provide "very valuable" information about American immigration. Commissioner Jeremiah Jenks and staffer W. Jett Lauck enthusiastically agreed. The investigation, "thoroughly and scientifically carried out, furnished a real basis for judgment on most of the questions connected with immigration." This contrasted with the conjecture, and "far too often . . . prejudice," that had dominated previous discussion. Lodge, who credited much of the effort to the "experts" who had staffed the commission, anticipated that the report of their impressive work, eventually filling forty-one volumes and over twenty thousand pages, would make "very interesting" reading.[1]

The full Dillingham Commission report, titled *Reports of the Immigration Commission,* might best be described as three, or perhaps four, interrelated summaries of the three-year investigation. Thirty-nine of the volumes provide an extensive review of the commission's work and a compilation of its findings, arranged according to the various lines of inquiry. The first two volumes abstract the full reports in the other thirty-nine, and because they were presented to an eagerly awaiting Congress as an introduction to the commission's findings, they would play a key part in influencing public policy. Finally, the abstracts' first fifty pages offer a prefatory condensation, at the end of which are the commission's controversial recommendations. The recommendations take up only four pages, a tiny fraction of the overall *Reports,* but because they deal with restrictions, they give the commission its most enduring legacy.

Commissioners LeRoy Percy and John Burnett reportedly worried that the sheer size of the *Reports* might overwhelm readers, and with the possible exception of those involved in their preparation, it is doubtful that anyone has ever read every report in its entirety. The full, unabridged volumes hold a treasure trove of historical information about American immigration, yet their immense size and technical style deters comprehensive reading. The text is generally dull, and a host of arcane statistics, graphs, and charts either dominate or wholly make up most of the volumes. Their verbosity has prompted most consultants to use the *Reports* only as an encyclopedic reference work. Subsequent researchers have rightfully raised questions about the nineteenth- and early-twentieth-century statistical methodology, yet there is no indication that the information in the *Reports* was inaccurately prepared or is deliberately biased. To the extent that historians can have any sense of the statistical past, the *Reports* offer a vast collection of valuable information.[2]

The commissioners had taken care to prepare the best possible document. Field agents wrote the initial drafts, then sent them to senior staffers, especially W. Jett Lauck and William Husband, who edited the reports and passed them on to the commissioners. Historian Oscar Handlin doubts whether the congressional commissioners even examined the manuscript volumes prior to their publication, but meeting minutes show that they gave them considerable scrutiny. Although not all members were present when every report came up for discussion, everyone collectively participated in the review process, and several members, including Representatives Lodge, John Burnett, and William Bennet, requested revisions or voiced objections. Several of the changes were volume and page specific. In the hectic final days the commission approved Bennet's motion to allow any commissioner to take up with the secretaries and statisticians matters of change in form and expression in any part of the report.[3]

The largest section, twenty-five volumes prepared by Lauck, deal with immigrants in industries and include information about 507,256 wage earners in twenty-one major and numerous minor industries in locations between the Atlantic coast and the Rocky Mountains. Many of the workers, especially recent hires, had not worked for wages in their native countries and therefore lacked industrial training, but in this they were not appreciably different from their northern and western European predecessors. Members of the older immigrant groups usually earned more than the recent arrivals and relied less on borders or lodgers for family income, but the reports acknowledged that their longer U.S. residence gave them certain financial advantages. The same applied to literacy rates. Analysis of home purchases posed a special problem because of the widespread use of "company houses" in some industries, but again, longer residence increased the likelihood of home ownership. Most national, or ethnic, groups tended to send their children to school rather than to work.[4]

Critics have since contended that the commission failed to consider "the whole question of duration of settlement" in assessing various groups, but this distinction is consistently made in the reports. In discussing citizenship among all industrial workers, it is noted that comparing new and old immigrants is not fair "unless the length of residence of each class of immigrants" is taken into account. The reports do emphasize significantly lower naturalization rates for newer groups, but the chart on the subject does break down the overall percentages into residency-length categories, showing that longer residency corresponded to higher rates of U.S. citizenship. Similar methodology and presentation of findings show that earlier-arriving bituminous-coal miners, both individually and as ethnic groups, currently earned more money than those who had come more recently. Also, while members of newer immigrant groups did have a higher propensity for accidents in that industry, the commission reports that this was due mainly to their lack of experience.[5]

Discussion of the potentially contentious issue of "racial displacement," the idea that low-paid recent arrivals took jobs away from natives and members of earlier-arriving groups presented a mixed assessment of the "new immigrants." As new immigrants' numbers increased after 1890, many natives and older immigrants had left certain industries, but those who remained tended "to attain to the more skilled and responsible technical and executive positions which required employees of training and experience." In a context of industrial expansion, new immigrants tended to push established workers up the economic scale, and sometimes new immigrants achieved significant upward mobility as well. However, the stigma of working in occupations dominated by southern or eastern Europeans had pushed some older employees into less financially rewarding positions. Those who remained in their old occupations were predominately "the thriftless, unprogressive elements of the original operating forces." Further, children of the older workers, whether native or immigrant, seldom pursued their fathers' trades; instead, they sought more socially desirable employment. These findings not withstanding, the *Reports* do not contain criticism of new immigrants for accepting lower wages or for taking away jobs.[6]

In places the *Reports* do indirectly distinguish between native workers and more newly arrived immigrants in manner unfavorable to the latter. The section covering New England cotton mills is a case in point. From the 1810s to the 1840s, the mills locally recruited what the reports' authors describe as laudable young men and women. The so-called Lowell Girls were "attractive and, as a rule, well educated," and the males were "sober, intelligent, and reliable." Coming from nearby farms, they seemed to be the very embodiment of virtue. The authors go on to describe their eventual replacement, due to increased demand for labor, by western Europeans, French Canadians, and ultimately southern and eastern Europeans. The descriptions of the latter groups are not negative, but they lack the salutations given the earlier-employed U.S. natives. This absence of any reference to their character or deportment suggests a belief that the immigrants lacked their predecessors' rectitude.[7]

Lauck's few surviving field notes, on immigrants working in Illinois coal mines, also present a mixed assessment. Employers' preference for immigrant workers provoked natives' concern. The natives feared that the new arrivals would work for lower wages or under less desirable conditions, but Lauck noted steadier immigrant work habits as another possible explanation for their concern. In some locations eastern Europeans had bad reputations, but in others they were viewed as good workers. Overall, Lauck found low levels of frictions between immigrants and natives, with antiradicalism being the primary reason for anti-alien sentiments. Surprisingly, since one group was old and the other new, Germans and Slovaks received the strongest local rebuke, for their shared socialist leanings and their "persistence for the past two years of displaying their red flag at the spring festival." Not long before, this had sparked a "minor riot," and "more serious trouble will probably be encountered a year hence." Radicalism was thought to produce "recklessness," which was said to be on the rise among miners from both groups.[8]

The commission's Pacific Coast and Rocky Mountain investigation produced three volumes on "Japanese and Other Immigrant Races" working in area industries. Given the region's long-standing and ongoing antagonism toward Asians, the effort there, directed by Jeremiah Jenks, was aimed at learning about the nature and strength of local sentiments toward Pacific Coast immigration. Jenks's agenda had called for a thorough study of immigrants in the western states, including their social conditions, their geographic and occupational distribution, and the economic effects of their presence. The commission had opened a San Francisco office and hired Stanford University economist Henry H. Millis to direct fieldwork. Millis, like many of his Stanford colleagues, was not anti-Japanese; he believed that no nationality should be "unduly restricted," and he subsequently would propose a very lenient Asian immigration policy.[9]

Under Millis's leadership the commission prepared a balanced, generally objective evaluation of the region's immigrants that refuted the Western stereotype. Giving special attention to the recently controversial Japanese Americans, Millis's report included data on over thirteen thousand of the one hundred thousand immigrants and their children. Cooperation with consular officials, Japanese student-interpreters, and the immigrants themselves helped to ensure accuracy. Breaking with the commission's stated aversion to relying on personal impressions and observations, staffers also interviewed numerous employers and supervisors. Findings showed Japanese to be "ambitious" workers who "tended to rise rapidly" up the economic ladder even in the face of notable "race prejudice."[10]

Many immigrants—primarily southern and eastern Europeans, Mexicans, declining numbers of Chinese, and increasing numbers of Japanese—worked on western railways, and their ethnic diversity allowed for comparative assessments. Appraisals varied considerably. According to one unidentified official, the "sober, tractable, and industrious" Japanese made "the best" maintenance and construction workers. Others found them to be more peaceable than either Italians or Greeks, who had earned bad reputations for being hot-tempered and violent. Conversely, another railroad had discharged most of its Japanese workers, having found that they were "'more difficult to satisfy' than other races." Some supervisors disliked Japanese workers because of what they perceived as their "crafty" nature, and the Santa Fe Railroad paid them lower wages, contending that they "were less strong and less satisfactory than the Mexicans." Japanese workers for the Union Pacific Railroad earned less than those belonging to the "white races," but so too did Italians, Greeks, and Austrians. Overall, the commission found that the Japanese were among the lowest-paid laborers but that their wages had tended to rise over the past several years.

The investigation in the western states also documented the area's anti-Asian bias, and this likely influenced the commission's decision to endorse continued Asian exclusion despite the favorable findings about Asian immigrants themselves. A report titled "Pacific Coast Opinion of Japanese Immigration and the Desire for Asiatic Laborers" chronicled the region's historically "strong opposition" to Japanese immigrants and the objections to giving them the same rights and privileges as "the white races." The reports' authors also expressed concern that the proximity of Asians would negatively affect settlement of other groups. "The presence of Asiatics," they asserted, "has in some areas prevented the influx of other races," and a reduction of the former "would increase the influx of families from the East and Middle West."[11] Ramifications of this negative conclusion eventually appeared in policy recommendations.

One part of the reports' Pacific Coast findings shows the commission's controversial use of racial classification. Even as Boas was formulating contrary contentions, the authors of the reports consistently implied that inherent, immutable characteristics defined immigrant types. For example, statistical tables showing what might be called ethnic breakdowns for particular industries used three broad categories: "Native White," "Foreign White," and "Colored," with the last including Negroes, Chinese, Japanese, and Indians. Perceptions of racial difference evidently outweighed the similarities in Asian and European immigrants' experience, but there was no rational reason except bigotry toward both groups for grouping overseas migrants with American Indians. Without evidence to the contrary, this can only be seen as the commissioners' desire to designate the Asians as non-white and therefore inherently undesirable.

Such classification problems were not confined to the study of Pacific immigrants. Group identification and definition continually bedeviled the commission. "A mere enumeration of the various races coming from Austria-Hungary," wrote Secretary William Husband, "would, it seems to me, convince any one of the necessity for a racial classification." In a discussion of how to classify Jews, he acknowledged that some nationalities preferred the term *people* and that others preferred the term *race* to designate particular groups. The commission had borrowed its general classification system from the Bureau of Immigration, and Husband wanted to eliminate any suggestion that the system was based on prejudice or anything other than mere classification for reasons of record keeping. In the case of Jews, he disavowed any notion that religion played a part in classification; *Jew* or *Hebrew* was intended to mean "a race or people, nothing more."

Others, including Commissioner William Wheeler, were skeptical of this distinction. At a hearing in December 1909, U.S. Jewish leaders asked the commission not to employ the Bureau of Immigration's racial classifications and to instead use country of origin for compiling immigration statistics. Simon Wolf, representing B'nai B'rith, and Julian W. Mack, with the American Jewish Committee, objected to the idea that *Hebrew* and *Jew* were racial terms; the leaders contended that they applied to religion, not race. Ironically, when Congress began considering restrictions ten years later, the parties would reverse themselves. Husband would then argue strictly in favor nationality as a means of immigrant classification, while Jewish leaders would see this as discriminatory. Husband had definitely reversed his position, but his behavior should not be taken as evidence of anti-Semitism; nor should it cast doubt on his sincerity in disclaiming religious and other prejudice while working for the commission.[12] Rather, it demonstrated the Progressive Era desire to establish certainty—an often elusive if not impossible goal.

The commissioners' adherence to notions of racial classification was displayed most blatantly in the reports' *Dictionary of Races or Peoples,* but that volume also demonstrates that the commission's conception of race involved social and cultural characteristics that later social scientists would associate with ethnicity. Franz Boas, Jeremiah Jenks, and others had talked about preparing such a volume in order to clarify and improve understanding of "the many ethnical [*sic*] names that were employed to designate various races or peoples" in the study. The dictionary was originally intended to aid agents doing fieldwork, but when that phase of the investigation came to an unexpectedly early end, Dr. Daniel Folkmar, who shared fellow anthropologist Franz Boas's interest in the study of physical characteristics, expanded the dictionary project to create an "authoritative" volume.

The commission both recognized the dictionary's potential to create controversy and sought to ensure its "accuracy and scientific value from an ethnological standpoint." William Husband acknowledged that there was "considerable disagreement as to various racial classifications," and that divers experts would not agree "upon every detail." Still, because there was nothing else like it written in English, the dictionary "would be valuable from a general, as well as a scientific viewpoint." Husband wanted to make every effort to prepare the best possible document, and he sought outside review from Franz Boas and others even though the work was considered "incidental to the work of the Commission as a whole."[13]

Folkmar used what he described as the "most generally accepted" ethnological conventions to classify groups "according to their language, their physical characteristics, and other such marks as would show their relationship to one another." He first separated humanity into five "physical or somatological" categories: Caucasian—white, Ethiopian—black, Mongolian—yellow, Malay—brown, and American—red. Further subdivision relied on linguistic differences. As the individual entries would show, cultural traits were often considered as well. Folkmar justified this methodological blending of natural and social sciences, on the grounds of "convenience": it worked for the practical grouping and counting of immigrants. An inspector, he reasoned, had neither the time nor the training necessary to determine whether an immigrant was "dolichocephalic or brachycephalic in type."

Examination of a few selected entries reveals the commission's complex understanding of race, showing it to involve an imprecise mixture of physical, cultural, and social characteristics—such as geographical proximity to other groups. For example, Albanians' use of both the Greek and Roman alphabets, along with their physical characteristics, gave them their distinct identity. Bohemians had greater "brain weight" than any other Europeans, "due to their native endowment as Slavs," but their civilization had been "profoundly modernized" by their contact with Germans. The Germans were those who used the German "mother tongue," and linguistics similarly "best defined" the Finns. "Language, physique, and character," as well as geography, separated the Italians into two groups, northern and southern. Hebrews were a mixed race, using several languages, and Slavs could be grouped according to many different subdivisions.

These questionable definitions, and more importantly the whole dubious notion of "ineradicable race distinctions" notwithstanding, the dictionary offers two positive examples of the commission's effort to provide a balanced and objective report. First, Folkmar acknowledged that the "classification of peoples" was an ongoing process and that ethnologists were still struggling with the relationship between nature and nurture. Second, the entries did not suggest the inherent inferiority of frequently disparaged groups. If the Slav was "still backward in western ideas, appliances and form of government, it is nonetheless conceivable that the time is not far distant when he will stand in the lead." Other new immigrants—Poles, Hebrews, and Magyars/Hungarians—were described in perfunctory, nonjudgmental ways. As for southern Italians, the dictionary critically characterized them as "impractical" and as having "little adaptability to highly organized society" and a greater propensity toward crime than their northern countryfolk; yet they were also "benevolent, religious, artistic, and industrious."[14]

Along with the *Dictionary* and the extensive industrial section, the reports cover many other topics as well. The European research makes up one volume, the Boas investigation another. Two other volumes contain the "statements and recommendations" submitted by various interested parties and a summary of U.S. legislation and court cases related to immigration. The volume titled *Statistical Review of Immigration, 1820–1910* was intended as a ready reference of relevant data culled from various government reports.

In another volume, Joseph A. Hill, a Census Bureau statistician, used his agency's records to study immigrant occupations, comparing the first and second generations of each ethnic group. Additional volumes covered immigrants in cities, children of immigrants in schools, and the immigration situation in other countries. All of them adhered to the commission's highly formal, statistical style.

The volume *Immigrants in Cities* demonstrates how the commission sought to examine what had "long been considered one of the most unfavorable features of the modern immigration problem." It studied "crowded quarters" in seven cities ranging in size and location from the immigrant port of New York to the Midwestern industrial center of Milwaukee, Wisconsin. By examining entire neighborhoods instead of just the poorest families in those areas, the commission learned that the majority lived cleanly, though often in poverty. Rather than producing their own poor living conditions, immigrants persevered "in spite of them." Most families could not afford better quarters, and some had to take in borders to pay for even modest housing. Immigrants, especially the recently arrived young men, did live in congested areas, but this tendency declined the longer they stayed in the United States. However, the commission warned that it was "not safe to conclude . . . that immigrants tend to reduce congestion in homes as the length of their residence in this country increases," as had been the case for northern Europeans. Here was a not-so-subtle jibe at the new immigrants.[15]

The study of immigrant children in schools provides an object lesson about the shortcomings of relying too heavily on statistics. The commission examined over two million pupils, ranging from kindergarten age to college age, to determine the extent to which "immigrant children are availing themselves of educational facilities and what progress they make in school work." Three volumes provide over fifteen hundred pages of arcane statistics, but the accompanying text offers scant interpretation. The reports leave unanswered the question of whether immigrants deserved criticism or praise when it came to the pursuit of education. Foreign-born children did tend to be found disproportionately in the lower grades, but as a group they may just have been younger—or they may have had a higher propensity to drop out as they reached their teenage years. The commissioners seemed more concerned with presenting an overabundance of numerical data than with trying to address such issues, and at the time of final approval, they deleted unspecified text. This may have been because of disagreement over some conclusion, but unfortunately, there is no way of knowing the content of the removed parts. Just the fact of removal, however, suggests that some degree of subjectivity would have provided insight into the authors' opinions of immigrant education.

They did make some criticism. Despite the immensity of the statistical record, the commissioners complained that secondary teachers did "not sufficiently explain what was desired" in regard to one particularly important matter, that of "retardation," the condition of students who were two or more years older than the normal age for their grade. Immigrants did show higher instances of this perceived malady, with southern Italians being the worst offenders, but the reports' authors explain did not explain why. The authors also avoided the issue of whether retardation demonstrated intrinsically diminished capacity among immigrant children or merely showed that they had received less formal education than their native-born peers. The closest the commissioners came to censure of immigrant children was the expected conclusion that "retarded" children were more frequently from homes where English was not the primary language.

The commissioners may have felt that they lacked sufficient information to make more subjective judgments, but it is more likely that they simply avoided such issues in the substantive volumes of the *Reports* because their progressive empiricism demanded hard evidence. The abundance of tables and numerical data suggests a belief that the statistics somehow would speak for themselves. The volumes dealing with children in schools do provide considerable information and positively indicate that many immigrant children living in various cities did go to school. Some groups performed better than others, and achievement by members of the same group varied by location. Still, the commissioners offered no definitive statement as to whether the educational information reflected positively or negatively on recent arrivals. Because nothing in the data suggests the latter, here is a place where the commission could have made a stronger pro-immigrant statement.[16]

The *Immigration and Crime* volume did make such a testimonial. "No satisfactory evidence has yet been produced to show that immigration has resulted in an increase in crime disproportionate to the increase in adult population," the report began. In fact, statistics showed that natives were more likely than immigrants to commit criminal acts. American-born children of immigrants did have higher instances of juvenile delinquency than those of native-born parents, but the commission found mitigating circumstances, such as the concentration of the former in urban areas. The criminality of these youth was "largely a product of the city." As to the greater questions of whether immigration increased crime in the United States, and if it did, which groups bore the greatest responsibility, "no one can answer . . . fully without a machinery much greater than that which the Immigration Commission has had at its disposal." What the commissioners could report contradicted prevalent nativist assertions regarding criminal propensity.[17]

The commission also sought to determine whether significant numbers of criminal immigrants were entering the United States. An existing statute excluded those convicted abroad of crimes involving moral turpitude, but many Americans doubted the law's effectiveness. Popular belief held that large numbers of Italian criminals were coming to the United States, and in a study confined to New York City, the commission found ample evidence that Italian convicts had entered the United States illegally. Nonetheless, most Italian Americans were "law abiding and industrious." Even this statement, though, had a negative spin. The fact that Italian immigrants themselves had become the principal targets of malicious compatriots cast "grave reflection upon the efficiency" of laws designed to ensure criminal exclusion and made clear the need for better regulation.[18]

The final volume of the *Reports* contains "Statements and Recommendations Submitted by Societies and Organizations Interested in the Subject of Immigration." The commission had received statements and recommendations from sixteen groups that had been asked to proffer their opinions. The groups ranged from the Sons of the American Revolution to the American Jewish Committee and B'nai B'rith. The selective invitations had been "confined to some of the more important societies" that had substantial involvement in national, as opposed to local or regional, immigration matters. Some, such as the Immigration Restriction League (IRL), advocated more stringent exclusions, while others, such as National Liberal Immigration League, opposed such measures. A third type of organization primarily promoted immigrant welfare; one group of this type was the North American Civic League for Immigrants.

The statements provide excellent synopses of the different groups' purposes and their positions on immigration, but it is doubtful that they had any influence on the commission's summations or recommendations. In the volume's brief introduction, the commissioners reiterated their intent to avoid hearings except where essential, but indicated that the information provided by the societies would "be of value in the study of the immigration question."[19] The commission's meeting minutes gives no indication that these petitions received even cursory examination, in contrast to the considerable attention given to the various statistical investigations.

While the unabridged volumes of the *Reports* provide a wealth of historical information and some admittedly debatable conclusions, to many contemporaries they were nothing more than elaborate and costly window dressing. Most of the interested parties wanted succinct analysis and remedial recommendations, and they wanted them quickly. As the deadline for the final report to Congress approached in the fall of 1910, Commission Secretary William Husband sought to meet this demand by preparing an abstract summarizing "the salient features of every part of the Commission's work." He planned for the abstract to be two hundred pages long, but it eventually filled two volumes totaling about sixteen hundred pages. He also asked project leaders to prepare synopses, in some cases condensations of previously submitted reports, which would be included in the summary volume. Central office staffers collected and edited the submissions, and each commissioner got an opportunity to review their work. The commissioners recognized the importance of the condensed reports, realizing that to "the average student of the immigration problem," it would be the summaries, not the thirty-nine volumes of full reports, that would convey the essence of the three-year, multimillion-dollar investigation.[20]

The summary abstracts characterized recently arrived groups more negatively than did the full reports. Rather than blatantly condemning the new immigrants, however, the abstracts tended to suggest their connection to U.S. socioeconomic problems, such as low standards of living. For example, in the "Manufacturing and Mining" summary, tables showing wages and income divide the immigrants by ethnic group, but do not give any consideration to length of residence in the United States. The more recently arrived groups did make less money, and tables elsewhere indicated their shorter tenure in the United States, which would explain their generally lower wages, but in the abstracts this information was not explicitly connected to earnings as it had been in the full reports. The text in the abstracts challenged the impression that certain groups inherently made less money, noting "that earning ability is more the outcome of industrial opportunity or conditions of employment than of racial efficiency and progress," but the tables conveyed a visually contradictory message. Elsewhere in the same section authors noted that "recent immigration was responsible for many social and political problems." These included the "passive opposition" to improvements in industrial wages and working conditions that resulted from the presence of large numbers of readily available low-wage workers.[21]

The brief introductory statement at the start of the abstracts, itself an overall summary prepared by Secretary Husband, emphasized the commission's positive findings about the new immigration's general effects on "the people, the industries, and the institutions of the United States." The new arrivals, although economically poor, "as a rule are the strongest, the most enterprising, and the best of their class." They came mainly to improve their situation, and their households were "usually found unexpectedly good," even though there was considerable room for improvement. Current laws, which overall worked well, had contributed to these positive findings by effectively excluding most physically and mentally unsound prospective immigrants and most paupers. Immigration of criminals continued to be a serious problem, but as a whole immigration did not appear to cause a notable increase in crime rates. The harshest criticism was that the presence of large numbers of immigrant laborers slowed industrial reform.[22]

Interestingly absent from the forty-one volumes was the bugaboo of radicalism. Surviving field notes mention it, but the commissioners neither highlighted it in the abstracts nor offered it as a justification for imposing new restrictions, even though Charles Neill, for one, had previously written about its dangers. Perhaps the commissioners had not found ample evidence of radicalism, or perhaps the absence nationally of notable labor unrest had muted the issue, enabling investigators' attention to be directed to other issues. Still, concerns about immigrant radicalism had not disappeared. The 1912 textile strike in Lawrence, Massachusetts, involving the Industrial Workers of the World would soon reemphasize that aspect of the immigration debate.

Husband's brief statement concluded with the long-awaited recommendations, the four pages that restrictionists realized would dominate future legislative efforts. As early as February 1909 Georgia representative Alexander Clay, a pronounced xenophobe who believed that immigration from Europe and Asia threatened the "peace, morality, and homogeneity of our race," wanted to see the investigation finished so Congress could turn its attention to doing something about the nation's most pressing problem. Some of the reports had been sent to Congress by that time, but not the all-important legislative recommendations. Lodge, who had been willing to postpone consideration of statutory revisions until the investigation's end, now urged his colleagues to begin working on them, but the majority decided to wait. They did release the reports on steerage and white slavery, both of which influenced the passage of new legislation, and this cause and effect suggested the weight to which Congress should give the commission's opinions. "It seems to me this is a crisis in our affairs," recognized IRL leader Joseph Lee as he and others awaited the final report, "and if we don't make good now we might as well quit": without a favorable recommendation, Congress would be reluctant to pass a restriction bill.[23]

Everything depended on the disposition of key members of the commission. Monitoring the situation closely, IRL lobbyist James Patten expressed belief that the commission would recommend a literacy test in its December 1910 reports, but in a bizarre twist he emphasized the need to put pressure on Henry Cabot Lodge. The senator had long been the leading congressional restrictionist, but Lee feared that instead of getting William Dillingham, Jenks, and perhaps even Wheeler to endorse the literacy test, Lodge would join the others in concluding that the commission's evidence showed no need for new restrictions. If he did so, Lee was prepared to "soak" him politically. Lee hoped to "stiffen his backbone" to prevent any "wobble." The eleventh-hour replacement of the deceased Anselm McLaurin with LeRoy Percy troubled restrictionists, who worried about Percy's earlier praise for Italian immigrants. Support from Wheeler also seemed like a long shot, but he was the commissioner from the strongly anti-Asian West, which might be enough for him to advocate general restriction.[24]

The commissioners fueled speculation by avoiding the controversial matter of legislative recommendations until December 1910 and by refusing to make any public comment. At the beginning of what became a frenetic final few days, they first approved a list of general principles, prepared by Jeremiah Jenks, that would serve as guidelines for making specific suggestions. These principles noted that while the United States historically had welcomed "the oppressed of other lands," it now had to take care to admit such "quantity and quality as not to make too difficult the process of assimilation." The reference to "the oppressed" was puzzling in that the commission had concluded elsewhere that most immigrants came for economic reasons, with relatively few seeking to escape adverse political conditions. Jenks emphasized this in his second principle, which called for basing admission standards on "the prosperity and economic well-being of our people." These declarations, which became part of the official *Reports,* opened the door for the endorsement of specific restrictions, but the next several principles indicated that the commission did not want to deprecate immigrants themselves.

In these next principles the commissioners took care to express compassion about the plight of industrial workers, a significantly immigrant class. A country's economic wealth must go beyond enabling business success and offer ample opportunity "to the citizen dependent on employment for his material, mental, and moral development." Slower business growth that "would permit the adaptation and assimilation of the incoming labor supply" was preferable to rapid growth, which encouraged the immigration of "laborers of low salaries and efficiencies, who imperil the American standard of wages and conditions of employment." This placed as much of the blame for existent social maladies on greedy businesspeople rather than on the immigrant laborers whom they attracted. As for the foreign-born, they received their strongest criticism for sending savings abroad and for discouraging other immigrants from pursuing naturalization. Those engaging in the first practice should be discouraged, and those engaging in the latter deported.[25]

Attention then shifted to the drafting of specific recommendations. William Bennet, the acknowledged antirestrictionist, suggested allowing for the deportation of any immigrant who became a public charge within three years of admission, and Charles Neill advised excluding all working-class males not accompanied by family members. The commission endorsed Bennet's proposal, but noted Neill's proposition only as a "suggested" exclusion. Dillingham secured approval for a plan to give the secretary of commerce and labor the authority to decide when, in the absence of suitable domestic workers, companies could import contract laborers. Neill then got his colleagues to take a further step toward restriction. On the basis of the conclusion that the United States had an oversupply of unskilled labor, the commission unanimously recommended that Congress pass "legislation which will at the present time restrict the further admission of such unskilled workers." At Bennet's urging and despite their favorable characterization of Asians elsewhere in the reports, the commission followed what they had found to be popular Western sentiment and endorsed the continuation of Asian exclusion. In their draft minutes the commissioners labeled such immigrants "undesirable," but that denigration was omitted from the published version.[26]

The key votes came on 4 and 5 December. Wishing to go beyond the commission's imprecise call for the restriction of unskilled laborers, John Burnett, who had emerged as the group's most adamant xenophobe, moved to add the specific recommendation of a literacy test, which remained restrictionists' method of choice. The subsequent role call produced interesting results. Only Burnett and Benjamin Howell voted in favor of the recommendation; all of the others, including Jenks and a "wobbling"

Lodge, voted against making such a precise recommendation. The others, with the exception of Bennet and Wheeler, did try to hedge, saying that they were not voting "against the specific test, but against the policy of recommending by a mere majority vote one method of restriction in preference to all the others." The commission instead adopted a more generic call for "restriction as demanded by economic, moral and social considerations" and offered, without indicating preference, a list of suggested means.[27]

Burnett was not through. He alone refused to accept the decision not to specify new restrictions, arguing that it was "an evasion of the purpose for which the Commission was created, in that it makes no recommendations as to the method of restriction." Going even further the next day, he threatened to present a minority report that would not only call for a literacy test but also assert that a majority of the commissioners favored such legislation. This would raise the question of why they had not recommended it, which could very well cast doubt on the veracity of the entire collection of reports. Then, at what one contemporary called the "psychological moment," Lodge called for a reconsideration of the previous day's vote. All of those present then voted to recommend the literacy test "as the single most feasible" means of restriction. Proponents of the literacy test would henceforth emphasize this recommendation, arguing that the test offered what the progressives sought: a workable means to an end.

The endorsement of the test supplemented, but did not replace, the broader call for exclusion on the basis of economic and social considerations, suggesting that the literacy requirement met those criteria. It would exclude enough immigrants to reduce the perceived overabundance of laborers and would promote better assimilation of those who continued to arrive. Interestingly, although those present at the meeting approved wording indicating that individual commissioners supported the test to "a greater or lesser degree," this wording did not appear in the final *Reports,* likely because the commissioners wanted to stress harmony and accord. Also, those present agreed that none of them would file a separate report and that all would say that the "Commission as a whole" concurred as to the conditions that should dictate the severity of exclusion. Consensus carried the day, but the commission's decision was not unanimous.[28]

Representative Bennet did not attend the 5 December meeting, but when he learned via telephone of the commission's decision, he asked, as he had been privileged to do, to prepare a minority report. He too stressed agreement, saying he was united with his colleagues in backing the commission's conclusions "so far as they are based on the reports," even when they differed from his previously held opinions. This included their conclusion about the need to reduce the immigration of unskilled laborers. He could not, however, recommend the literacy test, "for which no logical argument can be based on the report." Citing time limitations, he did not offer an "elaborate dissent," but he did minimally voice opposition to the test on the grounds of unfair selectivity. He also mentioned that the *Reports* contained "many excellent provisions," showing that even the commission's most ardent antirestrictionist found much to praise about the group's work.[29]

Bennet and his compatriots may have been especially pleased that the *Reports* did not contain an unqualified condemnation of immigrants themselves. The newcomers were not portrayed as inherently pernicious; rather, they were judged as dangerous because of their overabundance in basic industries, a condition that threatened all proletarians' quality of life. Votes on general principles and specific recommendations show that all of the members agreed with the basic premise of controlling immigration in such a way as to promote economic and social betterment. Even the commission's support for the exclusion of Asians, however unfair and misguided, focused on concerns about the allegedly deleterious effects of coolie labor on American wages and working conditions. Despite investigators' positive findings about Asian-immigrant laborers, the commissioners did separately and unequivocally recommend their continued exclusion, but at least they purged the unflattering personal description of "undesirable" that had been in their draft. James Patten, the IRL's ardent lobbyist, provided an immediate and insightful observation when he described how the commission had used the popular argument of labor and industrial effects, rather than the unpopular one of race discrimination, to support its recommendations.[30]

When the commission's full set of reports, with its call for reducing the number of unskilled laborers and its specific endorsement of the literacy test, reached Congress on 10 December, it rejuvenated the stagnant restrictionist movement. While it was being conducted, the investigation had sharply curtailed congressional action, which had been limited to sporadic calls for new restrictions and limited action on such matters as steerage accommodations. Now, with the *Reports* in hand, Congress was poised for change. Two of the commission's suggested means of increased restriction, the literacy test and numerical limitations, or quotas, would soon spark intense debate and lead to the passage of increasingly stringent prohibitions on immigration.

CHAPTER SEVEN

"Most Feasible Means"

"A MAJORITY OF THE COMMISSION favor the reading and writing test as the most feasible means of restricting immigration," proclaimed jubilant Immigration Restriction League (IRL) lobbyist James Patten. Through the years, the literacy test had remained the restrictionists' favorite proposed new means of exclusion, on the assumption that it would keep out undesirables and offered the best chance for the enactment of some type of general prohibition. Now, although supporters still faced challenges in getting legislative and presidential approval, Patten believed that they had won a key victory. Not only had the test received an important endorsement, but the commission had stressed the measure's feasibility for producing the desired positive result—the exclusion of immigrants who were unwanted for socioeconomic reasons. This was an appealing argument for progressives, who generally sought specific solutions that could be readily implemented.[1]

Congress would enact a literacy test over President Woodrow Wilson's veto in 1917, but not without another six years of contentious debate, much of it centering on the commission's work. Restrictionists took the recommendations as the long-awaited validation of their beliefs and concerns, believing that they would provide the impetus for what telephone inventor Alexander G. Bell called "the intelligent restriction of immigration." Others, such as industrialist Andrew Carnegie and Harvard University president Charles Eliot, remained unconvinced. Political pundits wondered how the commission's recommendations might affect foreign-born voters in subsequent elections, which in turn might influence congressional behavior. Others, notably key administrators in the executive branch, contended that the *Reports* and their recommendations did not call for any immediate action, especially none so drastic as harsh new restrictions.[2]

Reaction to the so-called white slave trade, the allegedly widespread, well-organized practice of forcing women into prostitution, gave an early indication of the commission's legislative influence. Much of the concern centered on the purported entrapment of young immigrants; charges were made that the practice involved ethnic group representatives at Ellis Island. The commission investigated this, "the most pitiful and the most revolting phase of the immigration question," and the results were surprising. While the depravity did involve a substantial number of waylaid innocents, the majority of imported prostitutes, likely numbering into the thousands, came as established practitioners. The Immigration Act of 1907 officially excluded them and set penalties for those who procured their services, but the commission recommended better collection of information about suspected prostitutes in Europe, more thorough inspection at U.S. entry points, and detention of questionable young women as ways of improving enforcement. The commission also advocated the elimination of time limits on deportation, the imprisonment of deportees who attempted to return to the United States, better expulsion procedures, and criminal prohibition of interstate transport of women for prostitution or other immoral purposes.[3] These recommendations, plus public testimony by Jeremiah Jenks, helped to secure passage of two related acts.

In December 1909, Dillingham commission member Representative Benjamin Howell and Illinois Republican senator James R. Mann each introduced a bill designed to curb white slavery. When the Howell bill, which called for preventing the entrance of alien prostitutes, came up for debate, restrictionists demanded more. Democrat Charles L. Bartlett of Georgia told his House colleagues that the crusaders against white slavery did not want the limited Howell bill, and others agreed. "This ceaseless flood of immigration," averred Republican Richard W. Austin of Tennessee, "good, indifferent, and worthless, with an annual average of more than a million people from the four corners of the earth, in my judgment means more to the peace and civilization of our country than any question upon which this body can legislate." Such sentiment did not carry the day. Senator Henry Cabot Lodge, likely remembering past difficulties with multifaceted bills, spoke for the majority when he urged disposal of the "white slave issue without any encumbrance." Taking that tack and "closely following" the commission's recommendations, Congress passed the Howell bill in March 1910.[4]

The Mann bill, which would make it a federal crime to transport women across state lines for immoral purposes, also engendered a spirited and far-reaching debate. Several representatives from the states-rights–oriented South opposed the measure on constitutional grounds, and they also questioned whether the bill followed the commission's recommendations. Many of the measure's opponents thought that general immigrant exclusion could accomplish the same end. Instead of trying to regulate the interstate transportation and harboring of aliens engaged in immoral conduct, critics wanted "to shut them out, all out if necessary." Clearly the bill's detractors believed that the nation's prostitution problem, like radicalism, owed its existence primarily to immigration, which therefore needed to be substantially reduced. The congressional majority, however, again followed the commission's recommendation, passing the unencumbered Mann Act in June 1910.[5]

Response to the commission's report on white slavery no doubt whetted the appetite of those looking forward to its broader recommendations, but the remainder of 1910 produced little more than watching and waiting. The IRL kept lobbyist James Patten at the Capitol, where he closely monitored commission and congressional activity and tried to coordinate various restrictionist voices, such as labor and nativist groups and other League contacts. Restrictionists, he believed, could do the most good by pushing William Dillingham and William Bennet to finish the commission's work. "The Senate Committee has had just one meeting this session," Patten jabbed Dillingham. "Industrious, energetic, conscientious, Dilly-Dally. . . . Shortly we will try a few well directed shots into it and him." As for Bennet, Patten reported rumors that the New York congressman had a secret plan to have the commission continue its work until 1913. This did not materialize, but Congress did grant the limited extension that gave the investigators until December 1910 to complete their task. After the extension was granted, an exasperated Joseph Lee suggested that it was time for direct confrontation between restrictionists and their opponents, especially the troublesome Bennet.[6]

Lee thought Bennet's work on the commission might give restrictionists a means by which to discredit him. Investigators had spent over $600,000 for research around the world, but they had not done a satisfactory job investigating the most important single location, Ellis Island. IRL investigators had conducted their own thorough study and had found station director Robert A. Watchorn to be incompetent. Shortly after the League charged Watchorn with graft and corruption, and amid press reports of his unsatisfactory performance, William Williams replaced the beleaguered station director. Lee believed that because Bennet had been on the immigration commission, which should have uncovered the problems at Ellis Island, he could be accused of either sloppy research or failure to make a full disclosure. In either case, his negligence in addressing the alleged abuses would show that he was no friend of the immigrant, and this would deprive him of key supporters. James Patten tried to raise some of these issues at a House immigration committee meeting, and the IRL published two pamphlets, "Congressman Bennet Not a Progressive" and "'Jews' Attention" to try to portray him as actually anti-immigrant.[7]

Correspondence between Patten and Lee, whose dogged IRL activism kept them in contact with many other prominent anti-immigrant groups, indicates their growing frustration and their realization of how important the commission's recommendations would be. A particularly agitated Lee warned against following the siren-like temptation to press side issues, such as the bonding of immigrants, which were currently under discussion in some congressional quarters. He tried to impress on Patten that "we don't want any two-for-a-cent compromise. We want a literacy test." The hesitancy on the part of some Republicans led Lee once again to suggest some form of confrontation. For instance, someone could tell the GOP lawmakers that they owed the IRL something in December because the congressional party leaders had not pushed for a vote on the literacy test that spring. Lee also thought that restrictionists should put more pressure on their longtime champion Henry Cabot Lodge. In this case, however, Patten urged restraint, explaining that their friends, including Lodge, agreed with the merits of restriction; they just wanted the matter held over until the next session because of political exigency. Lee agreed, but only grudgingly: "My feeling about restrictive legislation is that it is on the White Queen's plan of jam every other day,—that is, jam yesterday and jam tomorrow, but never jam today."[8]

Patten tried to balance his pleas for patience with plans for more aggressive efforts at the Capitol. Republicans had decided not to commit themselves to a restriction bill during the present session for political reasons, but the next session, after the election, looked promising. "It is better to make haste slowly," the lobbyist warned in an ironically worded prognostication. "The public need time to catch up, and unquestionably, it's on the catch!" Still, Patten was not opposed to taking a decidedly more confrontational tack in addition to more passive types of lobbying. "To be of importance here," he argued, "we simply must get into the political game, by taking a fall out of the dilly-dally Commission, getting closer to organizations, helping the other fellow where the fellow is 'agin' us etc." "We have got to inspire them [congressmen] with the idea that there is no use kicking against the restriction pricks." In November 1910, Patten relished both Bennet's defeat for reelection and the victory of Bennet's fellow Dillingham commissioner John Burnett, a solid restrictionist.[9]

The commission's near-unanimous endorsement of a literacy requirement abruptly squelched restrictionists' growing belligerence, and prudent moderation became their modus operandi. They especially sought to follow the commission's lead in calling for restriction on the basis of "economic, social, and moral considerations." Claims that made specific reference to Slavs and Italians or that suggested "race prejudice" were to be avoided. "The last argument [race] we are going easy on," Joseph Lee candidly pronounced. "I myself am doubtful whether it pays to use it. It is my favorite one, which makes the position more difficult." League activist Richards M. Bradley, a well-known health care reformer, criticized colleague Prescott Hall for his use of racial arguments, partly because they could engender hostility on the part of immigrants already in the United States. Racial references also tended to become personal.[10]

Restrictionists tried instead to link reduced immigration with the defense of American workers and the preservation of the nation's democracy. Low-priced European and Asian laborers threatened the nation's plentiful benefits. "The question here," Lee editorialized, "is not whether every man who can read and write is a saint and every illiterate man a sinner, but whether upon the whole the standard of American citizenship will be improved or lowered by the importation of illiterates from the Old World." He also wondered if the nation could permanently raise the standards of its laboring class, including their living conditions, if it put no limit on the number and type of workers pouring in from Europe. Preparing this message for publication, he heeded his own advice and deleted a reference to illiterate "races and the illiterate parts of races."[11]

As Richards Bradley critically noted, Prescott Hall and Robert Ward continued to use ethnically denigrating rhetoric, but they did try to strike a balance between progressivism and nativism. The literacy test, Hall asserted, would discriminate against "the less desirable races." "The leopard's spots cannot be changed, nor can bad racial stocks be changed to good," he argued. Furthermore, mixing of races had never produced anything but "mongrel types," and this had caused the downfall "of nearly every great nation." Yet he also contended that the inability to read went hand-in-hand with ignorance of trade, congregation in slums, spendthrift behavior, and indifference to assimilation and naturalization. Had the literacy test been in effect since 1885, Hall continued, there would have been "much less social unrest due to the struggle to compete with those having a lower standard of living, and much less extreme radicalism imported from Europe." Ward worried about "racial inter-breeding" and believed that it should be allowed only for the most mentally and physically capable.[12]

Ironically, author Madison Grant soon would use a decidedly progressive approach to convey overtly racist arguments. "The great lesson of the science of race," he wrote in the widely acclaimed *Passing of the Great Race,* first published in 1916, "is the immutability of somatological or bodily characteristics, which is closely associated with the immutability of physical predisposition and impulses." Here, at least in Grant's mind, was direct refutation of Franz Boas's commission findings, especially his implication that America was a success as a melting pot. Readers who had consulted the anthropologist's report, Grant advised, would do well to study Mexico, where race mixing had created a "type" that was engaged in demonstrating its incapacity for self-government. In the United States, the ongoing immigration of undesirable types, defined as "human flotsam," threatened to destroy the American race. Because race determined morality and intellect, immigration posed a threat to the nation's democracy and other attributes. Linking the progressive faith in science and expertise with restrictionist bigotry, these arguments soon would have their day, but in the campaign for the literacy test, leading advocates saw the value of putting such contentions aside.[13]

Along with reenergizing restrictionists, receipt of the commission's *Reports* also shook Congress from its lethargy. The House Committee on Immigration quickly agreed to consider a literacy test bill that would require all immigrants except certain family members and those from the western hemisphere to be able to read or write English or some other language, but intervening developments dashed any hopes that the bill would be considered during that session. "The House machine," Patten fumed, "has decided upon limiting legislation this session to the appropriation bills." Many of the lame ducks did not want to go on record either for or against restriction; they preferred that their successors bear the brunt of any criticism. Patten continued roaming the Capitol, looking for ways to sway the House leadership, but neither chamber took any further action that session.[14]

The ensuing showdown, complete with a host of strange twists and turns, took place in January 1912. The Senate immigration committee, chaired by Lodge, reported an administrative measure without a literacy test or any other new means of restriction. As Lodge had insisted upon having the test included in the commission's recommendations, this puzzled and angered its supporters. According to those close to the senator, he feared that attachment of the test would stir up greater opposition than had its inclusion in the 1906 bill. On the floor North Carolina Democrat Furnifold Simmons argued that information gathered by the Dillingham Commission had removed the many consequences of unrestricted immigration from the realm of conjecture. Numerous authorities and many ordinary Americans believed that a reading test offered the best solution to the immigration problem and that it belonged in the present bill. When Dillingham himself tried to explain that the test had been removed solely for the sake of expediency, Simmons countered that its consideration should not be postponed.[15]

Dillingham's balanced response drew on his commission experience. American immigration, he began, had changed after 1880, and rather than going to the nation's agricultural regions, the newer arrivals, primarily southern Europeans, had settled in urban areas. (This had actually had been the tendency for all immigrants since at least 1850.) Yet recent immigrants shared their predecessors' sense of purpose; they also came in the prime of life and sent their children to school. Contrary to popular belief, their native governments did not ship them across the Atlantic; nor did major companies actively recruit them. Instead, most received information about life in the United States from friends and relatives. One the negative side, the majority of the new immigrants came alone, single men without families. They sought only to earn the greatest possible income in the least amount of time, which often led them to accept lower-than-standard wages and to subordinate creature comforts to other considerations. According to the commission's estimate, they collectively sent home a minimum of $141 million per year. They also separated themselves into colonies, usually urban enclaves, showed no interest in putting down roots, and—here he contradicted his earlier remarks—showed little inclination to send their children to school.

Although these issues were serious, Dillingham concluded, they were not the reasons for tightening entrance requirements. The problem was not the immigrants themselves. Rather, as the commission had argued in its recommendations, the United States had reached a point where it could no longer assimilate an unlimited number of even the best men and women. It

no longer needed every able-bodied laborer who sought to work in its industries, and immigrants in excess of the number needed caused problems.
At the end of its extensive study, the commission had concluded that the
literacy test offered the most feasible means of sufficiently reducing the
oversupply of unskilled laborers and barring those least likely to assimilate
American ways. When the test's supporters then asked why it was not in
the current bill, Dillingham responded that he had not favored its removal.
Lodge then reversed himself, saying that the full Senate should decide on
its inclusion.[16]

Lodge's announcement produced a veritable donnybrook. Over two days
in April 1912, legislators engaged in vociferous debate, and not even
calamity was allowed to interrupt the proceedings. On Sunday, 14 April,
the White Star liner *Titanic* sank after hitting an iceberg, and over fifteen
hundred of its passengers drowned. The catastrophe shocked the world.
"There were those," James Patten reported, "who urged that the Senate ad-
journ as did the House . . . 'out of respect' and as a tribute to the memories
of those who lost their lives on the *Titanic*." Unswayed by such calls for
reverence, Lodge and other leaders insisted that the Senate keep to its task
and dispose of the immigration bill. So while nautical tragedy preoccupied
much of the nation, the upper house moved toward closure on legislation
that might well decide the future of many other seaborne travelers.[17]

Another sensational event may have helped the restrictionists cause. On
12 January, a strike led by the sometimes violent Industrial Workers of the
World (IWW) had broken out among textile workers in Lawrence, Massachusetts. Several commentators implied a connection between the city's
large immigrant population and the appearance of radical-directed labor
unrest. Explaining why the workers would follow the IWW's "profoundly
revolutionary leadership," one observer noted that "the mill-hands are for
the most part foreigners . . . all of them very remote from an environment
conducive to the best American citizenship." Former commission staffer W.
Jett Lauck also placed much of the blame on immigrant workers, specifically those from southern and eastern Europe, who "have resisted an improvement in conditions of employment because of their lack of permanent interest in the industry in which they are engaged." Senators alluded
to the Lawrence strike in their calls for a literacy test, and James Patten believed that the high percentage of immigrants among the strikers, and their
willingness to follow the IWW, boded well for the test's passage.[18]

Although it took several more months to reach agreement between the
Senate and House, Patten proved to be a good prognosticator. What had become the Dillingham-Burnett bill, appropriately named for two former
commissioners, included a literacy test, a head-tax increase, and, in a show
of racism, a Senate provision excluding Asians who were not eligible for citizenship. The commission had endorsed this type of discrimination, but
not the type in Mississippi senator John S. Williams's narrowly defeated
proposal to exclude all Negroes immigrants. The commission's concerns

about the feasibility of certifying emigrants in Europe also may have influenced the decision to drop a requirement that those arriving in the United States have "a certificate of good character." Illinois Democratic representative Adolph Sabath, one of the bill's most vocal opponents, dismissed the commission's findings as already outdated, but former member John Burnett and other literacy test supporters drew on the commission's work in bringing together a House majority.[19]

Attention now turned to President William H. Taft. Exactly what he would do with the Dillingham-Burnett bill remained in doubt, but for some time he and his administration had given indications of being antirestrictionist. In November 1910, Harvard University president A. Lawrence Lowell, an adherent to the notion of Anglo-Saxon superiority, had urged Taft to sign a literacy test bill. "Without the power to read assimilation is very difficult," wrote Lowell, "and the exclusion of illiterates would, therefore, seem to be a wise and proper thing." Joseph Lee called Taft's attention to the commission's literacy test endorsement. It would be best, he acknowledged, if inspectors could look into immigrants' souls and let in only the best, "but until an instrument for that purpose is perfected it seems to me the recommendation of the commission is the sound one." Others offered similar judgements.[20]

Taft claimed that he had been in favor of a reading test, but that after reviewing the congressional debates he was "not quite so clear in my mind." He also received a negative assessment from Secretary of Commerce and Labor Charles Nagel. "It is my opinion," Nagel advised, "that Dr. Lowell has given too much weight to the mere ability to read and write." Character and physical condition should be the test of an immigrant's desirability. Illiteracy was always one factor in deciding the question of admission or rejection, evidently because it was useful in judging the likelihood that an immigrant would become a public charge, but it was not the determining factor. Conversely, literacy in combination with America's foreign-language newspapers' tendency to promote "colonization" in congested urban areas retarded assimilation. As part of a completely different admission process, Nagel concluded, he possibly could support a literacy test, but for the present, a sound mind, a square look, and a willingness to work should be the measures of a desirable immigrant.

Nagel also found reason to downplay the commission's literacy test endorsement. The commission had recommended the test as the most feasible method of restriction, the single provision best designed to keep out large numbers of immigrants, but its efficiency was not a measure of its fairness or justice. As an absolute requirement it would no doubt exclude a large number of undesirables, but it would also bar many otherwise acceptable men and women who could provide valuable industrial labor. "The practical question," Nagel asserted, "is whether so broad a measure shall be resorted to upon the ground that the good result will outweigh the bad." A better requirement would weigh illiteracy as one negative presumption against an alien that could be overcome by an affirmation of the migrant's general fitness. As to the concerns of the IRL and other restrictionists, they would be better served by promotion of the admission of good immigrants through support of "those who are engaged in the enforcement of existing laws." The secretary reiterated these views to the president after Taft had received the Dillingham-Burnett bill.[21]

Fearing the worst, restrictionists tried to sway the seemingly disinclined president. "I venture to say," Prescott Hall wrote of the literacy test, "that there is no measure which the mass of the people more anxiously desire than this." Author Madison Grant, in a prelude to what he would say in his book *The Passing of the Great Race,* invoked the specter of race. The literacy test, he argued, would reduce significantly the number of immigrants from southern and eastern Europe, peoples who had never demonstrated that they could maintain a high degree of civilization. Others shied away from race, instead emphasizing the adverse effects of immigration on wages and American standards of living. Even Prescott Hall circulated such a petition, which highlighted immigrants' purported contributions to domestic distress. The Italian American Chamber of Commerce mounted an impressive counteroffensive, amassing eight thousand signatures in protest against a literacy requirement.[22]

One of the most interesting appeals came from former commissioner Jeremiah Jenks, who, after his commission service, had concluded that there should be "further restriction of immigration." First, he subtly distorted the commission's findings, asserting that investigators had found many instances in which newly arrived aliens had taken work away from natives and earlier immigrants. In reality, the reports stated that when immigrants who were willing to accept lower pay moved into a particular industry, older employees generally moved on to other locations or positions, where they enjoyed higher wages. Jenks also made specific reference to the literacy test's anticipated exclusion of southern and eastern Europeans, but the reports, while mentioning that the stereotypical low-paid immigrants came from those areas, did not mention any particular group or type in its call for more extensive restriction. In closing, Jenks said that neither he nor Commissioner Charles Neill would have supported the literacy test if they had believed that any other method could provide the same beneficial results. Yet the two had given their support only at the second commission meeting on the issue, when Burnett's opposition had threatened to undermine the entire investigation.[23]

Others, in a variety of ways, also made use of the commission's recommendations. When President Taft convened a public hearing, F. S. Katzenbach, representing the Junior Order United American Mechanics, argued that the Dillingham-Burnett bill had been drafted in accordance with the commission's recommendations and that its passage would ensure that the fruits of the three-year inquiry would not be lost. Professor Marion D. Learned, in an ironic twist, testified that the commission's focus on recent arrivals had obscured the extent to which earlier immigrants had assimilated and contributed to their adopted nation; the same could hold true for newer arrivals. Finally, former commissioner and representative William Bennet discussed the commission's generally positive findings about the newer immigrants: "We found them less frequently in hospitals, less frequently in the poor-houses, less frequently in the asylums, than either the native born or those of older immigration."[24]

In the end, one progressive tenet, that of treating people fairly and with a sense of social justice, won out over the equally progressive penchant for practicality. It may have been Nagel's assertions that swayed the president, but William Bennet would offer an additional explanation. Prior to Taft's nomination, New York City Republicans had arranged for him to have a social evening with labor and community leaders on the East Side. There, in almost exclusively foreign-born company, he had gotten to know "some of the leading east side people and formed a high opinion of them as citizens and got an entirely new view of the immigration question." Taft would later tell Bennet that that evening, and the positive opinions he had formed about the immigrant guests, "had been largely influential in causing him to veto the bill." These assertions came many years later, but they are consistent with evidence from other sources.

Taft's February 1913 veto message conveyed the difficulty of his situation. He noted his "great reluctance" to reject the bill's "many valuable amendments," which would clarify existing statutes and make it easier to exclude undesirable immigrants. He also praised the Dillingham Commission, noting that it had recommended the bill's literacy test and other provisions after conducting "an extended investigation" and arriving at "carefully drawn conclusions." Yet he agreed with Nagel, whose analysis was included with the veto message, that the test violated America's tradition of welcoming all desirable immigrants. One can only surmise whether those desirables included the men with whom he and Bennet had socialized that evening in New York City.[25]

Taft's veto and the House's failure to override it disheartened restrictionists. The commission's recommendation seemed to have provided the endorsement necessary for getting the literacy test passed. The recommendation had presented the test as a practical, progressive reform, and two former commissioners had shepherded the bill through Congress. Test supporters could not accept Taft's and Nagel's logic, and some wondered what more they could do. IRL leader Robert Ward proposed disbanding the League, thinking that its emphasis on restriction might be too negative and therefore offensive to otherwise supportive people. He suggested the formation of a national committee for regulating immigration as an alternative.[26] This did not happen, and restrictionists instead looked to the future, when a new president would occupy the White House.

In the aftermath of Taft's veto, president-elect Woodrow Wilson presented restrictionists with a conundrum: how to assess his beliefs about immigration and thereby anticipate how he would react to a general restriction bill. His background offered conflicting indications. Joseph Wilson, Woodrow's father, was the son of Scotch-Irish immigrants, and his mother, Janet Woodrow, had immigrated from England as a child. These familial ties suggested that Woodrow might feel a kinship with contemporary immigrants. As a member of the Jefferson Society at the University of Virginia, Wilson debated the issue of Chinese exclusion, but there is no record of his opinion. In his 1901 *History of the American People,* however, he harshly criticized recent arrivals. He argued that the Chinese subsisted on a handful of rice and worked for a pittance, but that they were "more to be desired" than the currently arriving Europeans, whom he described as "the lowest class from the south of Italy and men out of the ranks where there was neither skill nor any initiative to quick intelligence." The new European immigrants adhered to lifestyles never before known to American workers, who tolerated them only because they filled menial occupations. Elsewhere, Wilson wrote highly of America's putative Anglo-Saxon roots.[27]

During his 1912 presidential campaign ten years after he wrote those words, Wilson largely repudiated his nativist writings. When the opposition Hearst newspapers reprinted salient passages from Wilson's *History* in an effort to provoke antipathy among ethnic voters, Wilson responded in a much more immigrant-friendly vein. "I believe," he told a foreign-language editor, "in the responsible restriction of immigration, but not in any restriction which will exclude from the country honest, industrious, men, who are seeking what America has always offered—an asylum for those who seek a free field." When pressed about the passages in his book, Wilson explained that he had written about an earlier time when the worst sort of imported contract laborers, artificially induced to come to the United States, had dominated the immigrant stream. Present fears about "too much immigration" had not produced in him "the least uneasiness" as to their "being gripped as we have been gripped." Although Wilson often made such remarks to ethnic leaders and organizations, suggesting political expediency as much as deep-seated conviction, he clearly had changed his message.[28]

This recent behavior convinced restrictionists that Wilson would not sign a literacy test bill unless they could show him its merits. "I wish we could give W. W. some instruction on the subject of immigration," grumbled Prescott Hall, "from a source he would respect. All the people I have asked have side-stepped." The IRL's Joseph Lee believed that Wilson was "the kind of man who cannot be driven," but who could "be shown by people who really know." Lee hoped to meet with Wilson, at which time he planned to stress the Dillingham Commission's recommendations, especially its endorsement of restriction as a means of preserving America's wages and standard of living. Additionally, Lee thought, selected scholars should convey similar messages to the longtime academic. Such high-brow opinions might well convince the increasingly progressive new president of the literacy test's merits.[29]

One of those selected to approach the new president was Edward A. Ross, professor of sociology at the University of Wisconsin and a former student of Wilson's at Johns Hopkins University. An authority on immigration who believed that the flood of new arrivals was one of the nation's most serious problems, Ross had recently completed a series of articles on the subject for *The Century,* which were later issued collectively as *The Old World in the New.* His work derided recent immigrants, stressing both their negative characteristics and the adverse effects of their presence in the United States. Ross promoted restriction as a way of safeguarding America's "high standards of living, institutions, and ideals." He called Wilson's attention to the growing number of poor-quality immigrants, "more and more remote to the orbit of our civilization," and arranged to have proofs of the *Century* articles sent to the White House.[30]

In "a demonstration of force," a delegation of test supporters, including former commissioner Jeremiah Jenks and former staffer William W. Husband, took their case directly to the White House. They tried to show that the literacy test would provide a workable solution to the nation's immigration ills. The test would reduce the number of single males, "a potent cause of overcrowding and vice," and cut down the numbers of those most responsible for "low standards of living, temporary residence, etc." Without concurrent restriction, aids to immigrant distribution would only aggravate existing problems by attracting immigrants in even higher numbers. In one of the rare uses of ethnically based arguments, the delegates contended that only one out of every 130 Italians, Magyars, or Poles was a farmer and that the literacy test was a "good selective test for races." It would largely curtail the arrival of those "least habituated to democratic ideas and institutions."[31]

Wilson ultimately trumped restrictionists' progressive-oriented arguments based on the literacy test's expected efficiency and socially remedial results with arguments reflecting what has been called the cosmopolitan strain of liberal progressivism. In a letter to South Carolina senator Ellison D. Smith the president suggested taking a more positive course of action. "Could we not substitute," he wondered, "for that provision [the literacy test] a provision arranging for a careful inquiry by the government, through some proper instrumentality, as to the best plans for effecting an economic distribution of our immigrants after they arrive in this country, so as to relieve the congestion in cities, assist the industry in rural districts, and relieve the many problems which associate themselves with the arrival and residence here of unskilled workmen?" Wilson had begun to frame his belief that any immigration reform should incorporate assimilation and education, drawing on the nation's traditional ability to absorb desirable alien newcomers. He clearly did not think that greater restriction was an acceptable answer to immigration-related social problems.[32]

Wilson received his first literacy test bill in January 1915, and although he had promised to keep an open mind to the extent of emulating Taft by holding a public hearing, his opposition was widely assumed.[33] In the end, despite the measure's potential for "enhancing " the work of the Bureau of Immigration, inclusion of two unacceptable sections prompted Wilson's veto. The first was a provision that would extend the antiradical restrictions of the Immigration Act of 1903 by barring those opposed to organized government. The president objected to this because it did not exempt those convicted of purely political offenses, so it could, for example, exclude those who merely sought the recognition of unalienable rights. The literacy test itself was the second piece of which Wilson disapproved, saying that it would bar "those to whom the opportunities of elementary education have been denied, without regard to their character, their purpose, or their natural capacity."

Wilson's message emphasized America's ability to assimilate newcomers. Previously the United States had welcomed all but those specifically designated as undesirable, as judged by tests "of quality or of character or of personal fitness." Immigrants admitted under these rules had made America great. Now, as the United States stood "in fullness of our national strength and at the maturity of our great institutions," Congress proposed to alter this traditional open-door policy. Wilson left unstated, but certainly implied, a reiteration of his earlier contention that the country could continue to take in the masses and make of them valuable additions. Wilson stated directly that the literacy test bill aimed "at restriction, not selection," and that he could not accept such a change in policy. He also doubted that that was what the American people wanted.[34]

The House failed by only four votes to override Wilson's veto, then two years later, like Banquo's ghost, a similar bill passed Congress. The outbreak of World War I in Europe had reduced immigration, which could have been an inducement to postpone the enactment of any new exclusions, but restrictionists argued that the number of new arrivals would increase dramatically with the end of hostilities. "No man," wrote Representative Augustus Gardner of Massachusetts, echoing a Senate speech by Idaho's Republican senator William Borah, "can fail to realize that the termination of the European War will swamp this country with immigrants." Others suggested that restriction was an important part of military preparedness. It took seven days of marathon debate for the new restriction bill to pass the House, and four more in the Senate. It reached the president's desk in January 1917.[35]

Wilson once again refused to sign the proposed legislation. In his second veto message he repeated his opposition to the literacy requirement, calling it a "test of opportunity," not quality. As such, it was "radical change in policy" that was "not justified in principle." Again, Wilson framed the issue as a contest between "feasibility," which had been the commission's rationale for endorsing the test, and his notion of protecting and continuing America's tradition of welcoming all but the pernicious to its shores. He noted that many immigrants came to the United States seeking an education, implying his continued belief that the nation could safely provide this opportunity. Not even the looming specter of war, which he knew would unleash jingoistic patriotism, could shake his faith in assimilation—his conviction that the United States had the means to correct the social difficulties to which immigrants might contribute, that newcomers simply should not be excluded. He also found fault with the wording of an exemption for those fleeing religious persecution.[36]

The necessary two-thirds of each chamber disagreed with Wilson's arguments, and with only brief debate, Congress overrode the veto. "Senate passed the immigration bill over veto sixty-two to nineteen *Bill is now law*" wired an ecstatic James Patten, and it was cause for celebration. He urged Joseph Lee to host a dinner party for the League's executive committee, where they could bask in the glow of success and "fight it over again." Henry P. Fairchild, restrictionist author and one of Lee's guests, could hardly believe what had happened. "Can you realize," he wrote to the IRL leader, "that we actually have the literacy test at last?" Indeed, it had been a long time in coming, and the enactment of the test marked a turning point in the history of U.S. immigration policy.[37] Thereafter, the nation would exclude otherwise desirable immigrants, a fact that had been recognized even by some who had voted for the test.

Several factors accounted for this closing of the open door. Possible U.S. entrance into World War I had heightened concerns about the possibly social disruption, and some had concerns about the loyalty of "hyphenates." Equally important, most of the bill's supporters, even those who generally found no fault with the foreign-born themselves, had accepted the commission's assertion, albeit not necessarily supported by its *Reports*, that too many immigrants posed socioeconomic problems. Therefore, the time had come for the nation to find a practical means of reducing their numbers, and toward that end, Congress selected the commission's primary recommended method, the literacy test. True, the commission's endorsement had come about only through last-minute wrangling, but once the endorsement was in place, the commissioners had provided a "progressive" rationale for the test's passage.

This demonstrates one of the Progressive Era's great paradoxes: the use of negative means to promote progress. The literacy test was intended to exclude men and women deemed otherwise desirable, people who under different circumstances could well have contributed to the nation's well-being. Unlike those previously excluded, they did not have negative traits, but since the number of immigrants had to be reduced, it was better to take good literates than good illiterates. This logic assumed that doing something negative, in this case keeping desirable migrants out of the United States, would have overall beneficial results. The test would be beneficial because it would exclude unneeded and hard-to-assimilate foreign laborers. To some, this reliance on a negative measure may seem to compromise the progressives' commitment to social betterment, but it is better seen as an example of the era's often contradictory nature. Restriction's next chapter, which also would have a commission connection, offers an even more striking example.

Joseph Lee responded favorably to Patten's call for a celebration, but he also viewed the event as an opportunity for restrictionists to discuss their next step. "Now is the chance to try for some of those schemes you thought we should try instead of the illiteracy test," he wrote to Richards Bradley. "I have always thought that they would make a very good second." The Dillingham Commission, whose endorsement had kept the literacy test alive and had contributed significantly to its enactment, would provide that "scheme." Immediately below the literacy test in its list of recommendations, the commission noted numerical limitation as another possible means of restriction. This would become the even more drastic, and historically more controversial, "second."[38]

CHAPTER EIGHT

"Mathematical Certainty"

JOSEPH REVESZ PROBABLY NEVER HEARD of the Dillingham Commission, and almost certainly he never met its executive secretary, William W. Husband, but both, albeit indirectly, tragically affected Revesz's life. In November 1922 the Slavic immigrant learned that his family would not be joining him in the Chicago apartment he had been preparing for their arrival. Officials at Ellis Island had deported his wife, Teresa, and sons, Adam and Joseph. Upon their return to Europe, Adam was conscripted into the army, and Teresa decided to postpone another attempt at emigration until after her son had completed his military obligation. What had precipitated this sorrowful chain of events? When Joseph's family arrived in the United States, that year's Jugo-Slav immigrant quota already had been filled. Had Joseph been a citizen, his wife and family could have entered, but that was not the case.[1]

The quota system principally owed its inception and subsequent adoption, but not its final form, to the Dillingham Commission. Prior to the commission's recommendation of a quota system there had been periodic proposals for such a strategy. Usually vague, such as Henry Cabot Lodge's 1905 suggestion that the United States admit "so many from each country," these schemes had received minimal consideration.[2] That changed with the efforts of Husband and William Dillingham, who considered numerical limitation first as an alternative to the embattled literacy test, then as an additional means of checking the expected postwar surge in immigration. Initially enacted as a temporary measure in 1921, then made permanent in 1924, the quotas would remain a fixture in American immigration policy for almost half a century, until 1965.

Not surprisingly, historians have focused on the end result, an extreme and biased system, and have tended to interpret immigration quotas as a manifestation of the pervasive and often extreme conservatism that dominated the post–World War I era. The Red Scare, the Palmer raids, and the trial of immigrant anarchists Nicola Sacco and Bartolomeo Vanzetti stressed the idea of imported, "alien" radicalism. Joining those concerned about threats to American "patriotism," Senator Henry Cabot Lodge stressed the need to "prevent a flood of Bolsheviki" immigrants. The resurgence of a more nativist, as opposed to merely antiblack, Ku Klux Klan also indicated Americans' growing intolerance for elements that were perceived as disruptive, especially those viewed as foreign and un-American. "In a climate gray with dissolution," explains historian John Higham, "the occasion had arrived . . . for 'a genuine 100 per cent American immigration law.'" The setting of definitive limits on the number of alien arrivals, with exemptions for family members of naturalized citizens and for immigrants from the Western Hemisphere, offered a means for agitated Americans to defend their beleaguered society.[3]

This interpretation focuses primarily on the quota system's draconian final form, which disproportionately affected new and Asian immigrants, but it tends to ignore the scheme's progressive roots. As Americans entered the postwar era, they did succumb to heightened anxieties engendered by concerns about disruptive elements, but they retained their faith in precision and efficiency and their belief that expertise, if properly applied, could solve social problems. Emphasis on social control, with its inherent negativity, superseded more positive approaches to social betterment, but the assumed triumph of progress did not wane. For Husband, Dillingham, and many other quota supporters, the system's objectivity, certainty, and even fairness in reducing the number of immigrants were its most appealing features. This high-minded rationale does not excuse the system's eventual excesses, bigotry, and blatant discrimination. Even Husband admitted that his proposal would most affect southern and eastern Europeans, albeit not because of specifically directed ill-will. In its final form the quota system applied the negative agenda of Madison Grant with the positive precision of Franz Boas and the commission's *Dictionary of Races.*

In its final report, the commission had listed a Husband-drafted quota system among its suggested new means of restricting immigration: "The limitation of the number of each race arriving each year to a certain percentage of that race arriving during a given period of years." But the majority's endorsement of the literacy test and the ensuing struggle for its enactment tended to obscure the quota and other suggestions: the exclusion of single, unskilled laborers; annual limitations at each port; an increased head tax, with a lower assessment for men with families; and a money-in-possession requirement. There is little to suggest that the commission or the public paid the additional suggestions much more than cursory attention. Then President Taft's veto of the literacy test convinced some of its discouraged supporters, including by that time Dillingham, that alternative measures must now be explored. Dillingham directed Husband to return his attention to numerical restriction.[4]

After studying the report of population in the 1910 census, Husband concluded that "some percentage system based on the foreign-born population of the United States might afford a means of what was desired, which admittedly was to cut down the great influx of aliens from Southern and Eastern Europe without erecting any barrier against immigration on a normal basis from Western Europe." This rationale did target new immigrants, but it was not its author's last word. After calculating the projected quotas, Husband concluded that the system "would afford the desired solution of the troublesome problem without a logical suggestion of discrimination among the various nationalities concerned." His system would not show prejudice against eastern and southern Europeans on cultural or racial grounds; such people would be more affected because they made up a higher proportion of current arrivals, whose numbers would be reduced. This would help to alleviate immigration-connected economic problems, which had been the commission's major concern.[5]

Husband prepared a table demonstrating how his plan would change annual immigration from different countries, allowing for variance depending on the base percentage, and presented it to Dillingham. To Husband's chagrin, the senator did not enthusiastically endorse the proposal, but he did discuss it with former commissioner and Senate colleague Henry Cabot Lodge. Both men were hesitant to abandon the literacy test, but they agreed that Husband should put his "new and rather radical provision" in the form of a legislative bill, which Dillingham would then introduce. Although Husband's proposition "promised mathematical certainty instead of a theoretical result based on the extent of illiteracy among immigrant aliens," the quota bill got no further than the Senate immigration committee.[6]

Given the extent to which restrictionists had committed themselves to the literacy test, it was not surprising that they turned a cold shoulder to alternative proposals, but the lack of serious congressional consideration was not an outright rejection. Husband's proposal did receive notable support. Former commissioner Jeremiah Jenks believed that President Wilson would be more inclined to support a percentage plan with an Asian provision, and he suggested combining quotas with a literacy test. Immigration Restriction League (IRL) leaders Prescott Hall and Robert Ward also liked the numerical proposal, but they did not want to encumber their favored literacy test, to which they and most other restrictionists remained committed even in the face of Taft's veto. After the adoption of a literacy test provision there would be ample time to back the quota plan. Conversely, as late as 1916 James Patten viewed Husband's substitute with suspicion, believing that the advocates of numerical limitation really did not want any new exclusions. He thought they only hoped to complicate congressional consideration and thereby scuttle the passage of any restrictive legislation.[7]

Concurrent with the presentation of Husband's initial quota proposal, Dr. Sidney Gulick, former missionary to Asia and head of the National Committee on Constructive Immigration Legislation, drafted a similar scheme. Like Husband, Gulick intended his plan as a reform measure. He hoped to give Asians, then largely excluded by statute and gentlemen's agreement, the same opportunity as other immigrants by assigning all nationalities impartial quotas based on their numbers already in the United States. "The danger of overwhelming oriental immigration" Gulick contended, "can be obviated by a general law allowing a maximum annual immigration from any land of a fixed percentage of those from that land already here and naturalized." Gulick's phraseology is somewhat confusing, as Asians could not be "naturalized" under existing law, but he likely meant citizens, who would be the American-born descendants of immigrants. He also intended that that prohibition, along with the other forms of Asian exclusion, would be eliminated by the new Asian quotas. Gulick testified before the Senate immigration committee in January 1914, and while Husband's proposal became the basis for various Dillingham bills, the former commission secretary later gave consideration to Asian quotas, which he had omitted from his original plan. Husband also worked with Gulick to elicit support for their shared idea.[8]

While Congress focused most of its attention on the literacy test, Husband pursued a variety of immigration-related endeavors. In 1912 he joined the Department of Commerce and Labor's Contract Labor Division, the agency that oversaw the enforcement of laws prohibiting hiring abroad for jobs in the United States, and in 1916 he began editing the *Immigration Journal*. The journal covered a wide range of immigration topics and issues and contained reports of ethnic conferences, expert commentary and opinion, news about immigrants themselves, and information about related congressional activity. Several prominent immigration authorities contributed articles. Husband edited the journal for a little over a year, then World War I effectively cut off European emigration. Still, even this brief tenure provided him with ample opportunity to promote his ideas.[9]

Several *Immigration Journal* articles promoted the quota system. In the first edition, Husband lauded a Dillingham bill that combined numerical restriction with a literacy test. He maintained that quotas would exclude more immigrants than the literacy test and would offer definite rather than conjectural results. The two measures could work in tandem: the quotas would limit the number of immigrants, while the literacy test would cull those of lesser quality. A later edition of the journal featured an editorial by Gulick calling for a better Asian immigration policy, one that would not discriminate against people of particular nationalities. Gulick supported maximum limits on the immigration of males and unwed females that would be based on nationality. Each group's quota would be a percentage of its number who were U.S. citizens. Congress would review the quotas and consider changes after each decennial census and also set minimal quotas for groups that had little or no previous American immigration. This idea evidently appealed to Husband, who printed Gulick's address and encouraged those with comments to write the author.[10]

The end of World War I engendered new interest in immigrant quotas. The nation's first general exclusion measure, the literacy test, had already become law, but the November 1918 armistice removed war-related impediments to transatlantic migration, which restrictionists feared would quickly return to prewar highs. Former commissioner Jeremiah Jenks, for one, saw this as a serious problem, and William Husband discussed it in the *Immigration Journal*. Congress extended enforcement of a wartime passport requirement until March 1921, while growing fears about unprecedentedly high numbers of immigrants fleeing their recently ravaged nations pushed the lawmakers to consider new restrictions. Additionally, the previous winter's Red Scare had heightened America's distrust of immigrants. The combination of their growing numbers and their putative subversive intent all but ensured that Congress would enact new restrictions.[11]

Pundits offered a variety of opinions. Madison Grant simply wanted to "dictate just what social elements we would allow to enter," but he did not specify how this could or should be done. Prescott Hall and Henry P. Fairchild supported Dilllingham's percentage plan, but without Gulick's Asian quotas, which the senator had initially supported but eventually abandoned to increase the chances of passing a new restriction bill. Jeremiah Jenks did not have a problem with Asian quotas, since any allotments would be negligible. Conversely, the whole quota idea had little appeal to author John Commons, because the system of setting standards was "too mathematical and mechanical." It would be better, he believed, to "bring forward the physical and mental tests." Congressman Albert Johnson thought he might support the Gulick idea, based on a low percentage, but also worried that others would constantly work to raise it. Finally, he joined others in favoring an immigration moratorium.[12]

Suspension proposals attracted attention initially. North Carolina senator Lee Overman called for a five-year prohibition, while Representative Albert Johnson, who had emerged as a vocal xenophobe by connecting immigration restriction with antiradicalism, proposed a two-year ban with exemptions for government officials and certain family members of U.S. citizens. Johnson argued that the pending immigrant inrush constituted a national emergency, which warranted immediate passage of his bill. It would not target any specific group, but would help to combat imported radicalism. Attorney General A. Mitchell Palmer had recently stressed this growing threat, and Johnson contended that there was a clear connection between it and alien provocateurs. Johnson's activism was somewhat ironic, since the IRL had once described him as "talking restriction, but apparently for home consumption only." Now he was leading the fight for new and extreme exclusions.[13]

Longtime antirestrictionist Adolph Sabath condemned the proposal as the product of hysteria, and former commissioner William Bennet, although no longer in Congress, argued that the bill would exclude needed laborers. Frederick A. Wallis, commissioner of immigration at Ellis Island, agreed that large numbers of new arrivals posed an economic threat, but disapproved of a temporary suspension. Instead, he thought, America needed to skim off the cream of the immigrant crop. Johnson countered with warnings of a postwar immigrant influx, especially from central Europe, calling it an emergency the nation could not ignore but could avert. Others believed that the moratorium would give Congress time to conduct a thorough revision of all immigration laws while simultaneously providing an interim barrier against imported radicalism. Despite the protests, after reducing the suspension to fourteen months the House passed the Johnson bill on 13 December.[14]

The Senate then devoted its attention to various quota plans. Thomas Sterling of South Dakota offered a complicated system of ethnically based immigrant quotas. Designed by Sidney Gulick, it called for the creation of an immigration board made up of the secretaries of State, Labor, Commerce, Agriculture, and Interior, plus a chairman appointed by the president, which would "define and interpret the term 'ethnic group,' taking into consideration questions of race, mother-tongue affiliation, nationality, and such other relationships as tend to constitute group unity." Each April, the board would calculate the maximum number of each ethnicity who could be admitted to the United States during the next fiscal year. Determination would be based on various regions' need for labor, a particular group's "adaptability" to meet those needs, its demonstrated "assimilability," and maintenance of American wages and standards of living. No quota could exceed 10 percent of the group's combined number of naturalized citizens and native-born children of alien parents.[15]

Senator Dillingham offered a Husband-prepared alternative. The former commission administrator dismissed those, such as Representative Johnson, who warned of an immigrant disaster, although he shared their concerns about the number and types of arrivals returning to pre–literacy test levels. Better distribution, for which Dillingham had been arguing since 1906, could alleviate some of the problems, but the Johnson bill would serve no positive purpose. It would reduce immigration, but in a way that discriminated against northern and western Europeans. The fault was with the bill's exemption for family members. Since most southern and eastern Europeans had come to the United States recently, they were likely to have parents, siblings, or spouses still in Europe who wished to immigrate. This would be far less likely among the more established old immigrants. While the Johnson bill's prohibition would reduce immigration from this group to almost nothing, the more recently numerous new immigrants would continue to stream into the United States.

The better solution, Husband contended, would be to fix a reasonable limit on the amount of immigration from any one country. This would reduce the number of arriving southern and eastern Europeans, but not in a discriminatory way. Dillingham's and Sterling's bills both offered such a fix, but with notable differences. Sterling proposed limits based on "racial" status, which might be difficult to determine, especially with the postwar shifting of national borders. Although Husband admitted that in some cases a combination of nationality and ethnicity might work best, he preferred a simpler method. The Dillingham bill, which Husband had prepared, would base limitations on nationality and set the quotas at 5 percent of the number of each group residing in the United States. It would reduce immigration from southern and eastern Europe by about two-thirds, and it would allow for the doubling of that coming from northern and western Europe.[16] No one, of course, challenged the plan's flagrant prejudice by suggesting that if the United States had to reduce immigration, itself a debatable proposition, it simply could set an overall limit and give out the slots indiscriminately until they were gone.

Husband's allusion to using quotas based on a combination of nationality and ethnicity touched on the contentious matter of classifying eastern European Jews. In the precision-oriented Progressive Era, this presented a problem. With Husband's approval, the immigration commission had given Russians, Poles, Lithuanians, and Hebrews separate designations, even though many Jews lived in and had adapted the cultural characteristics of Russia, Poland, and Lithuania. In theory, the Sterling bill emulated the commission's thinking in that its method of racial categorization would provide Jews with their own separate quota, but Husband proposed lumping together all immigrants from a particular country. The New York *Jewish Daily Forward* decried this practice in the case of Russia, claiming that it would unjustifiably curtail Jewish immigration; others, however, promoted the restriction's necessity by raising the specter of a massive influx of Europe's most impoverished Jews.[17]

New York Republican congressman Isaac Siegel and other Jewish American leaders objected to such a negative prognostication, claiming that there was no threat of such an immigrant invasion. An addendum to a House report supporting the Johnson suspension bill, which drew on the observations of an anti-Semitic State Department official, emphasized concerns about undesirable Jewish immigrants, especially from Poland. Critics countered that most Jews, except family members seeking to join earlier immigrants, wanted to stay in Poland and that the previous fall's onrush had resulted from a desire to escape Bolshevism. Supported by confirmation from Secretary of State Charles Evans Hughes, they also argued that congestion and the slow issuance of passports at Warsaw had given the impression of a Polish Jewish onslaught on immigration offices there, when in fact the same people were coming day after day trying to surmount bureaucratic impediments.[18]

Although Representative Siegel and other antirestrictionists assiduously pressed their case, the Dillingham bill continued to draw favor. Husband's testimony, coupled with numerous criticisms of Johnson's temporary suspension plan, convinced the Senate immigration committee to replace Johnson's plan with a quota system. Nationality-based limits would be equal to 5 percent of each group's foreign-born U.S. population according to the 1910 census. The temporary quotas would exclude primarily southern and eastern Europeans and thereby quiet public anxiety about a pending "flood of immigration." The Senate unanimously passed the revised bill and immediately called for a conference with the House, which subsequently agreed to the Senate bill, with significant changes.[19]

The conference committee provoked controversy when it reduced the quotas, still based on the 1910 census, to 3 percent, but the disagreements did little to impede the bill's ultimate passage. Isaac Siegel condemned the percentage reduction and argued that Dillingham disapproved of the change. Under questioning, however, he refused to elaborate on the Vermont senator's position. The use of the 1910 instead of the 1920 census also prompted censure. Siegel claimed that the 1920 figures would be available shortly and that the use of the earlier enumeration was a deliberate attempt to discriminate against southern and eastern Europeans. Responding to this issue, Albert Johnson claimed that the final 1920 tabulations were not complete. New York Democrat Herbert C. Pell Jr. then asked whether such an important matter might be better postponed until the next Congress, which would have more time for careful consideration. Such protests failed to carry the day, and both the House, by an overwhelming 296 to 40 vote, and the Senate passed the bill. It then went to outgoing President Woodrow Wilson.[20]

As indicated by his previous vetoes of two literacy test bills, Wilson had consistently opposed drastic new immigration restrictions, and the ailing president, who had suffered a stroke while campaigning for the League of Nations Treaty, decided that he would not sign the Dillingham bill either. According to Secretary of the Navy Josephus Daniels, Wilson continued to believe in America's ability "to grip" those who were willing to embrace their new land. Longing for "an X ray to determine where ones [sic] heart was—in this country or some other," he wanted only "to send back those who were not Americans." Secretary of Labor William B. Wilson, after reviewing the bill and assessing prevailing conditions, advised the president: "No immigration emergency exists that would justify temporary legislation of this character." Additionally, the plan posed administrative difficulties, such as the enforcement of fixed quotas at multiple entry ports. Because Congress had adjourned, President Wilson did not have to specify his own objections; he simply killed the bill with a pocket veto.[21]

Wilson's disapproval only briefly stalled the quota bill's enactment. After the inauguration of President Warren G. Harding, a self-proclaimed restrictionist who had "voted for the most stringent form of immigration legislation," Congress met in a special session during which both senators and representatives introduced a host of restriction bills. Proposals ranged from numerical exclusion to a four-year moratorium on virtually all immigration. The House acted first, passing a 3 percent quota plan. Defying its critics, the immigration committee followed the more discriminatory course of using the 1910 rather than the 1920 census, arguing that the earlier count could provide "a substantial base established on what is known as the 'old immigration,' which has become more permanently fixed in the United States than the 'new immigration.'" The bill's fourteen months of operation would be enough time to determine the feasibility of using the newer census as the basis for permanent legislation. Perhaps as a signal to those so inclined, the committee forewarned that a decision to use the later census might require a lowering of the percentage rate in order "to restrict immigration to any marked degree."

By this time Congress did have a choice of using either the 1910 or the 1920 figures. On 15 April, W. M. Stewart, acting director of the U.S. Census, informed Representative Siegel that the requested 1920 statistics on America's foreign-born population would be ready by 23 April. They would have been available even earlier except for some unforeseen processing difficulties. Siegel conveyed this information to the House immigration committee, which nonetheless opted to base the quotas on numbers from 1910. Adolph Sabath and Massachusetts Republican Robert S. Maloney then joined Siegel in denouncing the committee's choice as a clear demonstration of the bill's injustice. Even if quotas were the best way to reduce the number of immigrants from the most prominent ethnic groups, the same end could have been achieved in a less discriminatory fashion, such as making an equal number of slots available for each group or a total number of annual slots available indiscriminately. Instead, what had begun as Husband's plan for certainty had become a tool for bigotry. Both houses of Congress eventually agreed to put the bill in essentially the same form in which it had gone to Wilson, and this time it met with presidential approval.[22]

President Harding also selected William Husband to be commissioner-general of immigration, appropriately putting him in charge of implementing the system he had devised. Upon accepting the position, Husband showed himself to be typically progressive, acknowledging concerns about immigration but not condemning the immigrants themselves. He viewed the quotas as a temporary safeguard that would facilitate the abatement of America's war-engendered distrust of foreigners. Believing that "our immigration problem is largely one of the distribution of immigrants," he advocated the creation of a new distribution division within the Immigration Service. Senator Dillingham had long championed this approach of matching new arrivals to the areas that wanted or needed them, but any such scheme would have to wait. The quota system now demanded Husband's undivided attention.[23]

By June 1921 problems had already appeared. How to circulate the current immigrant totals for each nationality to various entry stations and how to set quotas for the new postwar nations troubled the new commissioner-general. The latter problem has a certain irony given Husband's earlier criticism of Senator Sterling's "racial" quotas. Also, American councils in Europe would need to have up-to-date information about the numbers of arrivals so they would know how many visas to issue and could keep steamship companies abreast of how many immigrants they should transport. Italians and members of a few other nationalities had already filled their monthly quotas, set at 20 percent of their annual totals, and more continued to arrive. Husband blamed the steamship companies, accusing them of "open, bold, and deliberate" attempts to exceed monthly limits, and he demanded that they comply with the new law. In the end, he and Secretary of Labor James J. Davis did allow an excess of almost 12,000 in the June quotas, but since that marked the end of the fiscal year, they charged them against the 1922 allotments. The commissioner wanted Congress to make steamship lines legally responsible for such quota overruns.[24]

In spite of these administrative problems, Husband never wavered in his support of the quotas' intent and purpose. He praised the act's operation, including its tacit discrimination against the new immigrants. "I do not hesitate to say," he wrote in August 1922, "that this per centum law has accomplished the purpose for which it was obviously enacted with a degree of success which few anticipated." Nations of northwestern Europe had not exhausted their quotas, and they now supplied a greater percentage of America's total immigration. Instead of what would have been an almost certain increase in the amount of immigration from southern and eastern Europe, the numbers from these regions had decreased by about 20 percent. Hence, Husband concluded that the law had shown itself effective in "keeping immigration down to an amount that the United States can absorb." It tended "to introduce to this country people who, as past experience has shown, assimilate very rapidly." However, after the first five months of its operation, he declined to tell a congressional committee whether the law should be extended.[25]

In 1924, as Congress debated making the quota system permanent, Husband reversed his earlier contention that it should be only a temporary expedient. He had come to doubt whether any other method could provide as effective restriction. He did, however, suggest several remedial changes. The quotas, he believed, should be counted overseas, with final reviews or inspections taking place in the United States. Initially accepted immigrants would receive a "quota certificate" good for six months; this would let them know before they sold their property or otherwise prepared to move that they would have the opportunity to enter the United States if they could meet all other entrance requirements. Husband also advocated dividing the quotas equally over twelve months and letting minor children take the nationality of their parents regardless of their own birth country.[26]

Congress did make the quota system permanent 1924, and this time it made Husband's tool for mathematical certainty excessively discriminatory. The first phase lowered the percentage from 3 to 2 and applied it to foreign-born totals from the 1890 census. The second phase, intended for 1927 but not implemented until 1929, called for even more discriminatory quotas.

Called the National Origins System, it assigned national quotas derived from arcane and highly suspect statistical analysis of the entire 1920 U.S. population, going back for data to the 1790 census. For example, experts determined that 44 percent of Americans were of British origin, so that nation recieved a quota of 44 percent of the 150,000 overall total; Italians received less than 4 percent. These were deliberate attempts to utilize population samples including fewer southern and eastern Europeans. The result, admittedly skewed by the onset of the Great Depression, which made the United States a less appealing destination, was the near elimination of immigration from the groups that had dominated U.S. immigration since the turn of the century. Husband had not recommended the congressional changes, but if he had any strong reservations, he did not voice them in his annual report. His only complaint concerned what he believed to be redundant language regarding Chinese exclusion.[27]

The making of the permanent quota system marked the immigration commission's final chapter. The commission's inclusion of numerical limitations among possible means of restriction gave the measure legitimacy, and its emphasis on objective, statistical information certainly influenced William Husband, the quota system's principal author, proponent, and implementer. Husband's work exemplified the investigators' typically progressive search for certainty. He envisioned his plan as one that would place an absolute cap, an immutable limit, on the annual number of immigrants, thereby providing a definitive solution to a problem that had vexed the United States for over thirty years. Also, Congress could easily make changes to accommodate future exigencies by adjusting the determining percentages.

Whether it was deliberately discriminatory or merely the unbiased result of an effort to curtail the size of the most prevalent immigrant groups, even Husband's original proposal targeted new immigrants. By using ethnic divisions, even the most innocuous quota plans invited qualitative judgments based on place of origin. Husband, and later Congress, could have achieved the certainty by coming up with an overall total to be broken down into twelve equal monthly parts and filled on a first come, first served basis. Instead, he stressed that the various Dillingham bills "would result in a very material reduction in the movement from various countries of Southern and Eastern Europe." The 1921 act, he later claimed, had deterred "millions" of such immigrants.[28]

Treatment of Asians provides an even more glaring example of the quotas' discriminatory nature, as the various acts assigned a very small Asian allotment, and that only to the Japanese. This was blatant bigotry given that the previous exclusions had limited Asian immigration to the extent that so few would have been counted in each decennial census that Asians would have received only minimal quotas. This treatment is even more reprehensible because the commission had, overall, reported favorably on Asian immigrants in the western states. Husband had coordinated his push

TABLE 2

Country	1922 Quotas	Projected Quotas Using 10%	Annual Average, 1903–1912
Germany	68,039	250,398	35,139
Sweden	19,956	66,806	22,877
Italy	42,021	134,426	207,152
Russia	34,247	175,520	172,581

Source: Annual Report of the Commissioner General of Immigration to the Secretary of Labor, for the fiscal year ending 1921, 18; Husband, "Press Release," Husband Papers. The projected 10 percent quotas and annual averages are based on Husband's Press Release figures.

for numerical limitations with that of Asian advocate Sidney Gulick, and at least in the privacy of his own notes and papers, Husband had computed quotas for the various Asian groups. But anti-Asian bigotry was well-established by the time of the quota system's implementation, and in an era of heightened intolerance, it had no chance of being set aside.[29]

Husband, and by extension Dillingham and the immigration commission, cannot be excused for the quota acts' inequities, but many of those inequities were due primarily to the actions of congressional extremists. Husband's original plan had relatively liberal provisions. It had called for admitting up to 10 percent—the same figure Dillingham had used in his original, 1913, bill—"of the number of persons of such nationality resident in the United States," with a minimum of five thousand for any admissible group. With quotas based on the 1910 census, this determinant would have eased the discrimination against southern and eastern Europeans. No western European group with an annual prewar average of over five thousand would have approached its quota limit under Husband's 10 percent plan, or the 1921 Quota Act, for that matter, and the Husband plan would have treated Slavs, Poles, Italians, and Russian Jews more generously than did the act that was finally passed (see table 2).[30]

Another display of congressional partiality was in the choice of census. Husband called for using the "United States census next preceding" as the base to which the Bureau of Immigration would apply the selected percentage. This method would have been a least at little more favorable toward those who had recently arrived in large numbers (see table 3). After 1890 more southern and eastern Europeans had appeared in each successive enumeration. Although immigrant-friendly congressmen Sabath, Siegel, and Maloney opposed the entire 1921 Dillingham bill, they did urge the more numerous restrictionists to designate the 1920 census as the basis for quota allocations. To do otherwise, the dis-

TABLE 3—SAMPLE 1920S QUOTA OPTIONS

Nation	1922 Quotas Based on 1910 Census	1922 Quotas Based on 1920 Census	1929 Quotas Based on National Origins Act
Germany	68,039	50,583	25,957
Sweden	19,956	18,767	3,314
Italy	42,021	48,303	5,802
Poland	20,019	31,199	6,524
Russia	34,247	42,015	2,784

Source: U.S. Department of Commerce, Bureau of the Census, *Fourteenth Census of the United States Taken in the Year 1920* (Washington, D.C.: Government Printing Office, 1922), 3:47–48; U.S. Senate, 70th Congress, 2nd Session, Senate Document 259. The population figures in the 1920 census were multiplied by 3 percent to derive the quotas. Had the Immigration Service used this enumeration, it would have had to make adjustments, allowable under the law, to account for shifting European borders. Poland, for example, did not exist as a nation-state in 1910, the census year chosen for setting the quotas, but Poles did receive a quota.

senters argued, would be to discriminate against people "who have so conclusively shown their worth to the nation." Congress instead opted to use the 1910 census for the temporary measure, then the 1890 enumeration for the permanent one.[31]

Finally, Husband's plan can be compared to the near prohibition proposed by Albert Johnson. It would have been much more draconian, ensuring the separation of families and the wholesale denial of migration opportunity. Johnson's plan received enough support to pass the House of Representatives, and there is no reason to doubt that President Harding, the champion of "normalcy," would have signed it. The question of what would happen after the fourteen-month moratorium is open to speculation, but given the repressive social climate of the early 1920s, it is at least highly probable that it would have been extended and perhaps even made permanent along the lines of Chinese exclusion. Even with only a minimal fourteen-month tenure, it would have reflected far greater xenophobia than the alternative. The quotas did discriminate, but they let in at least some immigrants from all European nations.

The Quota Acts stand as a testament to both the laudable aspects of progressivism and its most pernicious manifestations. Progressives such as William Husband and the members of the Dillingham Commission sought practical solutions, often involving legislative remedies, to America's most pressing problems. This included searching for a practical means of dealing with large numbers of new immigrants and resolving the problems to which they reputedly contributed. By the early 1900s, it meant finding a way to reduce their numbers. William Husband developed the quota system as a sensible and mathematically certain method for curtailing immigration. One commentator described it as "too logical, if anything" as a means of restriction.[32]

Athough subsequent analysis clearly shows that it discriminated in favor of northern and western Europeans, its initial advocates believed that it avoided the ticklish question of an immigrant's desirability. William Husband consistently tried to make this argument. "I am convinced," he publicly pronounced, "that the immigration problem cannot be settled on the basis of superiority or inferiority of the races involved, but . . . can be solved, in large part at least, if due weight is given to its purely economic aspects." No one could substantiate personal convictions about the "relative worth" of various ethnic groups "to the satisfaction of an impartial tribunal." Even immigrants, Husband averred, would support additional restrictions that were based on economic self-defense, as opposed to those based on the idea that targeted groups were the dregs of humanity. Further, to the extent that specific groups were affected, it was because of their large numbers, which posed an economic threat.

Husband's remarks made him an appropriate Dillingham Commission spokesman. Although he, like a majority of the commissioners, ultimately came to advocate restriction, he saw restriction as positive, as a reform. Unlimited immigration threatened to reduce the conditions of U.S. workers to the level of the worst conditions of workers in Europe, replete with "barefooted American mothers" carrying "bricks and mortar" through the streets. But Husband did not foresee such a catastrophe. "I believe," he said in support of the commission's recommended restrictions, "the problem will be solved in such a way that we will get the good the immigrants bring to us without getting the evils that many of us believe would come from an unrestrained immigration of the classes now coming to these shores."[33] Unfortunately, the quota system, whatever may have been its originators' good intentions, did not achieve this lofty goal.

Assessing the End of an Era

THE DILLINGHAM COMMISSION EXEMPLIFIED both the best and the worst of Progressive Era reform. It accomplished what the nation expected its leaders and experts to accomplish. Between 1907 and 1910, the commissioners attempted to investigate literally every aspect of American immigration, and had time and money allowed, they would have done more. Armed with the belief that objective research would lead to the implementation of enlightened public policy, the commissioners set out in search of the factual, as opposed to the speculative, immigrant. With every mile the commissioners traveled through Europe, with every blank their staff filled with pertinent information, with every new fact acquired in any part of the investigation, they saw themselves as getting that much closer to knowing the alien, to understanding how these men and women collectively fit into their American milieu. Upon completion of this thorough inquiry, they sought to make recommendations based on fair and objective criteria.

As to the attainment of these lofty goals, the commission met with only partial success. They did collect an impressive array of factual information, and while critics legitimately question some of their findings, even those who elsewhere reprove the commission's work cite information from its reports.[1] The commissioners consistently strived to conduct an objective investigation, and with the possible exception of Representative John Burnett, those principally involved reached generally positive conclusions about immigrants. To the extent they recommended restriction, they did so on economic rather than social, cultural, or racial grounds. Yet the commission also contributed substantially to the closing of America's theretofore open door.

The literacy test, the quota system, and the resulting decline in European immigration all bore the stamp of commission-engendered progressive reform. Immigrant totals declined from 805,000 in 1921 to 280,000 in 1929, and they fell below 100,000 during the Depression and World War II years. They would not reach their former high levels until the end of the twentieth century. At that time different ethnic groups, primarily from Asia and the western hemisphere, would predominate. Ellis Island Immigration Station, the principal entry point for European arrivals, eventually closed due to lack of need. Phrases such as *old country* ceased to be common parts of the American vocabulary. Future generations would maintain some of their ethnic heritage, but for those of European ancestry, implementation of the quota acts ushered in the end of an era.[2]

Its connection with the dramatic curtailing of immigration, however, does not alone condemn the commission, or even restriction, to classification as part of progressive reform's dark side. By the early twentieth century, Americans legitimately could ask whether their nation should continue to welcome a virtually unlimited number of immigrants, or if the time had come to set reasonable limits. The tragedy of the eventual restrictions has been said to have been their underlying basis, that of ethnic bigotry, but perhaps even more tragic was the misappropriation of the commission's commitment to objectivity and feasibility for purely nativist goals.[3] Without question, in the early 1920s Congress could have developed a more fair and equitable system for reducing the number of immigrants.

In the end, restrictions that the commissioners believed should not unnecessarily burden any otherwise acceptable immigrant became a glaring testament to America's capacity for racially and ethnically motivated intolerance and bias. Congress designed and then modified the statutes to exclude non–western European types, first southern and eastern Europeans, and then others considered to be incompatible with "white America." This was the legacy of Madison Grant. Former commissioner William S. Bennet, writing at mid-century, offered a telling example of this. The original quotas did not apply to the western hemisphere, except for European colonies, whose immigrants were included in the mother country's total. At that time the entire Jamaican population could have entered under the British quota, but later revisions effectively excluded the Caribbean island's inhabitants. Bennet blamed the change on fear of the "immigration of negroes from Jamaica," a veiled intent that he decried for both its substance and its method.[4]

Whatever the commission's culpability for this deplorable turn of events, it must be shared by some of the larger society's most well-intentioned elements. The commission did its work at a time when Americans had great faith that the combination of science and technology would be the key to meaningful reform. Industrialization had radically changed American society, but it also held the key to making it better for all involved. Aviation hero Charles Lindbergh, who had come of age during the Progressive Era, offered keen insight into this faith in America's capacity for positive change. "Like most of modern youth," he later wrote, "I worshiped science." He was "awed by its knowledge" but later would see the day when that same science, along with his personally beloved technological innovation, the airplane, would threaten to destroy "the civilization I expected them to serve."[5] The same could be said by many Progressive Era social scientists, who consistently demonstrated the belief that acquisition of the appropriate knowledge, the proper facts, would allow them to make the right decisions and promote social justice.

World War I and the subsequent Red Scare significantly redirected this faith. The nation retained progressivism's commitment to efficiency and governmental remedy but changed the desired result from altruistic betterment to control. Those who did not fit traditional white, Anglo-Saxon American norms became the targets of mistrust, suspected malefactors whose potential for disruption had to be checked. Progressive methods, often based on the quest for some form of absolute certainty, offered effective means by which to eliminate or control these dangerous elements. The Dillingham Commission supplied an absolute means of reducing immigration, and avowed nativists then applied it to their own malevolent agenda. Science that was intended to promote progress had been hijacked.

Such was the ambiguity of progressive reform. When Jeremiah Jenks took part in a detailed study of industrial conditions with the aim of resolving the attendant problems, including those connected with big business, the effort was intended to improve society. When Charles P. Neill went to Chicago to investigate the veracity of Upton Sinclair's *The Jungle,* at least those parts connected to the stockyards and slaughterhouses, it aided in the enactment of pure food and drug laws, and it was intended to make life better. When some of the same men took part in a similar investigation of immigration, they pursued objective truth with the same high-minded goals. In the first two cases, the outcomes have been consistently lauded, but not so in the last. The overriding goal was the same, but the results were far different.

William Bennet, the last surviving commissioner, provides a fitting closing. Writing in response to congressional discussion of revising the 1952 McCarren-Walter Immigration Act, which included quota provisions, he dismissed as "idle" the talk of repealing all existing immigration legislation: "That would mean that we would have no immigration law at all. Besides, there are some good things in the law, advances over the previous legal situation which ought to be preserved."[6] Control of immigration is not itself the problem. The problem—in the early 1900s, in 1953, and in days yet to come—is finding a fair, effective, and just means to control immigration. The story of the Dillingham Commission, failures and all, is the story of the Progressive Era effort to find such a means.

NOTES

INTRODUCTION: THE DILLINGHAM COMMISSION AND PROGRESSIVE REFORM

1. Memorandum for the Secretary [of Commerce and Labor], 14 April 1909, Immigration and Naturalization Service, Record Group 85, File 53108/70, National Archives, Washington, D.C.; U.S. Immigration Commission, *Reports of the Immigration Commission*, vol. 1: *Abstracts of Reports of the Immigration Commission* (Washington, D.C.: U.S. Government Printing Office, 1911), 9–21.

2. David P. Thelen, "Social Tensions and the Origins of Progressivism," *Journal of American History* 56 (September 1969); Steven J. Diner, *A Very Different Age: Americans of the Progressive Era* (New York: Hill and Wang, 1998), 3–13; Daniel T. Rogers, *Atlantic Crossings: Social Politics in a Progressive Era* (Cambridge: Harvard University Press, 1998), 1–7 and passim; John Whiteclay Chambers II, *The Tyranny of Change: America in the Progressive Era, 1900–1917* (New York: St. Martin's, 1980), v–vii and passim; William L. O'Neill, *The Progressive Years: America Comes of Age* (New York: Harper & Row, 1975), v–vii; Arthur S. Link and Richard McCormick, *Progressivism* (Arlington, Heights, Ill.: Harlan Davidson, 1983), 1–3, 21–25, and 71–72. O'Neill interprets the era as one more of modernization than of reform, but he does acknowledge the latter's significant presence.

3. O'Neill, *Progressive Years,* 76; Arthur S. Link, "What Ever Happened to the Progressive Movement in the 1920's?" *American Historical Review* 64 (Winter 1959), 847; Morton Keller, *Regulating a New Society: Public Policy and Social Change in America, 1900–1933* (Cambridge: Harvard University Press, 1994), 223–25; Elizabeth Sanders, *Roots of Reform: Farmers, Workers, and the American State, 1877–1917* (Chicago: University of Chicago Press, 1999), 350–53. In contrast to these interpretations, John Buenker has noted the persistent historiographical disagreement about the "progressiveness" of immigration restriction; see *Urban Liberalism and Progressive Reform* (New York: Charles Scribner's Sons, 1973), vii.

4. Oscar Handlin, *Race and Nationality in American Life* (Boston: Little, Brown, 1948), 93–138; Matthew Frye Jacobson, *Whiteness of a Different Color: European Immigrants and the Alchemy of Race* (Cambridge: Harvard University Press, 1998), 78–79; Matthew Frye Jacobson, *Barbarian Virtues: The United States Encounters Foreign Peoples at Home and Abroad, 1876–1917* (New York: Hill and Wang, 2000), 71–72; Bernard A. Weisberger, *Many People, One Nation* (Boston: Houghton Mifflin, 1987), 225; John Higham, *Send These to Me: Immigrants in Urban America*, rev. ed. (Baltimore: Johns Hopkins University Press, 1984), 45; James S. Pula, "The Progressives, the Immigrant and the Workplace: Defining Public Perceptions,

1900–1914," *Polish American Studies* 52 (Autumn 1995). Other studies that have reached negative conclusions about the commission include Lawrence H. Fuchs, "Immigration Reform in 1911 and 1981: The Role of Select Commissions," *Journal of American Ethnic History* 3 (Fall 1993), and James S. Pula, "American Immigration and the Dillingham Commission," *Polish American Studies* 27 (Spring 1980).

In *Barbarian Virtues,* Jacobson does examine the connections between progressivism and immigration, but he presents the Dillingham Commission's concern for economic matters as a pause in its more general focus on "the menacing shift in U.S. immigration toward the problematic races of Southern and Eastern Europe" (71). To a large extent, however, this focus was the result of economic concerns.

5. William F. Blackman, "The Immigration Problem," *Yale Review* 10 (February 1902); John Higham, *Strangers in the Land: Patterns of American Nativism, 1860–1925* (1955; reprint, New York: Atheneum, 1978), 4; Lewis L. Gould, *America in the Progressive Era, 1890–1914* (Harlow, England: Pearson, 2001), 13, 60, and 107.

6. Commission Special Agent W. Jett Lauck, cited in the Buffalo, New York, *Express,* 6 April 1909, Scrapbook, Box 29, and Commission Questionnaire Blank used by field investigators, Box 80, William Jett Lauck Papers (4742), University of Virginia Library, Charlottesville, Virginia (hereafter, Lauck Papers); Immigration Commission Reports, *Abstracts,* 15–21. John Higham makes a similar assessment of progressives, concluding that they had little use for nativism and did not "seek foreign sources of America's problems." However, he discusses only minimally the extent to which progressives saw immigrants as part and parcel to those domestic ills and thereby made them a target of reform; see *Strangers,* 116–23.

7. Bruce G. Trigger, "Early Native North American Responses to European Contact: Romantic versus Rationalistic Interpretations," *Journal of American History* 77 (March 1991).

8. Jacobson, *Whiteness,* 6, 78–83; U.S. Immigration Commission, *Reports of the Immigration Commission,* vol. 5: *Dictionary of Races and Peoples* (Washington, D.C.: Government Printing Office, 1910), passim.

9. "Explanation of Outline," n.d., Lauck Papers; U.S. Immigration Commission, *Dictionary,* passim; Thomas G. Dyer, *Theodore Roosevelt and the Idea of Race* (Baton Rouge: Louisiana State University Press, 1980), 21–44; Fuchs, "Immigration Reform," 62; Theodore C. Blegen, *Norwegian Immigration to America: 1825–1850* (Northfield, Minnesota: Norwegian-American Historical Society, 1931), 352.

10. Finley Peter Dunne [Martin Dooley], "On Anglo-Saxon," in *Mr. Dooley in Peace and in War* (Boston: Small, Maynard & Company, 1914), 53–58. Matthew Frye Jacobson came to similar conclusions in preparing *Whiteness of a Different Color;* see pp. ix–x.

11. Roger Daniels, *Coming to America: A History of Immigration and Ethnicity in American Life* (New York: HarperCollins, 1990), 183–84; U.S.Immigration Commission Reports, *Abstracts,* 12–14.

12. National Archives, Legislative, Judicial, and Fiscal Branch, Civil Archives Division, "Reference Report, Location of Records of the United States Immigration Commission," unpublished memorandum, Washington, D.C., n.d.

13. Handlin, *Race and Nationality,* 137–38; Oscar Handlin, *The Uprooted,* 2nd edition (Boston: Little, Brown and Company, 1973), 3.

14. Cushman K. Davis to Henry Cabot Lodge, 9 September 1894, Henry Cabot Lodge Papers, Massachusetts Historical Society, Boston (hereafter, Lodge Papers); Robert Ward to Joseph Lee, 3 December 1905, Joseph Lee Papers, Massachusetts His-

torical Society, Boston (hereafter, Lee Papers); Immigration Restriction League, "Forcible Demand of the Press for the Further Restriction of Immigration by the Educational Test," IRL Pamphlet #23, ca. 1898, Immigration Restriction League Publications, Widener Library, Harvard University, Cambridge (hereafter, IRL Publications). For a history of the League, see Barbara M. Solomon, *Ancestors and Immigrants: A Changing New England Tradition* (1956; reprint, Boston: Northeastern University, 1989).

15. Richmond Mayo-Smith, *Emigration and Immigration* (New York: Charles Scribner's Sons, 1890), 69–73; Jacob Riis, *How the Other Half Lives: Studies among the Tenements of New York* (New York: Charles Scribner's Sons, 1890), 21; U.S. Department of Commerce, Bureau of the Census, *Historical Almanac of the United States, Colonial Times to 1970*, bicentennial edition (Washington, D.C.: U.S. Government Printing Office, 1975), 105–9.

16. U.S. Department of Commerce, Bureau of the Census, *Historical Almanac;* Mayo-Smith, *Emigration,* 132; William H. Jeffrey, "Immigration," *Journal of Political Economy* 1 (June 1893): 433–35; Robert DeC. Ward, "The Present Aspect of the Immigration Problem," IRL Pamphlet #1, 2nd edition, 1894, IRL Publications.

17. Mayo-Smith, *Emigration,* 135; Francis A. Walker, "Immigration," *Yale Review* 1 (August 1892): 134; Andrew Gyory, *Closing the Gate: Race, Politics, and the Chinese Exclusion Act* (Chapel Hill: University of North Carolina Press, 1998), 50–53; Immigration Restriction League, miscellaneous publications, 1894–1900, IRL Publications.

18. Elizabeth M. Howe to Joseph Lee, 18 March 1910, Lee Papers; Francis A. Walker, "Restriction of Immigration," *Atlantic Review* 77 (June 1896): 822–29; Hjalmar J. Boyesen, "The Dangers of Unrestricted Immigration," *Forum* 3 (March 1887): 532–42; Thelen, "Social Tensions"; Buenker, *Urban Liberalism,* vii–viii.

19. "Object Lesson in Municipal Government," *Century* 39 (March 1890): 154; Daniels, *Coming to America,* 121–264; Henry P. Fairchild, *Immigration: A World Movement and Its American Significance* (New York: Macmillan, 1913), 229–32; Tyler Anbinder, *Five Points: The 19th-Century New York City Neighborhood that Invented Tap Dance, Stole Elections, and Became the World's Most Notorious Slum* (New York: Free Press, 2001); Higham, *Send These,* 34–43; Riis, *How the Other Half,* 3 and passim.

20. Fairchild, *Immigration,* 233–368; Solomon, *Ancestors,* 136–43; Higham, *Strangers,* 116–23; Link and McCormick, *Progressivism,* 72–84. For a discussion of the settlement house movement, see Rivka Shpak Lissak, *Pluralism and Progressives: Hull House and the New Immigrants, 1890–1919* (Chicago: University of Chicago Press, 1989), passim; Eleanor J. Stebner, *The Women of Hull House: A Study of Spirituality, Vocation, and Friendship* (Albany: State University of New York Press, 1997), 27–47.

21. "The Menace of Immigration," *Gunton's Magazine* 16 (March 1899); Terence V. Powderly, "A Menacing Irruption," *North American Review* 147 (August 1888); "Immigration and Wages," *The Nation* 47 (30 August 1888); Richard T. Ely, "A Program for Labor," *Century* 39 (April 1890). Immigration Restriction League, "Annual Report of the Executive Committee for 1895"; "Whence Our Immigrants Come, and Where They Go," IRL Pamphlet #34, ca. 1901–1902; and "Demand of American Labor for Restriction of Immigration and an Illiteracy Test," IRL Pamphlet #35, ca. 1902, IRL Publications. Nick Salvatore, *Eugene V. Debs: Citizen and Socialist* (Urbana: University of Illinois Press, 1982), 104–6. Sally M. Miller, "For White Men Ony: The Socialist Party of America and Issues of Gender, Ethnicity, and Race," *Journal of the Gilded Age and Progressive Era* 2 (July 2003): 295–96.

22. Herman V. Ames, Dean, University of Pennsylvania, to Prescott Hall, 21 March 1910, Immigration Restriction League Papers (42), Houghton Library, Harvard University, Cambridge (hereafter, IRL Papers); *Congressional Record,* 54th Congress, 1st session (20 May 1896): 5476; John P. Diggins, *The American Left in the Twentieth Century* (New York: Harcourt Brace Jovanovich, 1973), v. and passim; Oz Frankel, "What Ever Happened to 'Red Emma'? Emma Goldman, from Alien Radical to American Icon," *Journal of American History* 83 (December 1996): 904.

23. John Chetwood Jr., *Immigration Fallacies* (Boston: Beacon Library Series, 1896), 108; Francis A. Walker, "Restriction of Immigration," in *Discussions in Economics and Statistics,* ed. Davis R. Dewey (New York: Henry Holt and Company, 1899); William Preston, Jr., *Aliens and Dissenters: Federal Suppression of Radicals, 1903–1933* (Cambridge: Harvard University Press, 1963), 1–10; Robert V. Bruce, *1877: Year of Violence* (Chicago: Ivan R. Dee, 1989), 225–43; Paul Avrich, *The Haymarket Tragedy* (Princeton: Princeton University Press, 1984), 215.

24. Ray Allen Billington, *The Protestant Crusade, 1800–1860* (1938; reprint, New York: Rinehard & Company, 1952), 407–12; Tyler Anbinder, *Nativism and Slavery: The Northern Know Nothings and the Politics of the 1850s* (New York: Oxford University Press, 1992), 127–42.

25. *Passenger Cases,* 7 Howard 283 (1849); Marcus Lee Hansen, *The Atlantic Migration, 1607–1860* (Cambridge: Harvard University Press, 1940), 257–61.

26. Higham, *Strangers,* 43–44; William S. Bernard, *American Immigration Policy: A Reappraisal* (New York: Harper and Brothers, 1950), 6–7; George A. Peffer, *If They Don't Bring Their Women Here* (Urbana: University of Illinois Press, 1999), 33–37 and 115–17; Gyory, *Closing,* passim; and Daniels, *Coming,* 271–72. Adam McKeown, "Ritualization of Regulation: The Enforcement of Chinese Exclusion in the United States and China," *American Historical Review* 108 (April 2003): 377–403.

27. John Chetwood, Jr., "Is It Practical to Regulate Immigration?" *Overland Monthly* 23 (February 1894); *New York Times,* 9 June 1890; Mayo-Smith, *Emigration,* 277–78; "Immigration and Wages," *The Nation;* and Henry Cabot Lodge, "The Census and Immigration," *Century* 46 (September 1893): 737–39.

28. Dr. A. Raynal to Senator William Chandler, 16 April 1893, William E. Chandler Papers, Library of Congress, Washington, D.C. (hereafter, Chandler Papers); Oswald Ottendorfer, "Are Immigrants to Blame?" *Forum* 11 (January 1891); J. H. Senner, "Immigration from Italy," *North American Review* 162 (September 1896); *The Nation* 62 (26 March 1896): 248–49; *New York Times* 29 March 1893 and 7 January 1898; Henry B. Leonard, "The Open Gate: The Protest against the Movement to Restrict Immigration," Ph.D. diss., Northwestern University, 1967.

29. Gustav H. Schwab, "A Practical Remedy for the Evils of Immigration," *Forum* 14 (February 1893).

30. Henry Rood, "The Mine Laborers in Pennsylvania," *Forum* 14 (September 1892): 110–22.

31. *Congressional Record,* 50th Congress, 1st session (12 July 1888): 6192–94 and 2nd session (19 January 1889): 999; House Report 3792 (Serial 2673), *To Regulate Immigration,* 50th Congress, 2nd session (19 January 1889).

32. House Report 3792, "Views of the Minority" (30 and 31 January 1889).

33. *Congressional Record,* 51st Congress, 1st session (22 January 1890 and 12 March 1890): 799 and 2159, respectively; House Report 3472 (Serial 2886), *Report of the Select Committee on Immigration and Naturalization, and Testimony Taken by*

the Committee on Immigration in the Senate and the Select Committee on Immigration and Naturalization of the House of Representatives under Concurrent Resolution of March 12, 1890, 51st Congress, 2nd session (15 January 1891); *New York Times,* 4 March 1892.

34. House Report 3472, 335–51, 679–83 and 844–46.

35. William E. Chandler, Memorandum, December 1890, Chandler Papers; House Report 3472, i–x.

36. Henry Cabot Lodge to L. B. Tuckerman, 10 December 1896, Lodge Papers; Peffer, *If They Don't,* 43–56; Edward W. Bemis, "Restriction of Immigration," *Andover Review* 9 (March 1888): 251–63.

37. Henry Cabot Lodge to Prescott Hall, 24 December 1896, and Lodge to [Jesse] Hayes, 15 February 1897, Lodge Papers; *The Nation* 62 (26 March 1896): 248–49; Immigration Restriction League, "The Present Aspect of the Immigration Problem," ca. 1894, and "Immigration: Its Effects on the United States," December 1896, IRL Publications; *Congressional Record,* 51st Congress, 2nd session (19 February 1891): 2955–58, and 54th Congress, 1st session (19 May 1896): 5533–34. Lodge concluded his 1891 congressional speech on the matter by asking that his recent article on immigration be reprinted in the *Congressional Record;* for the complete text, see Henry Cabot Lodge, "Restriction of Immigration," *North American Review* 152 (January 1891): 27–36.

38. *Congressional Record,* 51st Congress, 2nd session (25 and 27 February 1891): 3245 and 3428, respectively.

39. A. B. Nettleton, Acting Secretary of the Treasury, to Judson N. Cross, 4 May 1891, 11 May 1891, and 23 May 1891; Charles Foster to Cross, 18 May 1891 and 8 July 1891, Judson N. Cross Papers, Minnesota Historical Society, St. Paul, Minnesota (hereafter, Cross Papers); Immigration Restriction League, "Twenty Reasons Why Immigration Should Be Restricted," IRL Pamphlet #4, IRL Publications, ca. 1895. It is unclear whether Joseph Powderly was a relative of Knights of Labor activist Terence V. Powderly. In his autobiography, Terence wrote that he had seven brothers, but he did not identify them by name; see Terence V. Powderly, *The Path I Trod: The Autobiography of Terence V. Powderly,* ed. Harry J. Carman et al. (New York: Columbia University Press, 1940), 8.

40. Charles Foster to Judson N. Cross, 8 June 1891, Cross Papers. For background on the 1884 and 1891 laws, see Higham, *Strangers,* 48–49 and 100.

41. Judson N. Cross, "Data on Convict Immigrants from Liverpool England," 27 July 1891; Cross to A. B. Nettleton, 10 September 1891; and Cross, "Immigration Question," memorandum, May 1892, Cross Papers; *Minneapolis Tribune,* 7 December 1891; *Minneapolis Times,* 8 February 1892; *St. Paul Globe,* 8 February 1892; U.S. Commissioners of Immigration, *A Report of the Commissioners of Immigration Upon the Causes Which Incite Immigration to the United States,* Volume 1 of *Reports of the Commissioners* (Washington, D.C.: U.S. Government Printing Office, 1892), 127–28; John B. Weber and Charles S. Smith, "Our National Dumping Ground," *North American Review* 154 (April 1892): 424–38. Acting Secretary Nettleton did convey to the State Department Cross's concerns about convict migration; see Nettleton to Cross, 28 January 1892, Cross Papers.

42. Herman J. Schulties to Prescott Hall, 4 December 1896, IRL Papers (820); U.S. Commissioners of Immigration, *Report of the Commissioners,* 308; Herman J. Schulties, *Report on European Immigration to the United States of America and the Causes Which Incite the Same, with Recommendations for the Further Restriction of*

Undesirable Immigration and the Establishment of a National Quarantine (Washington, D.C.: U.S. Government Printing Office, 1893), 47.

43. *Congressional Record,* 52nd Congress, 1st session (6 June and 27 July 1892): 5052 and 6853; 2nd session (7 January–3 March 1893): 404, 901, 1894, 1941, 2002, 2468–75, and 2550. Untitled report, 52nd Congress, 1st session (6 June 1892); Senate Report 787 (Serial 2914), untitled Senate Immigration Committee Report, 52nd Congress, 1st session (6 June 1892); House Report 2206 (Serial 3104), *Immigration and the Contract-Labor Laws,* 52nd Congress, 2nd session (7 January 1893); William E. Chandler, "Shall Immigration Be Suspended?" *North American Review* 156 (January 1893): 1–8.

44. Henry Cabot Lodge to R. C. Parsons, 13 December 1891, and Lodge to E. E. Hamilton, 26 January 1891, Lodge Papers; Robert Ward, "An Immigration Restriction League," *Century* 49 (February 1895): 639; Immigration Restriction League Constitution, n.d.; Immigration Restriction League, "Annual Report of the Executive Committee (1138)," 14 January 1895; "The Educational Test as a Means of Further Restricting Immigration," IRL Pamphlet #6, 1895, IRL Publications; "What Does the American Press Say about the Further Restriction of Immigration?" IRL Pamphlet #10, ca. 1895, IRL Publications; "Newspapers Supporting the Educational Test," IRL Pamphlet #13, ca. 1895, IRL Publications.

45. *Congressional Record,* 54th Congress, 1st session (16 March 1896): 2817–20.

46. Reverend M. D. Lichleter et al., Board of Officers, Junior Order United American Mechanics, to President Grover Cleveland, 2 March 1897; General Executive Board, Knights of Labor, to Cleveland, 20 February 1897; P. J. McGuire, General Secretary, United Brotherhood of Carpenters and Joiners of America, to Cleveland, 20 February 1897; W. H. Allen to Cleveland, 19 February 1897; and Henry R. Smith to Cleveland, 20 February 1897, Grover Cleveland Papers, Library of Congress, Washington, D.C. The Cleveland Papers contain dozens of other pertinent letters and telegrams.

47. Senate Document 185 (Serial 3471), *"Immigration Laws." Message from the President of the United States, Returning to the House of Representatives Without His Approval, House Bill Numbered 7864, Entitled "An Act to Amend the Immigration Laws of the United States,"* 54th Congress, 2nd session, 2 March 1897.

48. Henry Cabot Lodge to Stephen Collins, 5 March 1897; Lodge to Robert Ward, 11 March 1897; and Lodge to Prescott Hall, 10 May 1898, Lodge Papers. William McKinley, Inaugural Address, 5 March 1897, in *Speeches and Addresses of William McKinley* (New York: Double Day and McClure, 1900), 10; "Immigration Restriction Defeated," *The Outlook* 60 (December 1898): 990; *Congressional Record,* 55th Congress, 3rd session (14 December 1898): 196–97. Lodge's outgoing correspondence for 1898 and 1899 indicates that immigration had markedly decreased in importance, having been replaced primarily by war-related matters.

49. Roger Daniels, *Asian America: Chinese and Japanese in the United States since 1850* (Seattle: University of Washington Press, 1988), 52–58.

50. S. N. D. North, "The Industrial Commission," *North American Review* 168 (June 1899): 708–19; The Oil City Derrick, comp., *Pure Oil Trust vs. Standard Oil Company, being the Report of an Investigation by the United States Industrial Commission* (Oil City, Pa.: Derrick Publishing Company, 1901); U.S. Industrial Commission, *Reports of the Industrial Commission: Including Testimony, with Review and Digest, and Special Reports* (1901; reprint, New York: Arno, 1970).

51. Cleveland, veto message (Senate Document 185 [Serial 3471]).

1: "AN EXHAUSTIVE INVESTIGATION"

1. Henry Cabot Lodge to Theodore Roosevelt, 30 September 1905, in Henry Cabot Lodge, ed., *Selections from the Correspondence of Theodore Roosevelt and Henry Cabot Lodge, 1889–1918*, 2 vols. (New York: Charles Scribner's Sons, 1925), 2:205.

2. William L. O'Neill, *The Progressive Years: America Comes of Age* (New York: Harper & Row, 1975); Steven J. Diner, *A Different Age: Americans of the Progressive Era* (New York: Hill and Wang, 1998).

3. Carl Schurz, "Restricting Immigration," *Harpers Weekly* 42 (January 1898): 27.

4. H. F. Bowers to Hall, 21 April 1910, Immigration Restriction League Papers (40), Houghton Library, Harvard University, Cambridge (hereafter, IRL Papers); Theodore Roosevelt, speech at Jamestown, 27 April 1907, Joseph Cannon Papers, Illinois Historical Society, Springfield, Illinois (hereafter, Cannon Papers); Theodore Roosevelt, "America Past and Present and the Americanization of Foreigners," *America: A Journal of Today* 14 (April 1888): 1–3, Theodore Roosevelt Collection, Widener Library, Harvard University, Cambridge (hereafter, Widener Roosevelt Collection); "Response of Theodore Roosevelt to the Toast 'Americanism and Immigration,'" Appomattox Day Banquet of the Hamilton Club of Chicago," 20 January 1893, Widener Roosevelt Collection.

5. Theodore Roosevelt to Prescott Hall, 26 March 1896, IRL Papers (801); Madison Grant to Hall, 18 November 1914, IRL Papers (469); and Roosevelt to Hall, 24 March 1920, IRL Papers (801); Roosevelt to Lodge, 19 March 1897, in Lodge, *Selections*, 1:259–60. For other interpretations of Roosevelt's views on immigration and ethnicity, see Edmond Morris, *Theodore Rex* (New York: Modern Library, 2002), 37; John M. Blum, *The Republican Roosevelt*, 2nd ed. (1954; reprint, New York: Atheneum, 1975), 28 and 113; John Higham, *Strangers in the Land: Patterns of American Nativism, 1860–1925* (1955; reprint, New York: Atheneum, 1978), 128; Gary Gerstle, "Theodore Roosevelt and the Divided Character of American Nationalism," *Journal of American History* 86 (December 1999): 1296 and passim; Thomas G. Dyer, *Theodore Roosevelt and the Idea of Race* (Baton Rouge: Louisiana State University Press, 1980), 123–42; and Roger Daniels, *Asian America: Chinese and Japanese in the United States since 1950* (Seattle: University of Washington Press, 1988), 122 and 122n45.

6. Prescott Hall, form letter to charity organizations, 30 June 1905, IRL Papers (1046); Henry Cabot Lodge to Theodore Roosevelt, 3 November 1902, in Lodge, *Selections*, 1:545; Fred L. Israel, *State of the Union Messages of the Presidents*, 4 vols. (New York: Chelsea House–Robert Hector, 1966), 2:2017–22. At that time, State of the Union Messages were delivered by proxy, not in person, but Roosevelt's messages did attract congressional attention; for example see, Morris, *Rex*, 70–76.

7. Israel, *State of the Union Messages*, 2:2059, 2078, 2127; Theodore Roosevelt to Henry Cabot Lodge, 23 May 1904, in Lodge, *Selections*, 2:77–8; Charles M. Peffer to Joseph Cannon, 20 June 1906, Cannon Papers. For background on these political considerations, see A. James Reichley, *The Life of the Parties: A History of American Political Parties* (New York: Free Press, 1992), 174–79; and Paul Kleppner, *Continuity and Change in Electoral Politics, 1893–1928* (New York: Greenwood, 1987), 110–11.

8. Morris, *Theodore Rex*, 229, 243–45, 253–54, and 354.

9. Madison Grant to Prescott Hall, 15 November 1915, IRL Papers (468); Israel, *State of the Union Messages*, 3:2177–79 and 2223; Theodore Roosevelt to Joseph Cannon, 27 May 1906, in Elting E. Morrison, ed., *Letters of Theodore Roosevelt, 6*

vols. (Cambridge: Harvard University Press, 1952), 5:285–86; Henry Cabot Lodge to Roosevelt, 12 August 1906, and Roosevelt to Lodge, 15 August 1906, in Lodge, *Selections,* 2:227.

10. James B. Reynolds to Theodore Roosevelt, 28 November 1906, Immigration and Naturalization Service, Central Office Correspondence, Record Group 85, File 52903/29A (hereafter, INS Correspondence); Joseph Lee to Robert Ward, 29 December 1906, and Ward to Lee, 7 January 1907, Joseph Lee Papers, Massachusetts Historical Society, Boston (hereafter, Lee Papers); Henry Cabot Lodge to Roosevelt, 18 August 1906, Henry Cabot Lodge Papers, Massachusetts Historical Society, Boston (hereafter, Lodge Papers). Robert Bacon, acting secretary of the Department of Commerce and Labor also wrote Roosevelt about the literacy test, noting that the exemptions for Canada, Mexico, and Cuba would conflict with the favored-nation clauses of treaties with those nations (19 June 1906, INS Correspondence, Record Group 85, File 52903/29A). For background on Reynolds, see Barbara M. Solomon, *Ancestors and Immigrants: A Changing New England Tradition* (1956; reprint, Boston: Northeastern University Press, 1989), 196–97.

11. Theodore Roosevelt to Joseph Cannon, 12 January 1907, 19 January 1907, and 27 June 1906, in Morrison, *Letters of Theodore Roosevelt,* 5:322–23, 494, and 557; Gary M. Fink, ed., *Biographical Dictionary of American Labor Leaders* (Westport, Conn.: Greenwood, 1974), 292–93; Lewis Gould, *The Presidency of Theodore Roosevelt* (Lawrence: University of Kansas Press, 1991), 167–68; Blum, *Republican Roosevelt,* 20.

12. Henry Cabot Lodge to Mr. Smith, 21 February 1898; Lodge to Prescott Hall, 14 March 1898; Lodge to J. Q. A. Walker, 23 January 1900; Lodge to W. E. Claflin, 3 January 1900; Lodge to Prescott Hall, 27 May 1902; Lodge to Robert Ward, 28 November 1902; Lodge to Wilson Mitchell, 3 February 1903; and Lodge to William Shaw, 4 February 1903, Lodge Papers. Lodge to Prescott Hall, 20 March 1903 (608); Hall, "Open Letter to Members," 25 November 1899 (1139); Immigration Restriction League, "Report of the Executive Committee for 1898, 1899, 1900," ca. 1901 (1138), IRL Papers. *The Outlook,* 58 (26 February 1898): 508–9. *Congressional Record,* 57th Congress, 2nd session (9 December 1902, 27 February 1903, and 28 February 1903): 128–44, 2749–53, and 2804–2809, respectively, and (2 March 1903): 2894–95, 2949–50, and 3010–11; and 58th Congress, 2nd session (20 February 1905): 2890. Senate Report 2119 (Serial 4264-9), *Regulation of Immigration: Statements before the Committee on Immigration, United States Senate, on the Bill (H.R. 12199) To Regulate the Immigration of Aliens into the United States,* 57th Congress, 1st session (27 June 1902); A. Wesley Johns, *The Man Who Shot McKinley* (New York: A. S. Barnes and Company, 1970); John Lombardi, *Labor's Voice in the Cabinet* (New York: Columbia University Press, 1942), 44–58.

13. Samuel Gompers to Joseph Cannon, 7 April 1906 and 30 October 1906, Cannon Papers. Joseph Lee, Speech Draft, 1906; Lee to D. F. McMahon, 14 December 1905, Lee to A. W. Gutridge, 6 December 1905, Lee Papers.

14. Daniels, *Asian America,* 106–26, 116 (Rowell quote).

15. Biographical Sketch, Guide to the Lee Papers; Prescott Hall, "Selection of Immigration," *Annals of the American Academy of Political and Social Science* 24 (July 1904); Henry P. Fairchild, "Distribution of Immigrants," *Yale Review* 16 (November 1907); John R. Commons, "Social and Industrial Problems," *The Chautauquan* 39 (May 1904): 13–32; James E. Whelply, "International Control of Immigration," *World's Work* 8 (September 1904): 5254–59. The phrase "Loss of Confidence" comes from a chapter title in Higham, *Strangers,* 158–82. Therein, Higham emphasizes the number of "new immigrants" when explaining the upsurge in restrictionist activity.

16. *Congressional Record,* 59th Congress, 1st session (15 February 1906, 22 May 1906, and 23 May 1906): 2524, 7212–34, and 7280–7300, respectively; Senate Report 2186 (Serial 4905), *Immigration of Aliens into the United States,* 59th Congress, 1st session (29 March 1906). Senator Dillingham's background and views on restriction are developed more fully in chapter 2.

17. James Patten to Joseph Lee, 8 March and 17 March 1906, Lee Papers; Jesse Taylor to All Brothers, Junior Order United American Mechanics, 3 April 1906 (563), Taylor to Pennsylvania Brothers, 20 June 1906 (563), Thos. H. Canning, Secretary-Treasurer, Knights of Labor, to Members of Congress, 22 June 1906 (578), and H. R. Fuller, Legislative Representative, Railroad Brotherhoods, to All Lodges, 22 June 1906 (438), IRL Papers; Henry Cabot Lodge to Theodore Roosevelt, 30 September 1905, in Lodge, *Selections,* 2:205.

18. Information about these representatives' lineage comes from U.S. Congress, *Biographical Directory of the American Congress* (Washington, D.C.: U.S. Government Printing Office, 1928).

19. Jesse Taylor, National Council, Junior Order United American Mechanics, form letter to "Brother Recording Secretary," 27 May 1906, IRL Papers (563); *Congressional Record,* 59th Congress, 1st session, 40:9152–57; House Report 4588 (Serial 4908), *Immigration of Aliens into the United States,* 59th Congress, 1st session (29 May 1906), 1–37; House Report 4912 (Serial 4908) *Immigration of Aliens into the United States,* 59th Congress, 1st session (11 June 1906), 1–37. Both reports contain views of the minority. Taylor's letter arouses speculation that some sort of deal was made among Cannon, Bennet, and Dalzell, but I have found no clear evidence for one. Unfortunately, there are no known Dalzell papers for that period; see U.S. Congress, House, *A Guide to Research Collections of Former Members of the United States House of Representatives* (Washington, D.C.: U.S. House of Representatives, 1988), 95.

20. Samuel Gompers to Prescott Hall, 10 January 1898, IRL Papers; Joseph Cannon to L. W. Busbey, 12 June 1907, Cannon Papers; Higham, *Strangers,* 128–29; L. White Busbey, *Uncle Joe Cannon: The Life of A Pioneer American* (New York: Henry Holt, 1927), 1–140 and 243–81; Blair Bolles, *The Tyrant from Illinois: Uncle Joe Cannon's Experiment with Personal Power* (New York: W. W. Norton, 1951), 66–77; Herbert F. Marqulies, "James R. Mann's Apprenticeship in the House of Representatives," *Congress and the Presidency* 26 (Spring 1999): 21–40; Gould, *Presidency of Theodore Roosevelt,* 110 and 147–71. For an example of Cannon's willingness to embrace certain reforms, as exemplified by a possible deal with Theodore Roosevelt regarding railroad regulation, see Blum, *Republican Roosevelt,* 79–82. For a more detailed examination of how Cannon's background influenced his supportive actions on the Dillingham immigration bill and in the commission's creation, see my "Hayseed Immigration Policy: 'Uncle Joe' Cannon and the Immigration Question," *Illinois Historical Journal* 88 (autumn 1995).

21. St. Louis *Globe,* 30 March 1908.

22. Joseph Cannon, "Response to H. R. Fuller," memorandum, ca. 1906, Cannon Papers; *Congressional Record,* 54th Congress, 2nd session (27 January 1897): 1229.

23. *Congressional Record,* 57th Congress, 1st session (21 May 1896): 5774–78 and 59th Congress, 1st session (25 June 1906): 9194–95. Biographical information for Grosvenor comes from a sketch prepared for the Charles H. Grosvenor Papers, Alden Library, Ohio University, Athens Ohio, and the 1928 edition of the U.S.

Congress, *Biographical Directory of the American Congress.* Unfortunately, the Grosvenor Collection does not have the types of materials that would give more insight into his beliefs and actions.

24. A. B. Nettleton, Assistant Secretary-Department of the Treasury, to Judson N. Cross, 4 May 1891; Nettleton to Cross, 11 May 1891; and Charles Foster to Cross, 8 June 1891, Cross Papers. Unfortunately, the contents of the Cannon Papers are very meager for the 1890s, and they contain no record of this event.

25. *Congressional Record,* 59th Congress, 1st session (25 June 1906), 40:9166. New York Immigration League, "The Original Insurgency, June 25, 1906" (New York: New York Immigration League, [ca. 1910]), copy in Cannon Papers. In this pamphlet the New York Immigration League reprinted the comments of H. R. Fuller, which the *Danville Press* had reported on 31 October 1906. Cannon prepared a response to Fuller's criticism, but he neither dismissed the accusations of tyranny nor offered a contrary version of the day's events; see Memorandum, Response to H. R. Fuller, ca. 1906, Cannon Papers.

26. William S. Bennet to James E. Watson, 19 November 1947; William S. Bennet Papers, Special Collections Research Center, Syracuse University, Syracuse, New York (hereafter, Bennet Papers).

27. Stenographic report of debate on immigration policy (likely for inclusion in the *Congressional Record*), ca. 1902; Citizens of New York to Watson, 26 May 1902; "An American" to Watson, May 1902, James E. Watson Papers, Indiana State University Library, Indianapolis, Indiana.

28. Theodore Roosevelt to Joseph Cannon, 15 August 1906, Cannon Papers. Charles Edgerton to Prescott Hall, 16 March 1906, Lee Papers. Henry Cabot Lodge to Roosevelt, 18 August 1906, Lodge Papers. William Loeb Jr., Secretary to the President, to Lodge, 11 August 1906; Lodge to Roosevelt, [12 August 1906]; and Roosevelt to Lodge, 15 August 1906, in Lodge, *Selections,* 2:226–27. Secretary of Commerce and Labor Oscar Straus conveyed concerns about the literacy test as a political liability as early as May and June 1906; see Higham, *Strangers,* 128.

29. *Congressional Record,* 59th Congress, 1st session (25 June 1906), 40:9195.

30. Samuel Gompers to Joseph Cannon, 19 January 1907; Rev. G. E. Redeker, National Committee on Legislation, Patriotic Order Sons of America, to Cannon, 10 October 1906; J. G. A. Richter, Junior Order United American Mechanics, Ohio Council, to Cannon, 10 October 1906, Cannon Papers.

31. Jesse Taylor to Joseph Cannon, 25 and 30 October 1906, Cannon Papers.

32. James Patten to Prescott Hall, 20 and 22 March 1910, and Patten to Joseph Lee, 16 May 1910, Lee Papers.

33. Henry Cabot Lodge to Theodore Roosevelt, 18 June 1906, in Lodge, *Selections,* 2:157; Daniels, *Asian America,* 113–28.

34. Daniels, *Asian America;* Oscar S. Straus, *Under Four Administrations* (Boston: Houghton Mifflin Company), 217–21; George E. Mowry, *The Era of Theodore Roosevelt and the Birth of Modern America, 1900–1912* (New York: Harper & Row, 1958), 186–88; William H. Harbaugh, *Power and Responsibility: The Life and Times of Theodore Roosevelt* (New York: Farrar, Straus, and Cudahy, 1961), 298–300; Philip C. Jessup, *Elihu Root,* 2 vols. (New York: Dodd, Mead, 1937), 2:3–33; Israel, *State of the Union Messages,* 3:2225–26; Andrew Gyory, *Closing the Gate: Race, Politics, and the Chinese Exclusion Act* (Chapel Hill: University of North Carolina Press, 1998), 7–53.

35. William S. Bennet to Clare Boothe Luce, 28 June 1943; Bennet to George E. Sokolsky, 7 April 1953; Bennet to William Mertens Jr., 13 April 1949; Bennet to Elihu

Root (the secretary of state's son), 11 February 1937, Bennet Papers. Oscar Handlin, *Race and Nationality in American Life* (Boston: Little, Brown, 1948), 99.

36. Response to Fuller, Cannon Papers; Theodore Roosevelt to Joseph Cannon, 12 January 1907 and 19 January 1907, in Morrison, *Letters of Theodore Roosevelt*, 5:494 and 557.

37. Theodore Roosevelt to Charles P. Neill, 28 June 1906, in Morrison, *Letters of Theodore Roosevelt*, 5:322–23; Frederick C. Croxton, "Autobiography," 47, Frederick C. Croxton Papers, Herbert Hoover Presidential Library, West Branch, Iowa (hereafter, Croxton Papers).

38. Croxton, "Autobiography," Croxton Papers.

39. Bennet to *Reader's Digest*, 28 August 1952, Bennet Papers.

40. Prescott Hall, Immigration Restriction League, to Elihu Root, 8 May 1912, and Root to Madison Grant, 13 May 1912, Elihu Root Papers, Library of Congress, Washington D.C.; Jessup, *Elihu Root*, 2:4; Richard W. Leopold, *Elihu Root and the Conservative Tradition* (Boston: Little, Brown, 1954), 3–23.

41. William S. Bennet to Clare Boothe Luce, 28 June 1943, and Bennet to William Mertens Jr., 13 April 1949, Bennet Papers; Henry Cabot Lodge to Henry White, 23 February 1907, and Lodge to Henry Higginson, 18 February 1907, Lodge Papers; *Congressional Record*, 59th Congress, 2nd session, 41:2808–11 and 3449.

42. *Congressional Record*, 59th Congress, 2nd session, 41:2808–11, 2939–52, 3017–39, 3083–99, 3210–22, 3261, 3283, 3514.

43. Robert Ward to Joseph Lee, 17 February 1907, Lee Papers.

44. Curtis Guild Jr. to Prescott Hall, 27 December 1905, IRL Papers (483).

45. Joseph Lee to Jeremiah Jenks, 9 August 1906; Lee to Ralph M. Easley, Executive Committeeman of the National Civic Federation, 1 May 1906; and Lee to L. T. Chamberlain, National Civic Federation, 29 May 1906, Lee Papers.

46. William S. Bennet, speech delivered to the Liberal Immigration League, 19 February 1907, Lee Papers.

47. Robert Ward to Joseph Lee, 17 February 1907, Lee Papers.

2: "NO MAN AFRAID OF THE FACTS"

1. Joseph Lee to Charles Nagel, 31 December 1910, Joseph Lee Papers, Massachusetts Historical Society, Boston (hereafter, Lee Papers); [Commission staffer W. Jett Lauck], "Memorandum for the President in Favor of the Reading Test Provision of the Burnett Immigration Bill," April 1914, Box 80, William Jett Lauck Papers (4742), University of Virginia Library, Charlottesville, Virginia (hereafter, Lauck Papers); William W. Husband, "Address to the Fifth Congress of the National Federation of Religious Liberals," 23 February 1915, William W. Husband Papers, Chicago Historical Society (hereafter, Husband Papers). Lauck and Husband both reported that the commissioners' views were initially moderate. This and subsequent evidence challenges those who contend that the commission was anti-immigrant from its inception; for example, see Oscar Handlin, *Race and Nationality in American Life* (Boston: Little, Brown, 1948), 100–2, and James S. Pula, "The Progressives, the Immigrant, and the Workplace: Defining Public Perceptions, 1900–1914," *Polish American Studies* 52 (autumn 1995), 62–65.

2. Steven J. Diner, *A Very Different Age: Americans of the Progressive Era* (New York: Hill and Wang, 1998); John Whiteclay Chambers II, *The Tyranny of Change:*

America in the Progressive Era, 1900–1917 (New York: St. Martin's, 1980); Peter G. Filene, "An Obituary for the Progressive Movement," *American Quarterly* 22 (spring
1970). Filene argues against the idea that there was any well-defined "progressive
movement."

3. Joseph Lee to Charles Nagel, 31 December 1910, Lee Papers.

4. Theodore Roosevelt to Jeremiah Jenks, 14 March 1907, Theodore Roosevelt
Papers, microfilm edition, Library of Congress, Washington, D.C., series 2, 71:338
(hereafter, Roosevelt Papers, LOC). Roosevelt sent the official letters of appointment
on 1 April 1907; see Roosevelt to Jenks, to Neill, and to Wheeler, 1 April 1907, Roo-
sevelt Papers, LOC, series 2, 72:19–21; Roosevelt to Francis J. Henry, 21 July 1908,
Roosevelt Papers, LOC, series 2, 82:52; Handlin, *Race,* 101; *Dictionary of American Bi-
ography,* vol. 5, part 2, 52–53; Jeremiah W. Jenks, *Citizenship in the Schools* (New York:
Henry Holt, 1909), 9–10 and 26; Jeremiah W. Jenks, *The Trust Problem* (New York:
McClure, Phillips & Company, 1900), 3–9; Clarence E. Wunderlin, Jr., *Visions of a
New Industrial Order: Social Science and Labor Theory in America's Progressive Era* (New
York: Columbia University Press, 1992), 15–22 and 96–100. There is nothing to sug-
gest that Roosevelt's disparaging remark about professors indicated that he did not
want a full and objective inquiry, the type that professors likely would demand.

5. Jeremiah W. Jenks, "The Racial Problem in Immigration," *The Social Welfare
Forum: Official Proceedings* 36 (1909): 215–22. Barbara M. Solomon cites the same
sources and contends, in contrast to my conclusions, that Jenks belonged to a group
of young economists who endorsed nativism and had much in common with the
New England restrictionists. See Barbara M. Solomon, *Ancestors and Immigrants: A
Changing New England Tradition* (Boston: Northeastern University Press, 1989),
127–28 and 197–98.

6. Jeremiah Jenks to the editor of the "Industrial Removal Office Bulletin," 28
May 1915, Industrial Removal Office Papers, American Jewish Historical Society,
Waltham, Massachusetts.

7. Charles Neill to Richard T. Ely, 16 January 1904, 17 March 1905, 7 November 1905, and 17 August 1906; and Neill to John R. Commons, 9 May 1906, Richard
T. Ely Papers, State Historical Society of Wisconsin, Madison. Telegrams, James B.
Garfield to Theodore Roosevelt, 31 July 1906, and Roosevelt to Garfield, 31 July
1906, Record Group 174, File 62153, Immigration and Naturalization Service, Central Office Correspondence, National Archives, Washington, D.C. *The National Cyclopedia of American Biography* (New York: James T. White & Company, 1948), 33:182;
Oscar S. Straus, *Under Four Administrations* (Boston: Houghton Mifflin, 1922), 214;
American Monthly Review of Reviews 34 (January 1905): 9.

8. *National Cyclopedia; American Monthly Review of Reviews* 35 (July 1906): 34;
John Lombardi, *Labor's Voice in the Cabinet* (New York: Columbia University Press,
1942), 167.

9. Charles P. Neill, "Anarchism," *American Catholic Quarterly Review* 27 (January 1902).

10. Ibid.; Solomon, *Ancestors,* 127.

11. William Wheeler to Benjamin I. Wheeler, 28 November 1904 and 11
February 1905, Benjamin I. Wheeler Papers, Bancroft Library, University of Cali-
fornia, Berkeley; and Wheeler to Hiram W. Johnson, 16 January 1911, Hiram
Johnson Papers, Bancroft Library, University of California, Berkeley (hereafter,
Johnson Papers); *Who Was Who in America* (Chicago: Marquis Publications,
1968), 1:1329; Eric Foner, *The Story of American Freedom* (New York: W. W. Norton

and Company, 1998), 141. No evidence suggests whether Williams had any prior association with his eight colleagues.

12. Theodore Roosevelt to William Wheeler, 19 March and 1 April 1907 and 24 February 1909, Roosevelt Papers, Series 2, 71:401, 72:20, and 91:397.

13. William Wheeler to Hiram Johnson, 11 February 1911, and Wheeler to Charles A. Nagel, 19 January 1911, Johnson Papers.

14. "Senator William Paul Dillingham," *Vermonter* 6 (November 1900): 51–53. Henry S. Wardner, William P. Dillingham, "President McKinley: An Address before the Vermont Commandery, Loyal Legion," 19 November 1901; "William Paul Dillingham: An Appreciation," n.d., ca. 1923; and William P. Dillingham, "Address of Hon. William P. Dillingham, before the Joint Assembly, State of Vermont, October 15, 1902," William P. Dillingham Miscellaneous Papers and Printed Materials, Assorted Collections, Waterbury Historical Society, Waterbury, Vermont. W. P. Dillingham to Polly [Pauline Dillingham], 4 February 1911, Box 2, Folder 5; W. P. Dillingham to Colonel [Charles Dillingham], 25 April 1914, 22 November 1914, 5 February 1916, and 6 May 1916, Box 2, Folder 6, Dillingham Family Papers, Woodson Research Center, Rice University, Houston, Texas.

15. [Prescott Hall] to Henry Cabot Lodge, 18 January 1906, Immigration Restriction League Papers (608), Houghton Library, Harvard University, Cambridge; F. P. Sargent to William Dillingham, 5 February 1907, Immigration and Naturalization Service, Central Office Correspondence, Record Group 85, File 51517/132; John M. Lund, "Vermont Nativism: William Paul Dillingham and U.S. Immigration Legislation," *Vermont History* 63 (Winter 1995); Roland Sanders, *Shores of Refuge: A Hundred Years of Jewish Emigration* (New York: Henry Holt and Company, 1988), 279.

16. New Brunswick *Daily Home News,* 17 February 1930.

17. Jesse Taylor, Junior Order United American Mechanics, to Joseph Cannon, 30 October 1906, Joseph Cannon Papers, Illinois Historical Society, Springfield. *Congressional Record,* 54th Congress, 1st session (28 January 1896): 1064; and 59th Congress, 1st session (21 December 1905, 21 and 24 January 1906, and 22 February 1906), 672, 1461, 1594, and 2881, respectively. John Higham, *Strangers in the Land: Patterns of American Nativism, 1860–1925* (1955; reprint, New York: Atheneum, 1978), 118. It should be noted that Jesse Taylor made his assertion about Howell at a time when the various lobby groups were trying to persuade Joseph Cannon to support the Lodge literacy test.

18. Henry Cabot Lodge to Prescott Hall, 31 July 1894; Lodge to Charles K. Landis, 26 March 1896; and Lodge to Thomas Higgonson, 24 January 1907, Henry Cabot Lodge Papers, Massachusetts Historical Society, Boston (hereafter, Lodge Papers); *Congressional Record,* 54th Congress, 1st session (16 March 1896): 2817–20.

19. Henry Cabot Lodge, *Early Memories* (New York: Charles Scribner's Sons, 1920), 19, 72, 126, 203–5; Louis A. Coolidge, "Hon. Henry Cabot Lodge, LL.D.," *New England Historical and Genealogical Register* 79 (July 1925); Charles G. Washburn, "Memoir of Henry Cabot Lodge," *Proceedings of the Massachusetts Historical Society* 58 (April 1925). See also John Garraty, *Henry Cabot Lodge: A Biography* (New York: Alfred A. Knopf, 1953), 3–128.

20. Lodge to R. W. Gilder, 9 December 1890, Henry Cabot Lodge Papers, American Academy and Institute of Arts and Letters, New York; Gilder to Lodge, 4 April 1891, Lodge Papers; Henry Cabot Lodge, "The Distribution of the Abilities in the United States," *The Century* 42 (September 1891). Lodge biographer John Garraty contends that the *Century* article "had nothing directly to do with his dislike

of the 'new' immigration" and that Lodge had developed those beliefs after the publication of "Abilities" (Garraty, *Henry Cabot Lodge,* 144). Lodge's concluding remarks, however, show a clear connection between his views on race and his fear of new immigrants.

21. See works by Henry Cabot Lodge: "A Word More on the Distribution of Ability," *The Century* 49 (July 1892); "The Census and Immigration," *The Century* 46 (September 1893); "Restriction of Immigration," *North American Review* 152 (January 1891); and "Lynch Law and Unrestricted Immigration," *North American Review* 152 (May 1891).

22. James Patten to Joseph Lee, 31 May 1910; Lee to A. Lawrence Lowell, 4 August 1910; Lowell to Lee, 9 August 1910; and Patten to Lee, 25 November 1910, Lee Papers; Curtis Guild to William Bellamy, 23 January 1911, Lodge Papers.

23. Invitation to B. J. Barbour to join Virginia Immigration Society, 28 May 1867, Barbour Family Papers (1486), University of Virginia Library, Charlottesville; Alex. J. Bondurant to William A. Anderson, 3 September 1888, Anderson Family Papers (38–96), University of Virginia Library, Charlottesville; Alabama Commercial and Industrial Association to James Patten, 21 June 1905, Lee Papers; *Biographical Directory of the American Congress* (Washington, D.C.: U.S. Government Printing Office, 1928), 764; Allen J. Going, *Bourbon Democracy in Alabama, 1874–1890,* 2nd ed. (Tuscaloosa: University of Alabama Press, 1992), 120–25. Burnett remains largely an enigma. Although he served in Congress for twenty years, he evidently left no collection of papers, and very little has been written about him. Attempts to find more information about his life and career have proven to be futile; Victor Nielsen, Alabama Department of Archives and History, to author, 29 July 1993.

24. *Congressional Record,* 59th Congress, 1st session (25 June 1906): 9164 and 9192–93.

25. *Congressional Record,* 59th Congress, 2nd session (18 February 1907): 3227–28 and 3232.

26. Note of personnel changes, *Commission Report,* 1:2; *Biographical Directory of Congress,* 1206; J. C. Hemphill, ed., *Men of Mark in South Carolina* (Washington, D.C.: Men of Mark Publishing Company, 1907), 1:214–17; *Cyclopedia of Eminent and Representative Men of the Carolinas of the Nineteenth Century* (1892; reprint, Spartanburg, South Carolina: The Reprint Company, 1972), 1:637–38; Francis B. Simkins, *Pitchfork Ben Tillman, South Carolinian* (Baton Rouge: Louisiana State University Press, 1944), 390; Robert M. Burts, *Richard Irvine Manning and the Progressive Movement in South Carolina* (Columbia: University of South Carolina Press, 1974), 32–33.

27. *Congressional Record,* 59th Congress, 2nd session (15 February and 2 March 1907): 3023 and 4413; Senate Report 7331 (Serial 5061-D), House Committee on Immigration and Naturalization, *Immigration Station at Charleston, S.C.,* 59th Congress, 2nd session (2 March 1907); Charles F. Kovacik and John J. Winberry, *South Carolina: A Geography* (Boulder, Colo.: Westview, 1987), 125–26; Stephen D. Kantrowitz, *Ben Tillman and the Reconstruction of White Supremacy* (Chapel Hill: University of North Carolina Press, 2000); Simkins, *Pitchfork Ben Tillman,* 517–18.

28. Commission Minutes, 20 February 1908, Husband Papers; *Congressional Record,* 59th Congress, 1st session (22 and 23 May 1906): 7215, 7289–91.

29. Commission Minutes, 20 February 1908, and Commission Record, p. 2, Husband Papers; *Biographical Directory of Congress,* 1272; Richard A. McLemore, ed., *A History of Mississippi* (Hattiesburg: University and College Press of Mississippi, 1977), 2:29; William F. Holmes, *The White Chief: James Kimble Vardaman* (Baton Rouge:

Louisiana State University Press, 1970), 62–69, 76; Bradley G. Bond, *Political Culture in the Nineteenth-Century South, 1830–1900* (Baton Rouge: Louisiana State University Press, 1995), 270–72 and 284.

30. John C. Willis, *Forgotten Time: The Yazoo Mississippi Delta after the Civil War* (Charlottesville: University of Virginia Press, 2000), 123; James C. Cobb, *The Most Southern Place on Earth: The Mississippi Delta and the Roots of Regional Identity* (New York: Oxford University Press, 1992), 93–95; McLemore, *History of Mississippi,* 49–51; Holmes, *White Chief,* 182, 203–5, 212.

31. James Patten to Joseph Lee, 8 and 25 November 1910, Lee Papers; *Congressional Record,* 59th Congress, 1st session (22 June 1906): 9194; Cobb, *Most Southern Place,* 93 and 109–11.

32. William Bennet to *Reader's Digest,* 28 August 1952; Bennet to George E. Sokolsky, 7 April 1953, William S. Bennet Papers, Arents Research Library, Syracuse, New York; *Congressional Record,* 59th Congress, 1st session (6 April and 25 June 1906): 4882–83 and 9162–63, respectively; *Biographical Directory of Congress,* 673; "William S. Bennet," Biographical Sketch in Bennet Papers; *New York Times,* 3 December 1962. Bennet later served as immigrant attorney before Boards of Special Inquiry, and in 1952 he urged President Harry Truman to veto the McCarren Immigration Act.

33. Henry Cabot Lodge to Theodore Roosevelt, 26 July 1908, in Henry Cabot Lodge, ed. *Selections from the Correspondence of Theodore Roosevelt and Henry Cabot Lodge, 1889–1918* (New York: Charles Scribner's Sons, 1925), 2:306–7.

34. Jesse Taylor to Joseph Lee, 1 February 1907; Robert Ward to Lee, 17 February 1907; Lee to Henry Cabot Lodge, 5 February 1907; Prescott Hall to James Patten, 4 February 1907; Ward to Lee, 26 January 1910; and Patten to Lee, 11 July 1910, Lee Papers; *Congressional Record,* 61st Congress, 2nd session (25 January 1910): 967; Solomon, *Ancestors,* 196–97.

35. Henry Cabot Lodge to Theodore Roosevelt, 19 February 1907, Lodge Papers, III; Lodge to Roosevelt, 26 July 1908, Lodge, *Selections,* 2:306-307

36. Senator [John C.] Spooner to Henry Cabot Lodge, 13 March 1907; Morton Crane to Lodge, 23 May 1907; and Lodge to Ambassador Henry White, 4 June 1907, Lodge Papers; Theodore Roosevelt to Jeremiah Jenks, 14 March 1907, Series 2, 71:338, Roosevelt Papers; Frederick C. Croxton, "Autobiography," 54–55, Frederick C. Croxton Papers, Herbert Hoover Presidential Library, West Branch, Iowa; William Husband to Franz Boas, 13 February 1909, Franz Boas Papers, microfilm edition, American Philosophical Society Library, Philadelphia; Roosevelt to Lodge, 4 September 1907, in Elting E. Morrison, ed., *Letters of Theodore Roosevelt* (Cambridge: Harvard University Press, 1952), 5:783; Lodge to Roosevelt, 26 July 1908, Lodge, *Selections,* 2:306–7. For the accusation made against Crane, see Handlin, *Race,* 101.

37. *National Cyclopaedia,* 34:264; *New York Times,* 13 March 1921; Croxton, "Autobiography," 54–55, Croxton Papers. Funding for the staff and salaries for the presidential appointees initially came from the head tax–supported Immigration Fund. A memo sent to President Roosevelt sought clarification of the salary for his appointees, which was set at $7,500 per annum; Commission Minutes, 22 and 24 April 1907, and Executive Order on Commissioners' Salary, 7 May 1907, Husband Papers; *Washington Star,* 27 September 1908.

38. [W. Jett Lauck], "Record of Work Done, 1907–," Box 25; Charles Neill, Memorandum on the Subcommittee on Statistics, 2 April 1908, Box 80; "Memorandum for the President in Favor of the Reading Test Provision of the Burnett

Immigration Bill, April 1914, Box 80; Jeremiah Jenks to Lauck, 10 October 1921, Box 37; Suzanne Broomshall to Lauck, 12 December 1922, Box 37; [Lauck] to the National Committee for Constructive Immigration Legislation, 19 February 1924, Lauck Papers.

39. Croxton, "Autobiography," Croxton Papers.

40. Theodore Roosevelt to Henry Cabot Lodge, 12 March 1908, and Lodge to Roosevelt, 13 March 1908, Lodge Papers, III.

41. Joseph Lee to Charles Nagel, 31 December 1910, Lee Papers; [W. Jett Lauck], "Memorandum for the President in Favor of the Reading Test Provision of the Burnett Immigration Bill," April 1914, Box 80, Lauck Papers; William W. Husband, "Address to the Fifth Congress of the National Federation of Religious Liberals," 23 February 1915, Husband Papers; *Congressional Record*, 61st Congress, 2nd session (25 January 1910): 966. Lauck and Husband both reported on the commissioners' initially moderate views, challenging the position that the commission was anti-immigrant from its inception; for examples, see Handlin, *Race*, 100–2 and Bernard A. Weisberger, *Many People, One Nation* (Boston: Houghton Mifflin, 1987), 225.

3: "EVERY PART OF EUROPE"

1. U.S. Immigration Commission, *Reports of the Immigration Commission*, vol. 4: *Emigration Conditions in Europe* (Washington, D.C.: U.S. Government Printing Office, 1911), 3–5; Henry Cabot Lodge to W. Sturgis Bigelow, 8 May 1907; Lodge to Henry White, 18 May 1907; and Morton Crane to Lodge, 23 May 1907, Henry Cabot Lodge Papers, Massachusetts Historical Society, Boston (hereafter, Lodge Papers). Birds of passage had provoked considerable discussion in the 1890s, and prohibition of their practice had been part of the bill vetoed by President Cleveland; see *Congressional Record*, 54th Congress, 1st session (19 May 1896): 5418–19.

2. Commission Minutes, 22 and 24 April 1907, William W. Husband Papers, Chicago Historical Society (hereafter, Husband Papers).

3. Mss. Report—Northern Italy, France, Switzerland, and Germany Sub-Committee (hereafter, Mss. Howell Report), 1, Benjamin F. Howell Papers, Alexander Library, Rutgers University, New Brunswick, New Jersey; William S. Bennet to Frank P. Sargent, 28 June 1907, Immigration and Naturalization Service, Central Office Correspondence, Record Group 85, File 51411/46, National Archives, Washington, D.C. (hereafter, INS Correspondence).

4. U.S. Immigration Commission, *Emigration Conditions*, 3–5; Oscar S. Straus, Bureau of Immigration and Naturalization, to William Bennet, 18 June 1907, INS Correspondence, Record Group 85, File 51411/46. Terence Powderly, testimony before the Chandler Committee, 16 April 1890; Robert Watchorn, testimony before the Senate Committee on Immigration, 18 June 1902, Senate Report 2119 (Serial 4264-9) *Regulation of Immigration of Aliens*, 57th Congress, 1st session, 149–51. President, Knights of Labor, to the Secretary of the Treasury, with Knights of Labor *Journal*, 22 April 1897; and Terence Powderly to W. H. Allen, 20 August 1897, Terence V. Powderly Papers, microfilm edition, Catholic University Library, Washington, D.C.; Oscar S. Straus, *Under Four Administrations* (Boston: Houghton Mifflin, 1922), 217–21.

5. U.S. Immigration Commission, *Emigration Conditions*, 3–5, 12, and 19. The commission divided the report into 5 parts: Part I—General Survey, 1–134; Part II—

Emigration Situation in Italy, 135–236; Part III—Emigration Situation in Russia, 237–348; Part IV—Emigration Situation in Austria-Hungary, 349–88; Part V—Emigration Situation in Greece, 389–415.

6. Meeting Minutes, 18 June 1907, Husband Papers; William Bennet to Oscar S. Strauss [*sic*], 1 June 1907, INS Correspondence, Record Group 85, File 51411/46; U.S. Immigration Commission, *Emigration Conditions*, 1–3 and 137–45; Donna R. Gabaccia, *Italy's Many Diasporas* (Seattle: University of Washington Press, 2000), 5 and 68–71; Thomas Kessner, *The Golden Door: Italian and Jewish Immigrant Mobility in New York City, 1880–1915* (New York: Oxford University Press, 1977), 3–23.

7. U.S. Immigration Commission, *Emigration Conditions*, 147–50 and 214–20.

8. Henry P. Fairchild, *Immigration: A World Movement and Its American Significance* (New York: Macmillan, 1913), 136–37; Donna Gabaccia, "Is Everywhere Nowhere? Nomads, Nations, and the Immigrant Paradigm in United States History," *Journal of American History* 86 (December 1999): 1120.

9. William Bennet to Joseph Cannon, 12 September 1907, Joseph Cannon Papers, Illinois Historical Society, Springfield; U.S. Immigration Commission, *Emigration Conditions*, 153–55 and 192.

10. Mss. Howell Report, 1–19.

11. U.S. Immigration Commission, *Emigration Conditions*, 135–235; Henry Cabot Lodge, "Lynch Law and Unrestricted Immigration," *North American Review 152 (May 1891)*; David A. Smith, "From the Mississippi to the Mediterranean: The 1891 New Orleans Lynching and Its Effects on the United States Diplomacy and the American Navy," *Southern Historian* 19 (1998); Gabaccia, *Italy's Many Diasporas*, 127–28; Alan M. Kraut, *The Huddled Masses: The Immigrant in American Society, 1880–1921* (Arlington Heights, Ill.: Harlan Davidson, 1982), 158–59. Kraut explains how people at the time completely misunderstood both the Mafia and various "black hand" groups.

12. U.S. Immigration Commission, *Emigration Conditions*, 113–20. American involvement began with enforcement of the U.S. Quarantine Law of 1893. In 1899, the United States sent a doctor to Naples to guard against the spread of plague from Egypt. The surgeon began inspecting U.S.-bound emigrants for signs of the plague. Later, under agreement with the Italian government, he started looking for any defect for which a person could be excluded under U.S. immigration law. At Naples, Americans conducted the medical examinations; at Palermo and Messina, Italian doctors conducted the examinations under the direction of the U.S. Public Health and Marine Hospital Service. Americans had no involvement at Genoa. Fiorello La Guardia, later a member of Congress and mayor of New York City, worked in 1903 at the Fiume Immigration Station, from which the Cunard Line had just started service to New York City. His autobiography describes the medical inspections and some of the problems with their administration. See *The Making of an Insurgent: An Autobiography, 1882–1919* (Philadelphia: J. B. Lippincott, 1948), 53–61.

13. William Bennet to Frank Sargent, 28 June 1907; and Sargent to Bennet, 18 July 1907, INS Correspondence, Record Group 85, File 51411/46. Prescott Hall to Sargent, 13 June 1903; and Sargent to Hall, 19 June 1903, INS Correspondence, Record Group 85, File 52903/29A. Gary M. Fink, ed., *Biographical Dictionary of American Labor Leaders* (Westport, Conn.: Greenwood, 1974), 318–19.

14. Mss. Howell Report, 25–29 and 34–36.

15. Mss. Howell Report, 19–21; U.S. Immigration Commission, *Emigration Conditions*, 105–6.

16. U.S. Immigration Commission, *Emigration Conditions,* 90–91, 102–3, and 105–6; and Mss. Howell Report, 34–36.

17. Mss. Howell Report, 37–49; U.S. Immigration Commission, *Emigration Conditions,* 93–102. For a description of trachoma and other common immigrant maladies, see Fairchild, *Immigration,* 209–11.

18. U.S. Immigration Commission, *Reports of the Immigration Commission,* vol. 37: *Steerage Conditions* (Washington, D.C.: U.S. Government Printing Office, 1911), 1–29.

19. U.S. Immigration Commission, *Emigration Conditions,* 92–93, 111–13, and 349–88.

20. Ibid., 289–348; 93–102.

21. George L. von Meyer, U.S. Ambassador at St. Petersburg, Russia, to Henry Cabot Lodge, 21 September 1906, Lodge Papers; U.S. Immigration Commission, *Emigration Conditions,* 289–348. The commission's minutes of 24 April 1907 and 17 September 1908 indicate Special Investigator Ralph H. C. Catterall went to Russia at a later date and that his findings augmented those of Dillingham and Wheeler (Husband Papers). For full coverage of the condition of Russian Jews, see Gerald Sorin, *Tradition Transformed: The Jewish Experience in America* (Baltimore: Johns Hopkins University Press, 1997), 34–60.

22. U.S. Immigration Commission, *Emigration Conditions,* 104–5 and 237–348.

23. U.S. Immigration Commission, *Emigration Conditions,* 389–415, with re-emigration figures on p. 414; Thomas Archdeacon, *Becoming American: An Ethnic History* (New York: Free Press, 1983), Table V-4, p. 139.

24. William Bennet to Frank P. Sargent, 13 July and 27 July 1907; John B. Jackson, American Legation, Athens, Greece, to Elihu Root, 11 July 1907; F. H. Larned, Acting Commissioner General, to Commissioners at Ellis Island, 30 July 1907; and Larned to Commissioners of Immigration at various U.S. ports, 19 August 1907, INS Correspondence, Record Group 85, File 51411/46; U.S. Immigration Commission, *Emigration Conditions,* 107–9.

25. William Bennet to Frank P. Sargent, 27 July 1907; and American Legation, Sinaia, Rumania, to Elihu Root, 9 August 1907, INS Correspondence, Record Group 85, File 51411/46; Bennet to Jacob Lochner Jr., 10 July 1951, William S. Bennet Papers, Special Collections Research Center, Syracuse University, Syracuse, New York; *Congressional Record,* 61st Congress, 2nd session (25 January 1910): 963–65.

26. *Congressional Record,* 61st Congress, 2nd session (25 January 1910): 963–65.

27. U.S. Immigration Commission, *Emigration Condition,* 3, 80–92, 109–11.

28. Extract from the unpublished one-page report of the subcommittee of the immigration commission to which was assigned the territory of northern Italy, France, Switzerland, Germany, and so on, 1907, INS Correspondence, Record Group 85, File 53108/70; U.S. Immigration Commission, *Emigration Conditions,* 82–90.

29. U.S. Immigration Commission, *Emigration Conditions,* 21–52.

30. Ibid., 69–80 and 120–35.

31. Ibid., 53–67.

32. Ibid., 120–35; Frank P. Sargent to William Bennet, 18 July 1907, INS Correspondence, Record Group 85, File 51411/46.

33. U.S. Immigration Commission, *Emigration Conditions,* 3–5 and 230; House Document 1489, *Statement Relative to the Work and Expenditures of the Immigration Commission,* 60th Congress, 2nd session, 1909, 10–11.

4: "Observations at Home"

1. Frank P. Sargent to William Bennet, 18 July 1907, Immigration and Naturalization Service, Central Office Correspondence, Record Group 85, File 51411/46; Commission Minutes, 22 April 1907, William W. Husband Papers, Chicago Historical Society (hereafter, Husband Papers).

2. Eric Rauchway, "The High Cost of Living in the Progressive Economy," *Journal of American History* 88 (December 2001); Theodore M. Parker, *Trust in Numbers: The Pursuit of Objectivity in Science and Public Life* (Princeton, N.J.: Princeton University Press, 1995), 20–37; U.S. Immigration Commission, *Reports of the Immigration Commission,* vols. 1 & 2: *Abstracts of Reports of the Immigration Commission* (Washington, D.C.: U.S. Government Printing Office, 1911), 1:12; Charlotte Erickson, ed., *Emigration from Europe, 1815–1914: Select Documents* (London: Adam & Charles Black, 1976), 91–92.

3. U.S. Immigration Commission, *Abstracts,* 1:20 and 2:651–727.

4. U.S. Immigration Commission, *Reports of the Immigration Commission,* vol. 19, *Immigrants in Industries, Part 23: Summary Report on Immigrants in Manufacturing and Mining* (Washington, D.C.: U.S. Government Printing Office, 1911), passim.

5. Commission Minutes, 22 April 1907, Husband Papers; "Act to Regulate the Immigration of Aliens into the United States," in U.S. Congress, *Statutes at Large of the United States of America, From December 1901 to March 1903* (Washington, D.C.: U.S. Government Printing Office, 1904).

6. Commission Minutes, 23 April 1907, Husband Papers. For background on the Progressive Era's reliance on empirical study, see Rauchway, "High Cost," 900–901, and Samuel Haber, *Efficiency and Uplift: Scientific Management in the Progressive Era, 1890–1920* (Chicago: University of Chicago Press, 1964).

7. Commission Minutes, 23 April, 7 December 1907, and 10 January 1908, Husband Papers. The minutes for the 7 December meeting in Vienna, Austria, note Dillingham's previous enlargement of the evasion committee's investigation.

8. Commission Minutes, 7 and 13 December 1907; Executive Committee Minutes, 18 January and 25 April 1908, Husband Papers.

9. Commission Minutes, 7 and 13 December 1907 and 1 April 1908; Executive Committee Minutes, 27 March and 1 April 1908, Husband Papers; *Dictionary of American Biography,* Supplement 4:584–88.

10. Immigration Restriction League to Theodore Roosevelt, 14 October 1905 (801), and James Patten, Letter to Newspaper Editors, 2 March 1908, Immigration Restriction League Papers, Houghton Library, Harvard University, Cambridge.

11. Commission Minutes, 7 and 13 December 1907, 10 January 1908, and 1 April 1908, Husband Papers. The executive committee approved Heard's appointment as superintendent of the southern investigation on 29 January 1908 (Executive Committee Minutes, 29 January 1908, Husband Papers).

12. Commission Minutes, 7 December 1907 and 10 and 18 January 1908, Husband Papers; Henry P. Fairchild, *Immigration: A World Movement and Its American Significance* (New York: Macmillan, 1918), 118–21.

13. Commission Minutes, 8 May, 22 May, and 17 December 1908, and Executive Committee Minutes, 22 May 1908, Husband Papers; U.S. Immigration Commission, *Reports of the Immigration Commission,* vol. 37, *Steerage Conditions* (Washington, D.C.: U.S. Government Printing Office, 1911), 1–13.

14. U.S. Immigration Commission, *Steerage Conditions,* 13–23.

15. Ibid., 24–29.

16. *Congressional Record,* 60th Congress, 1st session (21 February 1908, 27 May 1908): 2291–92 and 7054–60, respectively; 60th Congress, 2nd session (17 December 1908), 375–76.

17. Commission Minutes, 10 January 1908, Husband Papers; "Act to Regulate the Immigration of Aliens into the United States."

18. Commission Minutes, 22 April 1907 and 10 January 1908, Husband Papers; Henry Cabot Lodge to Jeremiah McCarthy, 13 March 1907 and 27 February 1908; McCarthy to Lodge, 26 February 1908, Henry Cabot Lodge Papers, Massachusetts Historical Society, Boston (hereafter, Lodge Papers).

19. Minutes, Executive Committee Meeting, 18 January 1908 and 14 February 1908; and Commission Minutes, 13 December 1907 and 1 April 1908, Husband Papers.

20. Commission Minutes, 29 May 1908, and Executive Committee Minutes, 14 February and 22 May 1908, Husband Papers.

21. Commission Minutes, 1 April, 8 May, and 15 May 1908; and 10 July 1910, Husband Papers; *Congressional Record,* 60th Congress, 1st session (6 and 31 January, 27 February, and 2 March 1908): 482, 1434, 2417, and 2746–52, respectively; House Report 1114 (Serial 5225), *Report to Accompany House Resolution 266,* 60th Congress, 1st session (28 February 1908).

22. Commission Minutes, 27 March, 1 and 24 April, and 10 July 1908; Executive Committee Minutes, 10 February 1908, Husband Papers.

23. Commission Minutes, 24 and 25 April 1908, including an "Outline of Investigations, Studies, and Compilations Now Underway or Proposed," which was presented to the commission on 24 April, Husband Papers; Frederick C. Croxton, "Autobiography," 54–55, in Frederick C. Croxton Papers, Herbert Hoover Presidential Library, West Branch, Iowa; "Explanation of Outline," n.d., William Jett Lauck Papers, University of Virginia Library, Charlottesville, Virginia (hereafter, Lauck Papers). The unsigned and undated "Explanation of Outline" was likely prepared by Croxton and was clearly intended to accompany the draft outline that Neill presented to the commission. The actual "Outline" is found in the Husband Papers. In his "Autobiography," Croxton discussed that he had been asked to prepare some sort of "Explanation" for the investigation's new organization, and this almost certainly is the "Explanation" found in the Lauck Papers.

24. "Outline of Investigation" and "Explanation of Outline," 3–11.

25. "Outline of Investigation" and "Explanation of Outline," 12–17.

26. "Outline of Investigation" and "Explanation of Outline," 18–23.

27. "Outline of Investigation" and "Explanation of Outline," 24–26.

28. "Outline of Investigation" and "Explanation of Outline," 27.

29. "Outline of Investigation" and "Explanation of Outline," 28–31.

30. "Outline of Investigation."

31. Commission Minutes, 8, 15, and 29 May, and 10 July 1908, and Executive Committee Minutes, 24 April and 8, 15, and 29 May 1908, Husband Papers. In September the executive committee hired a special agent for the school investigation; see Executive Committee Minutes, 17 September 1908.

32. Commission Minutes, 22 May, 10 July, and 17 September 1908, and Executive Committee Minutes, 22 May 1908, Husband Papers.

33. Commission Minutes, 10 July 1908, Husband Papers; William Husband to Whom It May Concern (noting Lauck's appointment as superintendent as of 19 July 1908), Lauck Papers.

34. W. Jett Lauck, memorandum to William Husband, "Opinions on the best methods of conducting a general investigation in the North, Middle West, and New England," n.d., Lauck Papers; Department of Labor, Individual Slip, copy in Lauck Papers; Plan for Field Investigation of Manufacturing Communities, n.d., Lauck Papers; *Buffalo Express*, 6 April 1909, copy in Lauck Papers.

35. Commission Minutes, 16 September and 12 November 1908, and Executive Committee Minutes, 9 January 1908, Husband Papers.

36. Commission Minutes, 17 September 1908 and 12 November 1908, Husband Papers.

37. Starr J. Murphy to John D. Rockefeller Jr., 10 November 1910, Record Group 2-P, Folder 313, Box 30, John D. Rockefeller Jr. Office Correspondence, Rockefeller Archives Center, North Tarrytown, New York; Commission Minutes, 12 November 1908, Husband Papers. The commission had previously decided not to have any of its members associate with the New York group; Commission Minutes, 25 April 1908, Husband Papers.

38. Commission Minutes, 22 February 1909, Husband Papers; *Congressional Record*, 60th Congress, 2nd session (18 February 1909): 2609–15.

39. *Congressional Record*, 60th Congress, 2nd session (27 February 1909): 3402–3403; House Document 1489 (Serial 5557), "Statement Relative to the Work and Expenditure of the Immigration Commission," 60th Congress, 2nd session (22 February 1909); *Congressional Record*, 60th Congress, 2nd session (24 January 1910): 930. The commission anticipated these problems and started discussing how best to respond to the funding changes in the fall of 1908; see Commission Minutes, 17 September, 12 November, and 17 December 1908, Husband Papers.

40. Commission Minutes, 16 and 25 March; 10 June; 19 October; and 1, 6, 19, and 11 December 1909; and Executive Committee Minutes, 16 March 1909, Husband Papers; *Congressional Record*, 61st Congress, 2nd session (24 January 1910): 930.

41. Commission Minutes, 16 March, 25 March, 10 June, and 19 October 1909, Husband Papers.

42. *Congressional Record*, 61st Congress, 2nd session (11 and 24 January 1910): 500 and 929–38, respectively; Senate Document 280 (Serial 5661), "Estimate of Appropriations for Continuing Work of the Immigration Commission," 61st Congress, 2nd session (11 January 1910).

43. Commission Minutes, 10 January 1910, Husband Papers; *Congressional Record*, 61st Congress, 2nd session (24, 25, and 38 January 1910): 929–38, 963–70, and 1216, respectively.

44. *Congressional Record*, 61st Congress, 2nd session (2, 4, 8, 10, 11, and 21 February 1910): 1369–72, 1493 and 1495, 1572, 1703–1722, 1756–57 and 1805–1806, and 2180–83, respectively.

45. Unknown correspondent to William Bennet, 12 August 1910, Lodge Papers. Unfortunately, only part of the letter became part of the Lodge Papers; the missing section probably indicates the author.

46. *Congressional Record*, 61st Congress, 2nd session (10 February 1910): 1703.

5: "Craniometry"

1. Franz Boas to Jeremiah W. Jenks, 19 and 23 March 1908, Franz Boas Papers, microfilm edition, American Philosophical Society Library, Philadelphia (hereafter, Boas Papers).

2. William Williams quoted in "Burdens of Recent Immigration in the State of New York," IRL Pamphlet #40, ca. 1903, Immigration Restriction League Publications, Widener Library, Harvard University. Joseph Lee to John M. Glenn, 20 April and 30 April 1907; Glenn to Lee, 23 April 1907; and Lee to John Graham Brooks, 11 July 1907, Joseph Lee Papers, Massachusetts Historical Society, Boston.

3. Martha Hodes, "The Mercurial Nature and Abiding Power of Race: A Transnational Story," *American Historical Review* 108 (February 2003), 85; George W. Stocking Jr., ed., *The Shaping of American Anthropology, 1883–1911: A Franz Boas Reader* (New York: Basic Books, 1974), 1–4 and 189–91; Matthew P. Guterl, *The Color of Race in America: 1900–1940* (Cambridge: Harvard University Press, 2001), 112–13.

4. Douglas Cole, *Franz Boas, the Early Years, 1858–1906* (Seattle: University of Washington Press, 1999), 280–82; Kevin MacDonald, *The Culture of Critique: An Evolutionary Analysis of Jewish Involvement in Twentieth-Century Intellectual and Political Movements* (Westport, Conn.: Praeger, 1998), 21–30; Marshall Hyatt, *Franz Boas, Social Activist: The Dynamics of Ethnicity* (New York: Greenwood, 1990), 1–99; Vernon J. Williams, *Rethinking Race: Franz Boas and His Contemporaries* (Lexington: University of Kentucky Press, 1996), 1–19.

5. Boas to Jeremiah Jenks, 19 and 23 March 1908, Boas Papers.

6. Boas to Jeremiah Jenks, 5, 19, and 23 March and 9 April 1908; Jenks to Boas, 11 and 26 March 1908, Boas Papers. The Boas Papers contain no correspondence between Jenks and Boas prior to 1908, but there may have been earlier letters that were lost. Boas does mention that he broached the subject of craniometric study in November 1907; see Boas to Jenks, 2 May 1908, Boas Papers.

7. Jeremiah Jenks to Boas, 8 and 14 April 1908, and Boas to Jenks, 7 April 1908, Boas Papers. Commission Minutes, 1 April 1908, William W. Husband Papers, Chicago Historical Society (hereafter, Husband Papers). The commission first reviewed Boas's proposal at the 1 April meeting, at which Representative Bennet asked for a postponement of its consideration. This suggests that he was the influential member to whom Jenks referred and that he later reversed himself on the full-funding vote. There is nothing else in the minutes that gives a clue as to the influential member's identity.

8. Boas to Jeremiah Jenks, 15 April 1908, Boas Papers.

9. Boas to Jeremiah Jenks, 28 April 1908, and Jenks to Boas, 29 April 1908, Boas Papers; Commission Minutes, 24 and 25 April, Husband Papers. Here again Bennet showed his uncertainty, but in a 1909 letter to Boas, Jenks would describe Bennet as a "strong" supporter; Jenks to Boas, 22 March 1909, Boas Papers. Perhaps by that time Bennet had come to realize that the results would be favorable to immigrants and had decided to support the project.

10. Jeremiah Jenks to Boas, 29 April 1908, Boas Papers.

11. Boas to Jeremiah Jenks, 2 May 1908, Boas Papers.

12. Commission Minutes, 8 and 15 May 1908, and Executive Committee Minutes, 15 May 1908, Husband Papers; Boas to Jeremiah Jenks, 12 May and 3 June 1908; Jenks to Boas, 20 May and 5 June 1908; and Jenks to Whom It May Concern, 5 June 1908, Boas Papers.

13. William Husband to Jeremiah Jenks, 6 June 1908, and Boas to Jenks, 8 and 26 June, 24 July, and 3 September 1908, Boas Papers.

14. Boas to Jeremiah Jenks, 3 September and 10 October 1908; Boas and C. Ward Crampton, 21 December 1908; Jenks to Boas, 12 August 1908; Memorandum of the Preliminary Findings, n.d., Boas Papers. Crampton presented the material to

the commission on 16 September and then sent a copy of his report to Boas; see Crampton to Boas, 16 December 1908, Boas Papers.

15. Jeremiah Jenks to Boas, 12 August, 20 November, and 12 December 1908; Boas to Jenks, 23 November and 4 December 1908; Morton Crane to Boas, 23 November 1908; Boas to Crane, 25 November 1908; Boas to C. Ward Crampton, 21 December 1908, Boas Papers; Commission Minutes, 12 November and 17 December 1908, Husband Papers.

16. Boas to William Husband, 4, 16, and 27 January and 12 June 1909; Jeremiah Jenks to Boas, 9, 23, and 26 January 1909; Husband to Boas, 12, 13, 14, 18, and 19 January 1909; Boas to Jenks, 18 November 1908 and 23 January and 8 March 1909, Boas Papers.

17. Boas to Jeremiah Jenks, 11 March 1909, Boas Papers.

18. Boas to Otto Koenig, 28 January 1909; Boas to Wilson Farrand, 28 January 1909; Boas to F. C. Lewis, 29 January 1909; Boas to William A. Hervey, 29 January 1909; Boas to Dr. A. B. Poland, 6 February 1909; and Boas to Jane E. Robbins, 10 February 1909, Boas Papers.

19. F. C. Lewis to Boas, 4 February 1909; A. B. Poland to Boas, 10 February 1909; Samuel T. Dutton to Boas, 10 February 1909; William A. Hervey to Boas, 6 February 1909; and Boas to William Husband, 6 February 1909, Boas Papers.

20. William Husband to Boas, 9 and 29 January 1909; Boas to Husband, 12 January and 1 February 1909, Boas Papers.

21. Boas to Jeremiah Jenks, 29 January 1909; Jenks to Boas, 30 January 1909; and Boas to William Husband, with attachment, 24 February 1908, Boas Papers.

22. Boas to Jeremiah Jenks, 3 and 16 April 1909; Jenks to Boas, 14 April 1909, Boas Papers.

23. Jeremiah Jenks to Boas, 6 March 1909, Boas Papers.

24. Boas to Jeremiah Jenks, 8 and 11 March 1909, Boas Papers.

25. Boas to Jeremiah Jenks, 30 March, 7 and 28 May, and 7 and 28 June 1909; Boas to William Husband, 19 April and 5 and 24 May 1909; Jenks to Boas, 8 and 29 June 1909, Boas Papers.

26. Boas to O. Schwarz, 2 July 1919; Boas to William Husband, 3 July 1909; Boas to Husband, 6 August 1909; Boas to Jeremiah Jenks, 6 August 1909; Jenks to Boas, 14 July and 12 August 1909, Boas Papers. Jenks warned Boas that it was unlikely that the commission would give him more money.

27. Boas to William Husband, 11 October 1909; Boas to Jeremiah Jenks, 23 September, 18 and 21 October, and 16 November 1909, Boas Papers.

28. Boas to Jeremiah Jenks, 2 December 1909, Boas Papers.

29. Jeremiah Jenks to Boas, 13 and 24 December 1909; Boas to William Husband, 15 December 1909; Husband to Boas, 17 December 1909; Boas to Jenks, 30 December 1909, Boas Papers.

30. Boas to Jeremiah Jenks, 31 December 1909, Boas Papers; Matthew Frye Jacobson, *Whiteness of a Different Color: European Immigrants and the Alchemy of Race* (Cambridge: Harvard University Press, 1998), 56–62; Guterl, *Color of Race*, 112–13.

31. Henry Cabot Lodge to Charles Francis Adams, 1 May 1906, and Lodge to Owen Wister, 30 April 1906, Henry Cabot Lodge Papers, Massachusetts Historical Society, Boston.

32. Boas to Jeremiah Jenks, 23, 24, and 31 December 1909, Boas Papers.

33. *New York Times*, 18 December 1909, and *Boston Evening Transcript*, 17 December 1909.

34. Boas to William Husband, 20 December 1909; Boas to Jeremiah Jenks, 21 December 1909; Boas to Morton Crane, 23 December 1909; Crane to Boas, 14 and 22 December 1909; and Boas to Jenks, 23 December 1909, Boas Papers.

35. Boas to Jeremiah Jenks, 23 and 28 February, 22 March, and 30 June 1910; Jenks to Boas, 28 February, 2 March, 4 and 13 June, and 30 July 1910; Morton Crane to Boas, 23 February 1910; Boas to Crane, 24 and 26 February, 7 and 29 March, and 25 May 1910, Boas Papers. From 1 July to 19 November 1910, Boas corresponded regularly with Crane and William Husband about preparing various aspects of the report for publication and writing up the summary abstract; their correspondence is in the Boas Papers.

36. U. S. Immigration Commission, *Reports of the Immigration Commission,* vol. 38, *Changes in Bodily Form of Descendants of Immigrants* (Washington, D.C.: U.S. Government Printing Office, 1911), 1–3.

37. Ibid., 1–115.

38. Ibid., 57, 76.

39. Jeremiah Jenks to Boas, 8 April 1910, Boas Papers.

40. Boas to Jeremiah Jenks, 14 and 21 March, 11 April, 2 June, and 14 November 1910; Jenks to Boas, 19 and 22 March and 12 and 20 April 1910; Boas to Henry Cabot Lodge, 29 November 1910, Boas Papers. Notation on the Boas to Lodge letter 29 November 1910 includes that it was forwarded to Smithsonian Secretary C. D. Wolcott on 5 December 1910, but the matter evidently died there.

41. Daniel J. Kevles, *In the Name of Eugenics: Genetics and the Use of Human Heredity* (Berkeley: University of California Press, 1985), 134–35; Carl Degler, *Culture versus Biology in the Thought of Franz Boas and Alfred L. Krolber* (New York: Berg, 1989), 3–4.

6: "VAST MASS OF VALUABLE FACTS"

1. Henry Cabot Lodge to Barrett Wendell, 13 April 1910; Lodge to Theodore Roosevelt, 4 August and 31 December 1910, Henry Cabot Lodge Papers, Massachusetts Historical Society, Boston; Jeremiah Jenks and W. Jett Lauck, *The Immigration Problem,* 5th ed. (New York: Funk and Wagnalls, 1924), xxiii–xxiv; U.S. Immigration Commission, *Reports of the Immigration Commission,* vol. 1: *Abstracts of Reports of the Immigration Commission* (Washington, D.C.: U.S. Government Printing Office, 1911), iv and 9.

2. Commission Minutes, 10 January 1910, William W. Husband Papers, Chicago Historical Society (hereafter, Husband Papers); James Patten to Joseph Lee, 25 November 1910, Joseph Lee Papers, Massachusetts Historical Society, Boston (hereafter, Lee Papers). James Patten claimed that commissioners Percy and Burnett worried that the voluminous *Reports* might overwhelm readers, rendering it less useful to the restrictionist cause. For a discussion of the problems of using historical statistics, see Jon A. Gjerde, "Appendix on Statistics," in *They Chose Minnesota,* ed. June D. Holmquist (St. Paul: Minnesota Historical Society, 1981).

3. "Community Notes on the Copper Country of Northern Michigan," William Jett Lauck Papers (4742), University of Virginia Library, Charlottesville (hereafter, Lauck Papers); Commission Minutes, 10 January; 5 and 22 February; and 21, 22, 23, and 25 November 1910, Husband Papers; Oscar Handlin, *Race and Nationality in American Life* (Boston: Little, Brown, 1948), 100.

4. U.S. Immigration Commission, *Reports of the Immigration Commission,* vol. 19, *Immigrants in Industries, Part 23: Summary Report on Immigrants in Manufacturing and Mining* (Washington, D.C.: U.S. Government Printing Office, 1911), passim.

5. Handlin, *Race,* 103; U.S. Immigration Commission, *Summary Report on Mining and Manufacturing,* 187–91; U.S. Immigration Commission, *Reports of the Immigration Commission,* vol. 6, *Immigrants in Industries, Part 1: Bituminous Coal Mining* (Washington, D.C.: U.S. Government Printing Office, 1911), 49–57 and 209–41.

6. U.S. Immigration Commission, *Bituminous Coal Mining,* 49–50.

7. Ibid., 54–60.

8. W. Jett Lauck, "Immigration to Coal Mines in Illinois," Lauck Papers.

9. Commission Minutes, 7 and 13 December 1907 and 1 April 1908, and Executive Committee Minutes, 27 March and 1 April 1908, Husband Papers; Henry A. Millis, *The Japanese Problem in the United States* (New York: Macmillan, 1915), xi–xii and 293–94.

10. U.S. Immigration Commission, *Reports of the Immigration Commission,* vol. 25, *Immigrants in Industries, Part 25: Japanese and other Immigrant Races in the Pacific coast and Rocky Mountain States* (Washington, D.C.: U.S. Government Printing Office, 1911), 1–32.

11. Ibid., 167–77.

12. Husband to Wheeler, 15 December 1908, and Commission Minutes, 1 and 4 December 1909, Husband Papers. The reports note that even among Jews themselves there was disagreement as to whether they should be considered a separate race; see Immigration Commission Reports, *Abstracts,* 1:18–20. The issue of Jews and the quota system is covered in chapter 8.

13. William Husband to Franz Boas, 29 September and 12 October 1909, and Boas to Husband, 9 October 1909, Franz Boas papers, microfilm edition, American Philosophical Society Library, Philadelphia (hereafter, Boas papers); Commission Minutes, 22 February 1909, Husband Papers; Daniel Folkmar, *Album of Philippine Types* (Manila: Bureau of Public Printing, 1904), passim; U.S. Immigration Commission, *Reports of the Immigration Commission,* vol. 5: *Dictionary of Races and Peoples* (Washington, D.C.: Government Printing Office, 1910), passim.

14. U.S. Immigration Commission, *Dictionary,* passim; Handlin, *Race,* 104–8.

15. U.S. Immigration Commission, *Reports of the Immigration Commission,* vol. 26–27, *Immigrants in Cities* (Washington, D.C.: Government Printing Office, 1910), passim.

16. Commission Minutes, 2 December 1910, Husband Papers; U.S. Immigration Commission, *Reports of the Immigration Commission,* vols. 29–33, *Children of Immigrants in Schools* (Washington, D.C.: Government Printing Office, 1910), 29:3 and 38.

17. U.S. Immigration Commission, *Reports of the Immigration Commission,* vol. 36, *Immigration and Crime* (Washington, D.C.: Government Printing Office, 1910), 1–2 and passim.

18. Ibid., 277–86.

19. U.S. Immigration Commission, *Reports of the Immigration Commission,* vol. 41, *Statements and Recommendations Submitted by Societies and Organizations Interested in the Subject of Immigration* (Washington, D.C.: Government Printing Office, 1910), 3 and passim.

20. William Husband to Franz Boas, 5 October 1910, Boas Papers; Commission Minutes, 17 November 1910, and Executive Committee Minutes, 18 October 1910, Husband Papers; U.S. Immigration Commission, *Abstracts,* 1:1.

21. U.S. Immigration Commission, *Abstracts*, 1:387, 491, 501, and 541.

22. Commission Minutes, 17 November 1910, Husband Papers; U.S. Immigration Commission, *Abstracts*, 1:9–44.

23. Henry Cabot Lodge to Prescott Hall, 29 January 1908, and Jeremiah Jenks to Hall, 3 March 1910, Immigration Restriction League Papers (608), Houghton Library, Harvard University, Cambridge (hereafter, IRL Papers); Commission Minutes, 16 and 22 March and 1 April 1909, Husband Papers; Joseph Lee to James Patten, 25 January 1910, Lee Papers; *Congressional Record*, 60th Congress, 2nd session (18 February 1909): 2609–15.

24. James Patten to Joseph Lee, 10 January; 15 March; 31 May; and 6, 8, 10, 25, and 29 November 1910; Lee to Patten, 20 and 25 January and 28 December 1910; Patten to Prescott Hall, 28 March 1910; Lee to A. Lawrence Lowell, 4 August 1910; Lowell to Henry Cabot Lodge, 9 August 1910, Lee Papers.

25. James Patten to Prescott Hall, 8 December 1910, Lee Papers; Jeremiah Jenks to Prescott Hall, 3 March 1910, IRL Papers (549); Commission Minutes, 3 December 1910, Husband Papers; U.S. Immigration Commission, *Abstracts*, 1:25 and 45.

26. Commission Minutes, 3 and 4 December 1910, Husband Papers; U.S. Immigration Commission, *Abstracts*, 1:45–48.

27. Commission Minutes, 4 December 1910, Husband Papers; U.S. Immigration Commission, *Abstracts*, 1:48. One week earlier Burnett had demonstrated his anti-immigrant bias by objecting "to statements relative to the peacefulness of South Italians in rural communities" in the *Recent Immigrants in Agriculture* report; see Minutes, 25 November 1910, Husband Papers.

28. Commission Minutes, 5 December 1910, Husband Papers. James Patten to Joseph Lee, 4 and 11 December 1910; Lee to Lodge, 13 December 1910; and Lee to Lawrence Lowell, 13 December 1910, Lee Papers; U.S. Immigration Commission, *Abstracts*, 1:45–48.

29. Commission Minutes, 5 December 1910, Husband Papers; U.S. Immigration Commission, *Abstracts*, 1:49.

30. James Patten to Lawrence Lowell, 13 December 1910, Lee Papers.

7: "MOST FEASIBLE MEANS"

1. James Patten to Joseph Lee, 4 and 10 December 1910, Joseph Lee Papers, Massachusetts Historical Society, Boston (hereafter, Lee Papers).

2. John J. D. Trenor, Republican League Clubs of New York, to John Hays Hammond, President, National Republican League, 4 March 1910, Immigration and Naturalization Service, Central Office Correspondence, Record Group 85, File 52903/29A (hereafter, INS Correspondence); Alexander G. Bell to Prescott Hall, 31 May 1911, Immigration Restriction League Papers (117) Houghton Library, Harvard University, Cambridge (hereafter, IRL Papers); Andrew Carnegie to Edward Lauterbach, 2 February 1911, and Charles Eliot to William Bennet, 10 January 1910, both printed at Bennet's request in the *Congressional Record*, 61st Congress, 1st session (14 January and 4 February 1911): 918 and 1951; Senate Document 251 (Serial 6174), *Amendment of Immigration Laws: Resolutions, Views, of Southern Governors, Newspaper Articles, and Hearings before the Committee on Immigration and Naturalization of the House of Representatives*, 62nd Congress, 2nd session, 11 January 1912; Senate Document 785 (Serial 6178), "Views on Immigration," 62nd Congress, 2nd session, 10 June 1912.

3. "White Slavery," *The Outlook* (22 January 1910): 131–32; Mark T. Connelly, *The Response to Prostitution in the Progressive Era* (Chapel Hill: North Carolina University Press, 1980), 57; David J. Langum, *Crossing over the Line: Legislating Morality and the Mann Act* (Chicago: University of Chicago Press, 1994), 35–36 and passim. U.S. Immigration Commission, *Reports of the Immigration Commission*, vol. 37: *Importation and Harboring of Women for Immoral Purposes* (Washington, D.C.: U.S. Goverment Printing Office, 1911), 57. The commission did not address the low level of women's wages, which some progressives thought was a more widespread cause of women turning to prostitution.

4. *Congressional Record*, 61st Congress, 2nd session (17 December 1909, 11 January 1910, 11 February 1910, and 28 March 1910): 245, 525, 1760, and 3855, respectively; U.S. Commission Report, *Importation and Harboring of Women*, 57.

5. James Patten to Joseph Lee, 3 and 10 January 1910, Lee Papers; *Congressional Record*, 61st Congress, 2nd session (6 December 1909, 26 January 1910, and 25 June 1910): 8, 1031–40, and 9037 and 9118, respectively; U.S. Commission Report, *Importation and Harboring of Women*, 93.

6. James Patten to Joseph Lee, 10, 19, and 28 February 1910; Lee to Patten, 28 February 1910; Patten to Miss Snow (Lee's secretary), 5 February 1910; and Lee to Patten, 9 February 1910, Lee Papers.

7. Joseph Lee to Prescott Hall, 1 March 1910; James Patten to Lee, 18 March 1910; Patten to Robert Ward, 21 March 1910; Mrs. Lucien Howe to Lee, 18 March 1910; and Lee to Howe, 23 March 1910, Lee Papers. *Boston Evening Transcript*, 19 May 1909; "Congressman Bennet Not a Progressive" and "'Jews' Attention," copies in Lee Papers.

8. Joseph Lee to James Patten, 20 January and 2 March 1910; Patten to Robert Ward, 6 March 1910; and Lee to Patten, 17 March 1910, Lee Papers.

9. James Patten to Joseph Lee, 12, 14, and 15 March; 6, 13, and 14 April; 13 and 21 May; 2 August; and 10 November 1910, Lee Papers. William B. Griffin, Junior Order United American Mechanics, to Lee, 20 December 1910; clippings from numerous southern newspapers, sent by Patten to Lee, summer 1910, Lee Papers.

10. James Patten to Joseph Lee, 11 January 1913; Richards M. Bradley to Lee, 16 March 1911; and Lee to A. Lawrence Lowell, 25 March 1911 and 1 January 1913, Lee Papers. In private Lee continued to discuss racial consequences and to generally praise the eugenics movement; see Lee to Mr. Ellis, 11 November 1911, Lee Papers. For background on Richards Bradley, see Marilyn Schultz Blackwell, "The Deserving Sick: Poor Women and the Medicalization of Poverty in Battleboro, Vermont," *Journal of Women's History* 11 (spring 1999).

11. B. S. Steadwell to James Patten, 16 March 1910; "Kentuckians on to St. Louis," 26 March 1910; Patten to Prescott Hall, 6 April 1910; Joseph Lee to Charles W. Hubbard, 25 March 1910; and Lee to the Editor of the *Boston Post*, 14 May 1912, Lee Papers. See also Henry P. Fairchild, "The Case for the Literacy Test," *Unpopular Review* 56 (January–March 1916).

12. Prescott Hall, "Educational Test of Immigrants," *Chamber of Commerce News*, 10 June 1912, and Robert Ward, *Boston Herald*, 16 August 1912; copies in Lee Papers.

13. Madison Grant, *The Passing of the Great Race*, rev. ed. (New York: Charles Scribner's Sons, 1918), xix (quote), 17, 89–94, and 226–27; Matthew P. Guterl, *The Color of Race in America: 1900–1940* (Cambridge: Harvard University Press, 2001), 14–67.

14. James Patten to Prescott Hall, 8 January 1911, Lee Papers. Patten to Joseph Lee, 11 December 1910; 21, 26, and 29 January; 1, 7, and 15 February; and 15 March 1911, Lee Papers. Lee to U.S. Representative George P. Lawrence, 8 February 1911, Lee Papers. *Congressional Record,* 61st Congress, 2nd session (15 December 1909): 180; 61st Congress, 3rd session (20 and 28 January 1911), 1209 and 1617, respectively. House Report 1956 (Serial 5847-1), *Immigration of Aliens into the United States,* 61st Congress, 3rd session (20 January 1911), and "Views of the Minority," part 2 (28 January 1911).

15. James Patten to Joseph Lee, 2 May 1911; Patten to Members of the IRL Executive Committee, 6 and 22 January and 18 March 1912; Patten to Lee, 22 and 25 January 1912, Lee Papers. *Congressional Record,* 62nd Congress, 2nd session (18 January; 1, 14, and 15 February; and 18 March 1912): 1060, 1614, 2040–41, 2080–84, 3531–47, respectively. Senate Report 208 (Serial 6120), *Regulation of Immigration,* 62nd Congress, 2nd session (18 January 1912). Patten thought Simmons's speech lacked tact and judgment, but Madison Grant praised the effort; see Madison Grant to Furnifold Simmons, 5 April 1912, IRL Papers.

16. *Congressional Record,* 62nd Congress, 2nd session (15 and 17 April 1912): 4781–82 and 4906–17, respectively. James Patten viewed Dillingham's speech as a positive development; see Patten to IRL Executive Committee, 17 April 1912, Lee Papers.

17. *Congressional Record,* 62nd Congress, 2nd session (18 and 19 April 1912): 4966–76 and 5017–33, respectively. James Patten to Joseph Lee, 19 April 1912, and Patten to IRL Executive Committee, 20 April 1912, Lee Papers; Michael Davie, *The Titanic* (London: Bodley Head, 1986), 1. The Senate did take time to appoint a committee to investigate the *Titanic* tragedy.

18. James Patten to IRL Executive Committee, 3 February 1912, and Patten to Joseph Lee, 28 December 1912, Lee Papers; William H. Wilder to Secretary Nagel, 27 February 1913, INS Correspondence, Record Group 85, File 53139/10L; Walter E. Weyl, "It Is Time to Know," *The Survey* 28 (April 1912); W. J. Lauck, "The Significance of the Situation at Lawrence," *The Survey* 27 (February 1912); *Congressional Record,* 62nd Congress, 2nd session (18 March 1912): 3541–45.

19. *Congressional Record,* 62nd Congress, 2nd session (18 and 19 April 1912): 4966–76 and 5017–33, respectively, and Appendix, 118–21; 3rd Session (14, 17, 18, and 19 December 1912; 2, 16, 17, 18, 20, 21, 25, 27, and 30 January 1913; and 1 February 1913), 650–91, 794–822, 861–67, 889–90, 939, 1645–46, 1672–94, 1706–13, 1763–79, 1840, 2016–46, 2080–88, 2283–2310, and 2220–28, respectively.

20. Joseph Lee to A. Lawrence Lowell, 3 November 1910; copy of Lowell to Taft, n.d., sent to Lee 4 November 1910; James Patten to Prescott Hall, 12 November 1910, Lee Papers. Lee to Presidential Secretary Charles Nagel, 22 and 31 December 1910; F. W. Alexander, National President—Patriotic Sons of America, to Taft, 25 November 1910; and John W. Hayes, General Master Workman—Knights of Labor, to Taft, 26 November 1910, INS Correspondence, Record Group 85, File 52903/29A.

21. William Howard Taft to A. Lawrence Lowell, 6 November 1910; Secretary Charles Nagel to President Taft, 7 December 1910; Charles D. Norton, Secretary to the President, to Lowell, with a copy of Nagel's letter to the President, 12 December 1910; Lowell to Joseph Lee, 21 December 1910; Nagel to Lee, 24 December 1910, Lee Papers. Nagel to Presidential Secretary Charles D. Hilles, 10 March and 6 April 1912, Record Group 85, File 52903/29A; and Nagel to Taft, 12 February 1913, INS Correspondence, Record Group 85, File 53139/10E. Nagel first responded to Taft on 8 No-

vember 1910; then, at the president's request of 11 November 1910, Nagel redrafted his letter. Nagel's new letter, dated 7 December 1910, was later sent to Lowell and subsequently sent to Lee. INS Correspondence, Record Group 85, File 52903/29A.

22. James Patten to Richards Bradley, 27 February 1912, and Patten to Joseph Lee, 28 December 1912, Lee Papers; Prescott Hall Petition, ca. summer 1912; Prescott Hall to Francis H. Atkins, 15 April 1912 (64); and Hall to Madison Grant, 13 April 1912 (468), IRL Papers; Hall to William H. Taft, 28 February 1912; Grant to Taft, 2 March 1912; Warren S. Stone, Brotherhood of Locomotive Engineers, to Taft, 1 March 1912; Italian Chamber of Commerce to Taft, 21 January 1913, INS Correspondence, Record Group 85, File 53453/43.

23. Jeremiah Jenks to William H. Taft, 8 February 1913, INS Correspondence, Record Group 85, File 53139/10; Jenks to Prescott Hall, 10 March 1913, IRL Papers (549); U.S. Immigration Commission, *Reports of the Immigration Commission,* vol. 1: *Abstracts of Reports of the Immigration Commission* (Washington, D.C.: U.S. Government Printing Office, 1911), 1:37–39 and 45–48.

24. Charles Hilles to Charles Nagel, 4 February 1913; William Williams to Nagel, 11 February 1913; Nagel to Howard H. Taft, 12 February 1913; Nagel to Rudolph Foster, 13 February 1913; and Hearings Before the President of the United States, 6 February 1913, INS Correspondence, Record Group 85, Files 53139/10E and 10F.

25. William Bennet to Dean Albertson, Columbia Oral History Project, 1 May 1950, William S. Bennet Papers Arents Research Library, Syracuse University, Syracuse New York. Charles Nagel to William H. Taft, 6 and 12 February 1913; Nagel to William Williams, 11 February 1913; Taft to the Senate, 14 February 1913, INS Correspondence, Record Group 85, File 53139/10. For a discussion of the quest for social justice as a progressive tenet, see Rivka Shpak Lissak, *Pluralism and Progressivism: Hull House and the New Immigrants, 1890–1919* (Chicago: University of Chicago Press, 1989), 13–24.

26. Robert Ward to Joseph Lee, 27 February 1913, Lee Papers; *Congressional Record,* 62nd Congress, 3rd session (19 February 1913): 3411–31.

27. Jefferson Society, Minutes of the Jefferson Society, 29 October 1880, University of Virginia, Charlottesville; John M. Mulder, *Woodrow Wilson: The Years of Academic Preparation* (Princeton: Princeton University Press, 1978), 3–5; Woodrow Wilson, *A History of the American People* (New York: Harper and Brothers Publishers, 1901), 5:185, 212–13; Woodrow Wilson, "Character of Democracy in the United States," *Atlantic Monthly* 64 (November 1889). Restrictionists looked favorably upon these writings and lamented Wilson's apparent change of heart; Prescott Hall to Jeremiah Jenks, 11 December 1914, IRL Papers.

28. "News Report," 22 July 1912, 24:563–64; "News Report to the Friendly Sons of St. Patrick of Montclair, New Jersey," 18 March 1912, 24:252; "A News Report of Three Addresses in Milwaukee," 24 March 1912, 24:259–61; "Three News Reports," 17 May 1912, 24:405–7; and "News Item about Wilson's Arrival in Fond du Lac, Wisconsin," 23 March 1912, 24:458, all in Arthur S. Link et al., ed., *Papers of Woodrow Wilson* (Princeton: Princeton University Press, 1966–1990).

29. Prescott Hall to Joseph Lee, 29 November 1912; Lee to James Patten, 3 May 1913; Lee to L. C. Marshall, 3 July 1913, Lee Papers. Hans Vought, "Division and Reunion: Woodrow Wilson, Immigration, and the Myth of American Unity," *Journal of American Ethnic History* 13 (spring 1994); Arthur S. Link, *Wilson: The Road to the White House* (Princeton: Princeton University Press, 1947). Link advances the

idea that Wilson became increasingly progressive during his successful quest for the presidency, and Vought sees Wilson as a "moderate progressive" who viewed immigration in the context of an effort to create "a homogeneous middle class."

30. Edward Ross to Woodrow Wilson, 19 November 1912; Franklin H. Giddings to Ross, 27 October 1912; Prescott Hall to Ross, 1 and 13 March 1913; and Robert U. Johnson to Ross, 18 May 1911 and 9 July 1912, Edward A. Ross Papers, State Historical Society of Wisconsin, Madison (hereafter, Ross Papers). Edward A. Ross, *The Old World in the New: The Significance of Past and Present Immigration to the American People* (New York: Century, 1914), ii and passim.

31. Joseph Lee to Edward A. Ross, 21 February 1914; Ross to Lee, 25 February 1914; Prescott Hall to Ross, 6 March 1914; Jeremiah Jenks to Woodrow Wilson, 27 March 1914; and Memorandum to the President, 14 March 1914, Ross Papers.

32. Remarks from press conferences on 29 January and 2 and 12 February 1914, 29:203, 29:213, and 29:240, respectively; Woodrow Wilson to Ellison D. Smith, 5 March 1914, 29:310–11, Woodrow Wilson Papers, Library of Congress, Washington, D.C. (hereafter, Wilson Papers). Lissak, *Pluralism*, 7–8.

33. James Patten to Edward A. Ross, 9 February 1915, Ross Papers; Transcript of a Hearing before the President of the United States on the Immigration Bill (H.R. 6060), Wilson Papers. *Congressional Record*, 63rd Congress, 3rd session (16 January 1915): 1733.

34. Woodrow Wilson to the House of Representatives, 28 January 1915, 32:142–44, Wilson Papers.

35. James Patten to Joseph Lee, 31 March and 11 April 1916, and Augustus Gardner to Lee, 23 June 1916, Lee Papers; *Congressional Record*, 63rd Congress, 3rd session (4 February 1915): 3013–78; 64th Congress, 1st session (30 March 1916), 5164–94; and 64th Congress, 2nd session (18 January 1917), 1658.

36. Woodrow Wilson to the House of Representatives, 29 January 1917, 47: 52–53, Wilson Papers. For examples of the feasibility argument, see C. J. Bullock to Wilson, 7 January 1915, IRL Papers; Memorandum for the President in Favor of the Reading Test Provision of the Burnett Immigration Bill (H.R. 6060), April 1914, Lee Papers, and Secretary William B. Wilson to Woodrow Wilson, January 1915, INS Correspondence, Record Group 85, File 53139/10R.

37. James Patten to Joseph Lee, telegram, 5 February 1917; Patten to Lee, 7 February 1917; Henry P. Fairchild to Lee, 7 February 1917, Lee Papers; *Congressional Record*, 64th Congress, 2nd session (1 and 5 February 1917): 2441–57, 2616–29.

38. Joseph Lee to James Patten 10 February 1917; Lee to Henry P. Fairchild, 12 February 1917; and Lee to Richards Bradley, 13 February 1917, Lee Papers; U.S. Immigration Commission, *Abstracts*, 1:47.

8: "MATHEMATICAL CERTAINTY"

1. Edith Abbot, ed., *Immigration: Selected Documents and Case Records* (Chicago: University of Chicago Press, 1924), 392–95.

2. Henry Cabot Lodge to Theodore Roosevelt, in Henry Cabot Lodge, ed., *Selections from the Correspondence of Theodore Roosevelt and Henry Cabot Lodge, 1889–1918* (New York: Charles Scribner's Sons, 1925), 2:157–58.

3. Henry Cabot Lodge to Prescott Hall, 18 October 1919, Henry Cabot Lodge Papers, Massachusetts Historical Society, Boston; Charles S. Bryan, Army and Navy

Club of America, to Hall, 6 November 1920, Immigration Restriction League Papers (195), Houghton Library, Harvard University, Cambridge (hereafter, IRL Papers); John Higham, *Strangers in the Land: Patterns of American Nativism, 1860–1925* (1955; reprint, New York: Atheneum, 1978) 308–9, and *Send These to Me: Immigrants in Urban America*, rev. ed. (Baltimore: Johns Hopkins University Press, 1984), 53–54; George M. Stephenson, *A History of American Immigration: 1820–1924* (Boston: Ginn and Company, 1926), 170–80; Roy L. Garis, *Immigration Restriction: A Study of Opposition to and Regulation of Immigration into the United States* (New York: McMillan, 1927), 142–68; William S. Bernard, *American Immigration Policy: A Reappraisal* (New York: Harper and Brothers, 1950), 18–21; Maldwyn A. Jones, *American Immigration* (Chicago: University of Chicago Press, 1960), 272–77; Thomas Archdeacon, *Becoming American: An Ethnic History* (New York: Free Press, 1983), 168–72; Elliott R. Barkan, *And Still They Come: Immigrants and American Society 1920 to the 1990s* (Wheeling, Ill.: Harlan Davidson, 1996), 9–15.

4. U.S. Immigration Commission, *Reports of the Immigration Commission*, vol. 1: *Abstracts of Reports of the Immigration Commission* (Washington, D.C.: U.S. Government Printing Office, 1911), 1:47–48; William Husband, "How the Quota System of Regulating Immigration Happened," Unpublished Manuscript, 1921, William W. Husband Papers, Chicago Historical Society, Chicago (hereafter, Husband Papers).

5. William Husband, "Quota" and "The Effects of Immigration upon the Standards of American Youth," Address to Mother's Club of Buffalo, New York, 11 March 1912, Husband Papers.

6. Ibid., Press Release, 2 June 1913, Husband Papers; *Congressional Record*, 63rd Congress, 1st session (2 June 1913): 1839.

7. Robert Ward to Joseph Lee, 3 December 1905; James Patten to Lee, 4 January 1914; and Lee to Patten, 7 January 1914, Joseph Lee Papers, Massachusetts Historical Society, Boston. William Kent to Prescott Hall, 27 March 1914 (571); and Jeremiah Jenks to Lee, 10 December 1914 (549), IRL Papers. William W. Husband, *Immigration Journal* 1 (July 1916): 9–10.

8. Sidney Gulick to Prescott Hall, 2 May 1914, IRL Papers (484); Sidney L. Gulick, *The American Japanese Problem* (New York: Charles Scribner's Sons, 1914), 281–307; Sandra C. Taylor, *Advocate for Understanding: Sidney Gulick and the Search for Peace with Japan* (Kent, Ohio: Kent State University Press, 1984), 111–66; Roger Daniels, *The Politics of Prejudice* (Berkeley: University of California Press, 1962), 79–95; Higham, *Strangers*, 302–3 and 393n27; House of Representatives, Hearings before the Committee on Immigration and Naturalization, "Percentage Plan for Restriction of Immigration," H230-15 (Y4.IM6/1:R31); 66th Congress, 1st session (June 1919), 1–88; and "Modified Percentage Plan for Restriction of Immigration," H230-2 (Y4.IM6/1:A14/8-3); 66th Congress, 2nd session (May 1920), 1–30; [S. Adele Shaw], "The New Immigration Commissioner," *Survey* 45 (March 1921). The question of whether Husband or Gulick conceived of the quota system first is of little importance. Most likely the two men independently and concurrently devised similar schemes, but Husband's position on the immigration commission allowed his plan to receive more and earlier public scrutiny.

9. *National Cyclopaedia of American Biography* (New York: James T. White & Company, 1948), 34:264; Husband, *Immigration Journal*.

10. William W. Husband, "Senator Dillingham's Bill," *Immigration Journal* 1 (March 1916); Sidney Gulick, "A Constructive Immigration Policy," *Immigration Journal* 1 (June 1916).

11. Jeremiah Jenks to Edward Ross, 14 April 1917, Edward A. Ross Papers, State Historical Society of Wisconsin, Madison; William Husband, "Immigration After the War," *Immigration Journal* 1 (May 1916): 35–38; Garis, *Immigration Restriction,* 142–68.

12. William Dillingham to Prescott Hall, 11 April 1917, 23 December 1920, and 6 May 1921 (363); Hall to Dillingham, 12 April 1917 (363); Henry P. Fairchild to Hall, 27 and 29 January 1919 and 8 May 1919 (451); Madison Grant to Albert Johnson, 23 November 1920 (469); Jeremiah Jenks to Hall, 8 January 1919 (549); John R. Commons to Hall, 22 October and 5 December 1918 (295); and Johnson to Hall, 14 and 20 May 1919, 27 November 1920 (552), IRL Papers.

13. Frank Morrison, Secretary, American Federation of Labor, to Robert Ward, 1 May 1919 (35); and Patten to Members of the IRL Executive Committee, 10 December 1913 (752), IRL Papers; *New York Times,* 12 January 1921; *Congressional Record,* 66th Congress, 3rd session (6, 7, 9, and 18 December 1920): 10, 27, 36 and 127–45, and 497, respectively; House Committee on Immigration, "Temporary Suspension of Immigration, with Views of the Minority," House Report 1109 (Serial 7776), 66th Congress, 3rd session (6 December 1920); U.S. Senate, Hearing before the Senate Committee on Immigration, "Emergency Immigration Legislation," S164-1-Part J (Y4.IM6/2:L52/1-10) and Part K (Y4.IM6/2:L52/1-11), 505–46, 66th Congress, 3rd session (January 1921); Higham, *Strangers,* 177–78.

14. *New York Times,* 12 January 1921; *Congressional Record,* 66th Congress, 3rd session (9, 10, 11, 13 December 1920): 127–45, 171–98, 225–50, and 285–87, respectively; House Committee on Immigration, "Temporary Suspension," H.Rept. 1109; Senate Committee on Immigration, "Emergency Legislation," S164-1, Part A: 7–40 and Part C: 143–90.

15. *Congressional Record,* 66th Congress, 3rd session (10 December 1920): 149; House Committee on Immigration, "Modified Percentage Plan," H230-2:2–10; Taylor, *Advocate,* 144 and 150–51.

16. Senate Committee on Immigration, "Emergency Legislation," S164-1, Parts J and K: 505–46.

17. *Literary Digest* 68 (26 February 1921), 7–9; Higham, *Strangers,* 309–10.

18. Charles Evans Hughes to Isaac Siegel, 20 April 1921, Isaac Siegel Papers, American Jewish Historical Society, Center for Jewish History, New York; *New York Times,* 5 January 1921; House Committee on Immigration, "Temporary Suspension"; and Higham, *Strangers,* 309–10 and 393n24.

19. *Congressional Record,* 66th Congress, 3rd session (15, 17, 19, and 21 February 1921): 3170, 3299–3302, 3442–64, 3564, respectively. Senate Committee on Immigration, "Emergency Immigration Legislation," 66th Congress, 3rd session (14 February 1921), S.Rept. 789 (Serial 7776).

20. *Congressional Record,* 66th Congress, 3rd session (22 and 26 February 1921): 3630 and 3964–73; House Committee on Immigration, "Temporary Suspension of Immigration," 66th Congress, 3rd session (22 February 1921), H.Rept. 1351 (Serial 7777). Husband reportedly supported the use of the 1910 census but not the reduction from 5 to 3 percent; see [Shaw], "New Immigration Commissioner."

21. From the diary of Josephus Daniels, 28 December 1920, 67:9, and William B. Wilson to the president, 1 May 1921, 67:178–81, Woodrow Wilson Papers, Library of Congress, Washington, D.C.

22. Warren G. Harding to Senator Frederick Hale, 18 March 1920, IRL Papers (497); House Committee on Immigration, "Restriction of Immigration, With Views of the Minority [including Stewart's April 15th letter to Siegel]," 67th Congress, 1st

session (19 April 1921), H.Rept. 4 (Serial 7920); Senate Immigration Committee, *Emergency Immigration Legislation,* 67th Congress, 1st session (28 April 1921), S.Rept. 17 (Serial 7918); House Conferees, *Immigration of Aliens,* 67th Congress, 1st session (12 May 1921), H.Rept. 62 (Serial 7920); *Minneapolis Journal,* 20 May 1921.

23. [Shaw], "New Immigration Commissioner," 914–15; *New York Times,* 13 and 15 March 1921.

24. "Racing Immigrant Ships," *Current History* 14 (September 1921); *New York Times,* 21 May and 7, 9, and 11 June 1921; Albert Johnson's extended remarks, *Congressional Record,* 67th Congress, 1st session (21 November 1921): 8934–41. When Congress extended the law in 1922, it heeded Husband's advice and imposed a $200 fine for each immigrant a steamship company brought over in excess of a filled quota; the law also required the company to refund the person's payment.

25. William W. Husband, "Immigration under the Per Centum Act," *Monthly Labor Review* 15 (August 1922); and "How Restricted Immigration Works," *Current History* 15 (January 1922); U.S. Department of Labor, Bureau of Immigration, *Annual Report of the Commissioner General of Immigration to the Secretary of Labor,* for the fiscal years ending 30 June 1921, 1922, 1923, and 1924 (Washington, D.C.: U.S. Government Printing Office, 1921–1924), 16–19, 3–8, 1–12, and 1–10, respectively. *Congressional Record,* 67th Congress, 1st session (19 April 1921): 8934–41.

26. [Geddes Smith], "Taking the Queue out of Quota: An Interview with W. W. Husband, Commissioner General of Immigration," *Survey* 15 (March 1924); Husband, "Immigration Under the Per Centum Act."

27. U.S. Department of Labor, Bureau of Immigration, *Annual Report* for the fiscal year ending 1924, 24–30.

28. William Husband, "Press Release, 2 June 1913," Husband Papers; William Husband, Speech to the Women's Section, National Civic Federation, reported in the *New York Times,* 17 February 1921; Husband, "How Restricted Immigration Works," 605.

29. William Husband, personal notes on "Press Release, 2 June 1913," Husband Papers; House Conferees, "Immigration of Aliens"; Roger Daniels, *Coming to America: A History of Immigration and Ethnicity in American Life* (New York: HarperCollins, 1990), 280.

30. Husband, "Press Release, 2 June 1913," ; U.S. Department of Labor, Bureau of Immigration, *Annual Report* for the fiscal year ending 1924, 18.

31. Husband, "Quota System," 1921, Husband Papers; House Immigration Commission, "Views of the Minority," 67th Congress, 1st session (19 April 1921), Report 4 (Serial 79230).

32. [Smith], "Taking the Queue out of Quota."

33. Husband, "Address to Buffalo Women's Club," ca. 1911, Husband Papers.

EPILOGUE: ASSESSING THE END OF AN ERA

1. Matthew Frye Jacobson, in *Whiteness of a Different Color: European Immigrants and the Alchemy of Race* (Cambridge, Harvard University Press, 1988), criticized several parts of the commission's *Dictionary of Races,* particularly its "political intent" (p. 80), but in *Barbarian Virtues: The United States Encounters Foreign Peoples at Home and Abroad, 1876–1917* (New York: Hill and Wang), 63, 68, and 70–72, he used information and statistics from other parts of the *Reports.*

2. For the postquota era of American immigration, see Barkan, *Still They Come.*

3. My conclusions here agree with those Roger Daniels offers in *Coming to America.* He strongly condemns the quota acts' underlying bigotry, but he also asserts: "In retrospect, without in any way endorsing his [Congressman Albert Johnson's] or others' theories about racial superiority and inferiority, it is easy to see that some kind of limitation on immigration was not only all but inevitable but probably desirable. There were and are limits to the number of immigrants a developed country can absorb" (284).

4. William Bennet to Arthur V. Watkins, 23 March 1953, William S. Bennet Papers, Special Collections Research Center, Syracuse University, Syracuse, New York (hereafter, Bennet Papers).

5. Lindbergh quoted in Brian Horrigan, "'My Own Mind and Pen': Charles Lindbergh, Autobiography, and Memory," *Minnesota History* 58 (spring 2002), 10.

6. William Bennet to Arthur V. Watkins, 23 March 1953, Bennet Papers.

BIBLIOGRAPHY

ARCHIVAL SOURCES

Anderson Family Papers. University of Virginia Library, Charlottesville, Va.

Barbour Family Papers. University of Virginia Library, Charlottesville, Va.

Bennet, William S., Papers. Special Collections Research Center, Syracuse University, Syracuse, N.Y.

Boas, Franz, Papers. Microfilm edition. American Philosophical Society Library, Philadelphia, Pa.

Cannon, Joseph, Papers. Illinois Historical Society, Springfield, Ill.

Chandler, William E., Papers. Library of Congress. Washington, D.C.

Cleveland, Grover. Papers. Library of Congress. Washington, D.C.

Cross, Judson N., Papers. Minnesota Historical Society, St. Paul, Minn.

Croxton, Frederick C., Papers. Herbert Hoover Presidential Library, West Branch, Iowa.

Dillingham Family Papers. Woodson Research Center. Rice University, Houston, Tex.

Dillingham, William P., Miscellaneous Papers and Printed Materials. Assorted Collections, Waterbury Historical Society, Waterbury, Vt.

Ely, Richard T., Papers. State Historical Society of Wisconsin, Madison, Wisc.

Grosvenor, Charles H. Papers. Alden Library, Ohio University, Athens, Ohio.

Howell, Benjamin F., Papers. Alexander Library, Rutgers University, New Brunswick, N.J.

Husband, William W., Papers. Chicago Historical Society. Chicago, Ill.

Immigration and Naturalization Service. Central Office Correspondence. National Archives, Washington, D.C.

Immigration Restriction League Papers. Houghton Library, Harvard University, Cambridge, Mass.

Immigration Restriction League Publications. Widener Library, Harvard University, Cambridge, Mass.

Industrial Removal Office Papers. American Jewish Historical Society, Waltham, Mass.

Jefferson Society. Minutes of the Jefferson Society. University of Virginia, Charlottesville, Va.

Lauck, William Jett, Papers. University of Virginia Library. Charlottesville, Va.

Lee, Joseph, Papers. Massachusetts Historical Society, Boston, Mass.

Lodge, Henry Cabot, Papers. American Academy and Institute of Arts and Letters, New York, N.Y..

———. Massachusetts Historical Society, Boston, Mass.

National Archives. Legislative, Judicial, and Fiscal Branch, Civil Archives Division.

Powderly, Terence V., Papers. Microfilm edition. Catholic University Library, Washington, D.C.
Rockefeller, John D., Jr., Office Correspondence. Rockefeller Archives Center, North Tarrytown, N.Y.
Roosevelt, Theodore, Collection. Harvard Widener Library, Cambridge Mass.
Roosevelt, Theodore, Papers. Microfilm edition. Library of Congress, Washington, D.C.
Root, Elihu, Papers. Library of Congress, Washington, D.C.
Ross, Edward A., Papers. State Historical Society of Wisconsin, Madison, Wisc.
Siegel, Isaac, Papers. American Jewish Historical Society, Center for Jewish History, New York, N.Y.
U.S. Congress. House of Representatives. Reports and Documents. Serial Set, 1888–1924.
Watson, James E., Papers. Indiana State University Library, Indianapolis, Ind.
Wheeler, Benjamin I., Papers. Bancroft Library, University of California, Berkeley, Calif.
Wilson, Woodrow, Papers. Library of Congress, Washington, D.C.

PERIODICALS

American Monthly Review of Reviews
Boston Evening Transcript
Boston Herald
Boston Journal
Buffalo Express
Chamber of Commerce News
Chicago *Daily Scandinavian*
Cincinnati Free Press
Fresno Republican
Jewish Daily Forward
Literary Digest
Minneapolis Times
Minneapolis Tribune
New Brunswick *Daily Home News*
New Orleans *Times Democrat*
New York Times
The Outlook
Philadelphia *Telegraph*
St. Louis *Globe*
St. Paul Globe
St. Paul Pioneer Press
Vermonter
Washington Star

BOOKS, ARTICLES, AND DISSERTATIONS

Abbot, Edith ed., *Immigration: Selected Documents and Case Records*. Chicago: University of Chicago Press, 1924.
Anbinder, Tyler. *Five Points: The 19th-Century New York City Neighborhood that Invented Tap Dance, Stole Elections, and Became the World's Most Notorious Slum*. New York: Free Press, 2001.

———. *Nativism and Slavery: The Northern Know Nothings and the Politics of the 1850s.* New York: Oxford University Press, 1992.

Archdeacon, Thomas. *Becoming American: An Ethnic History.* New York: Free Press, 1983.

Avrich, Paul. *The Haymarket Tragedy.* Princeton: Princeton University Press, 1984.

Barkan, Elliott R. *And Still They Come: Immigrants and American Society, 1920 to the 1990s.* Wheeling, Ill.: Harlan Davidson, 1996.

Bemis, Edward W. "Restriction of Immigration." *Andover Review* 9 (March 1888): 251–63.

Bernard, William S., ed. *American Immigration Policy: A Reappraisal.* New York: Harper and Brothers, 1950.

Billington, Ray Allen. *The Protestant Crusade, 1800–1860.* 1938. Reprint, New York: Rinehard & Company, 1952.

Blackman, William F. "The Immigration Problem." *Yale Review* 10 (February 1902): 430–32.

Blackwell, Marilyn Schultz. "The Deserving Sick: Poor Women and the Medicalization of Poverty in Battleboro, Vermont." *Journal of Women's History* 11 (Spring 1999): 53–74.

Blegen, Theodore C. *Norwegian Immigration to America: 1825–1850.* Northfield, Minnesota: Norwegian-American Historical Society, 1931.

Blum, John M. *The Republican Roosevelt,* 2nd ed. 1954. Reprint, New York: Antheneum, 1975.

Bolles, Blair. *The Tyrant from Illinois: Uncle Joe Cannon's Experiment with Personal Power.* New York: W. W. Norton, 1951.

Bond, Bradley G. *Political Culture in the Nineteenth-Century South, 1830–1900.* Baton Rouge: Louisiana State University Press, 1995.

Boyesen, Hjalmar J. "Dangers of Unrestricted Immigration." *Forum* 3 (March 1887): 532–42.

Bruce, Robert V. *1877: Year of Violence.* Chicago: Ivan R. Dee, 1989.

Buenker, John. *Urban Liberalism and Progressive Reform.* New York: Charles Scribner's Sons, 1973.

Burts, Robert M. *Richard Irvine Manning and the Progressive Movement in South Carolina.* Columbia: University of South Carolina Press, 1974.

Busbey, L. White. *Uncle Joe Cannon: The Life of a Pioneer American.* New York: Henry Holt, 1927.

Chambers, John Whiteclay, II. *The Tyranny of Change: America in the Progressive Era, 1900–1917.* New York: St. Martin's, 1980.

Chandler, William E. "Shall Immigration Be Suspended?" *North American Review* 156 (January 1893): 1–8.

Chetwood, John, Jr. *Immigration Fallacies.* Boston: Beacon Library Series, 1896.

———. "Is It Practical to Regulate Immigration?" *Overland Monthly* 23 (February 1894): 166–71.

Cobb, James C. *The Most Southern Place on Earth: The Mississippi Delta and the Roots of Regional Identity.* New York: Oxford University Press, 1992.

Cole, Douglas. *Franz Boas, the Early Years, 1858–1906.* Seattle: University of Washington Press, 1999.

Commons, John R. "Social and Industrial Problems." *The Chautauquan* 39 (May 1904): 13–32.

Connelly, Mark T. *The Response to Prostitution in the Progressive Era.* Chapel Hill: North Carolina University Press, 1980.

Coolidge, Louis A. "Hon. Henry Cabot Lodge, LL.D." *New England Historical and Genealogical Register* 79 (July 1925): 226–43.

Cyclopedia of Eminent and Representative Men of the Carolinas of the Nineteenth Century. 1892. Reprint, Spartanburg, S.C.: The Reprint Company, 1972.

Daniels, Roger. *Asian America: Chinese and Japanese in the United States since 1850.* Seattle: University of Washington Press, 1988.

———. *Coming to America: A History of Immigration and Ethnicity in American Life.* New York: HarperCollins, 1990.

———. *The Politics of Prejudice.* Berkeley: University of California Press, 1962.

Davie, Michael. *The Titanic.* London: Bodley Head, 1986.

Degler, Carl. *Culture versus Biology in the Thought of Franz Boas and Alfred L. Krobler.* New York: Berg, 1989.

Dictionary of American Biography, Supplement Four, 1946–1950. Edited by John A. Garraty and Edward T. James. New York: Charles Scribner's Sons, 1974.

Diggins, John P. *The American Left in the Twentieth Century* (New York: Harcourt Brace Jovanovich, 1973.

Diner, Steven J. *A Very Different Age: Americans of the Progressive Era.* New York: Hill and Wang, 1998.

Dunne, Finley Peter [Martin Dooley]. "On Anglo-Saxon." In *Mr. Dooley in Peace and in War.* Boston: Small, Maynard & Company, 1914.

Dyer, Thomas G. *Theodore Roosevelt and the Idea of Race.* Baton Rouge: Louisiana State University Press, 1980.

Ely, Richard T. "A Program for Labor." *Century* 39 (April 1890): 938–51.

Erickson, Charlotte, ed., *Emigration from Europe, 1815–1914: Select Documents.* London: Adam & Charles Black, 1976.

Fairchild, Henry P. "Case for the Literacy Test." *Unpopular Review* 56 (January–March 1916): 153-70.

———. "Distribution of Immigrants." *Yale Review* 16 (November 1907): 296–310.

———. *Immigration: A World Movement and Its American Significance.* New York: Macmillan, 1913.

Filene, Peter G. "An Obituary for the Progressive Movement." *American Quarterly* 22 (Spring 1970): 20–31.

Fink, Gary M., ed., *Biographical Dictionary of American Labor Leaders.* Westport, Conn.: Greenwood, 1974.

Folkmar, Daniel. *Album of Philippine Types.* Manila: Bureau of Public Printing, 1904.

Foner, Eric. *The Story of American Freedom.* New York: W. W. Norton and Company, 1998.

Frankel, Oz. "What Ever Happened to 'Red Emma'? Emma Goldman, from Alien Radical to American Icon" *Journal of American History* 83 (December 1996): 903–42.

Fuchs, Lawrence H. "Immigration Reform in 1911 and 1981: The Role of Select Commissions." *Journal of American Ethnic History* 3 (Fall 1993): 58–89.

Gabaccia, Donna R. "Is Everywhere Nowhere? Nomads, Nations, and the Immigrant Paradigm in United States History." *Journal of American History* 86 (December 1999): 1115–34.

———. *Italy's Many Diasporas.* Seattle: University of Washington Press, 2000.

Garis, Roy L. *Immigration Restriction: A Study of Opposition to and Regulation of Immigration into the United States.* New York: McMillan, 1927.

Garraty, John. *Henry Cabot Lodge: A Biography.* (New York: Alfred A. Knopf, 1953.

Gjerde, Jon A. "Appendix on Statistics." In *They Chose Minnesota,* ed. June D. Holmquist, 593–95. St. Paul: Minnesota Historical Society, 1981.

Going, Allen J. *Bourbon Democracy in Alabama, 1874–1890,* 2nd ed. Tuscaloosa: University of Alabama Press, 1992.

Gould, Lewis L. *America in the Progressive Era, 1890–1914.* Harlow, England: Pearson, 2001.

———. *The Presidency of Theodore Roosevelt.* Lawrence: University of Kansas Press, 1991.

Grant, Madison. *The Passing of the Great Race,* rev. ed. New York: Charles Scribner's Sons, Revised Edition, 1918.

Gerstle, Gary. "Theodore Roosevelt and the Divided Character of American Nationalism." *Journal of American History* 86 (December 1999): 1280–1307.

Gulick, Sidney L. *The American Japanese Problem.* New York: Charles Scribner's Sons, 1914.

———. "A Constructive Immigration Policy." *Immigration Journal* 1 (June 1916): 55–58.

Guterl, Matthew P. *The Color of Race in America: 1900–1940.* Cambridge: Harvard University Press, 2001.

Gyory, Andrew. *Closing the Gate: Race, Politics, and the Chinese Exclusion Act.* Chapel Hill: University of North Carolina Press, 1998.

Haber, Samuel. *Efficiency and Uplift: Scientific Management in the Progressive Era, 1890–1920.* Chicago: University of Chicago Press, 1964.

Hall, Prescott. "Selection of Immigration." *Annals of the American Academy of Political and Social Sciences* 24 (July 1904): 169–84.

Handlin, Oscar. *Race and Nationality in American Life.* Boston: Little, Brown, 1948.

———. *The Uprooted.* 2nd edition. Boston: Little, Brown and Company, 1973.

Hansen, Marcus L. *The Atlantic Migration, 1607–1860.* Cambridge: Harvard University Press, 1940.

Harbaugh, William H. *Power and Responsibility: The Life of Theodore Roosevelt.* New York: Farrar, Straus, and Cudahy, 1961.

Hemphill, J. C., ed. *Men of Mark in South Carolina.* Washington, D.C.: Men of Mark Publishing Company, 1907.

Higham, John. *Send These to Me: Immigrants in Urban America,* rev. ed. Baltimore: Johns Hopkins University Press, 1984.

———. *Strangers in the Land: Patterns of American Nativism, 1860–1925.* 1955. Reprint, New York: Atheneum, 1978.

Hodes, Martha. "The Mercurial Nature and Abiding Power of Race: A Transnational Story." *American Historical Review* 108 (February 2003): 84–118.

Holmes, William F. *White Chief: James Kimble Vardaman.* Baton Rouge: Louisiana State University Press, 1970.

Horrigan, Brian. "'My Own Mind and Pen': Charles Lindbergh, Autobiography, and Memory," *Minnesota History* 58 (Spring 2002): 2–15.

Husband, William W., "How Restricted Immigration Works," *Current History* 15 (January 1922): 604–609.

———. "Immigration under the Per Centum Act." *Monthly Labor Review* 15 (August 1922): 231–40.

———. "Senator Dillingham's Bill." *Immigration Journal* 1 (March 1916): 4–6.

———. "U.S. Commissioner General of Immigration Cites Need for Legislative Remedies." *Congressional Digest* (July–August 1923): 301–2.

————, ed. "Immigration after the War." *Immigration Journal* 1 (May 1916): 35–38.

————, ed. *Immigration Journal,* 1916–1917.

Hyatt, Marshall, *Franz Boas, Social Activist: The Dynamics of Ethnicity.* New York: Greenwood, 1990.

"Immigration and Wages." *The Nation* 47 (30 August 1888): 165–66.

Israel, Fred L., ed. *State of the Union Messages of the Presidents.* 4 vols. New York: Chelsea House–Robert Hector, 1966.

Jacobson, Matthew Frye. *Barbarian Virtues: The United States Encounters Foreign Peoples at Home and Abroad, 1876–1917.* New York: Hill and Wang, 2000.

————. *Whiteness of a Different Color: European Immigrants and the Alchemy of Race.* Cambridge: Harvard University Press, 1998.

Jeffrey, William H. "Immigration." *Journal of Political Economy* 1 (June 1893):433–35.

Jenks, Jeremiah W. *Citizenship in the Schools.* New York: Henry Holt, 1909.

————. "The Racial Problem in Immigration." *The Social Welfare Forum: Official Proceedings* 36 (1909): 215–22.

————. *The Trust Problem.* New York: McClure, Phillips & Company, 1900.

Jenks, Jeremiah, and W. Jett Lauck. *The Immigration Problem,* 5th ed. New York: Funk and Wagnalls, 1924.

Jessup, Philip C. *Elihu Root.* 2 Vols. New York: Dodd, Mead, 1937.

Johns, A. Wesley. *The Man Who Shot McKinley.* New York: A. S. Barnes and Company, 1970.

Jones, Maldwyn A. *American Immigration.* Chicago: University of Chicago Press, 1960.

Kantrowitz, Stephen D. *Ben Tillman and the Reconstruction of White Supremacy.* Chapel Hill: University of North Carolina Press, 2000.

Keller, Morton. *Regulating a New Society: Public Policy and Social Change in America, 1900–1933.* Cambridge: Harvard University Press, 1994.

Kessner, Thomas. *The Golden Door: Italian and Jewish Immigrant Mobility in New York City, 1880–1915.* New York: Oxford University Press, 1977.

Kevles, Daniel J. *In the Name of Eugenics: Genetics and the Use of Human Heredity.* Berkeley: University of California Press, 1985.

Kleppner, Paul. *Continuity and Change in Electoral Politics, 1893–1928.* New York: Greenwood, 1987.

Kovacik, Charles F., and John J. Winberry, *South Carolina: A Geography.* Boulder, Colo.: Westview, 1987.

Kraut, Alan M. *The Huddled Masses: The Immigrant in American Society, 1880–1921.* Arlington Heights, Ill.: Harlan Davidson, 1892.

La Guardia, Fiorello H. *The Making of an Insurgent: An Autobiography, 1882–1919.* Philadelphia: J. B. Lippincott, 1948.

Langum, David J. *Crossing over the Line: Legislating Morality and the Mann Act.* Chicago: University of Chicago Press, 1994.

Lauck, W. Jett. "The Significance of the Situation at Lawrence." *The Survey* 27 (February 1912): 1772–74.

Leonard, Henry B. "The Open Gate: The Protest against the Movement to Restrict Immigration." Ph.D. diss., Northwestern University, 1967.

Leopold, Richard W. *Elihu Root and the Conservative Tradition.* Boston: Little, Brown, 1954.

Link, Arthur S. "What Ever Happened to the Progressive Movement in the 1920's?" *American Historical Review* 64 (July 1959): 833–51.

———. *Wilson: The Road to the White House.* Princeton: Princeton University Press, 1947.

Link, Arthur S., and Richard L. McCormick. *Progressivism.* Arlington Heights, Ill.: Harlan Davidson, 1983.

Link, Arthur S., et al., ed. *Papers of Woodrow Wilson.* 64 Vols. Princeton: Princeton University Press, 1966–1990.

Lissak, Rivka Shpak. *Pluralism and Progressivism: Hull House and the New Immigrants, 1890–1919.* Chicago: University of Chicago Press, 1989.

Lodge, Henry Cabot. "The Census and Immigration." *The Century* 46 (September 1893): 737–39.

———. "The Distribution of the Abilities in the United States." *The Century* 42 (September 1891): 687–94.

———. *Early Memories.* New York: Charles Scribner's Sons, 1920.

———. "Lynch Law and Unrestricted Immigration." *North American Review* 152 (May 1891): 602–12.

———. "Restriction of Immigration." *North American Review* 152 (January 1891): 27–36.

———. "A Word More on the Distribution of Ability." *Century* 49 (July 1892): 477–78.

———, ed. *Selections from the Correspondence of Theodore Roosevelt and Henry Cabot Lodge, 1889–1918.* 2 vols. New York: Charles Scribner's Sons, 1925.

Lombardi, John. *Labor's Voice in the Cabinet.* New York: Columbia University Press, 1942.

Lund, John M. "Vermont Nativism: William Paul Dillingham and U.S. Immigration Legislation." *Vermont History* 63 (Winter 1995): 15–29.

MacDonald, Kevin. *The Culture of Critique: An Evolutionary Analysis of Jewish Involvement in Twentieth-Century Intellectual and Political Movements.* Westport, Conn.: Praeger, 1998.

Marqulies, Herbert F. "James R. Mann's Apprenticeship in the House of Representatives." *Congress and the Presidency* 26 (Spring 1999): 21–40.

Mayo-Smith, Richmond. *Emigration and Immigration.* New York: Charles Scribner's Sons, 1890.

McKeown, Adam. "Ritualization of Regulation: The Enforcement of Chinese Exclusion in the United States and China." *American Historical Review* 108 (April 2003): 377–403.

[McKinley, William.] *Speeches and Addresses of William McKinley.* New York: Double Day and McClure, 1900.

McLemore, Richard A., ed. *A History of Mississippi.* 2 vols. Hattiesburg: University and College Press of Mississippi, 1977.

"The Menace of Immigration, *Gunton's Magazine* 16 (March 1899): 166–70.

Miller, Sally M. "For White Men Ony: The Socialist Party of America and Issues of Gender, Ethnicity, and Race." *Journal of the Gilded Age and Progressive Era* 2 (July 2003): 283–302.

Millis, Henry A. *The Japanese Problem in the United States.* New York: Macmillan, 1915.

Morris, Edmond. *Theodore Rex.* New York: Modern Library, 2002.

Morrison, Elting E., ed. *Letters of Theodore Roosevelt.* 6 vols. Cambridge: Harvard University Press, 1952.

Mowry, George E. *The Era of Theodore Roosevelt and the Birth of Modern America, 1900–1912.* New York: Harper & Row, 1958.

Mulder, John M. *Woodrow Wilson: The Years of Academic Preparation*. Princeton: Princeton University Press, 1978.

National Cyclopaedia of American Biography. New York: James T. White & Company, 1948.

Neill, Charles P. "Anarchism." *American Catholic Quarterly Review* 27 (January 1902): 160–79.

North, S. N. D. "The Industrial Commission." *North American Review* 168 (June 1899): 708–19.

"Object Lesson in Municipal Government. *Century* 39 (March 1890): 154.

The Oil City Derrick, comp. *Pure Oil Trust vs. Standard Oil Company, being the Report of an Investigation by the United States Industrial Commission*. Oil City, Pa.: Derrick Publishing Company, 1901.

O'Neill, William L. *The Progressive Years: America Comes of Age*. New York: Harper & Row, 1975.

Ottendorfer, Oswald. "Are Immigrants to Blame?" *Forum* 11 (January 1891): 541–49.

Parker, Theodore M. *Trust in Numbers: The Pursuit of Objectivity in Science and Public Life*. Princeton, N.J.: Princeton University Press, 1995.

Peffer, George A. *If They Don't Bring Their Women Here*. Urbana: University of Illinois Press, 1999.

Powderly, Terence V. "A Menacing Irruption." *North American Review* 147 (August 1888): 165–79.

———. *The Path I Trod: The Autobiography of Terence V. Powderly*. Edited by Harry J. Carman et al. New York: Columbia University Press, 1940.

Preston, William, Jr. *Aliens and Dissenters: Federal Suppression of Radicals, 1903–1933*. Cambridge: Harvard University Press, 1963.

Pula, James S. "American Immigration and the Dillingham Commission." *Polish American Studies* 27 (Spring 1980): 5–31.

———. "The Progressives, the Immigrant, and the Workplace: Defining Public Perceptions, 1900–1914." *Polish American Studies* 52 (autumn 1995): 57–70.

"Racing Immigrant Ships," *Current History* 14 (September 1921): 932–33.

Rauchway, Eric. "The High Cost of Living in the Progressive Economy." *Journal of American History* 88 (December 2001): 898–924.

Reichley, A. James. *The Life of the Parties: A History of American Political Parties*. New York: Free Press, 1992.

Riis, Jacob. *How the Other Half Lives: Studies among the Tenements of New York*. New York: Charles Scribner's Sons, 1890.

Rogers, Daniel T. *Atlantic Crossings: Social Politics in a Progressive Era*. Cambridge: Harvard University Press, 1998.

Rood, Henry. "Mine Laborers in Pennsylvania." *Forum* 14 (September 1892): 110–22.

Roosevelt, Theodore. "America Past and Present and the Americanization of Foreigners." *America: A Journal of Today* 14 (April 1888): 1–3.

Ross, Edward A. *The Old World in the New: The Significance of Past and Present Immigration to the American People*. New York: Century, 1914.

Salvatore, Nick. *Eugene V. Debs: Citizen and Socialist*. Urbana: University of Illinois Press, 1982.

Sanders, Elizabeth. *Roots of Reform: Farmers, Workers, and the American State, 1877–1917*. Chicago: University of Chicago Press, 1999.

Sanders, Roland. *Shores of Refuge: A Hundred Years of Jewish Emigration*. New York: Henry Holt and Company, 1988.

Schulties, Herman J. *Report on European Immigration to the United States of America and the Causes Which Incite the Same, with Recommendations for the Further Restriction of Undesirable Immigration and the Establishment of a National Quarantine.* Washington, D.C.: U.S. Government Printing Office, 1893.

Schurz, Carl. "Restricting Immigration." *Harpers Weekly* 42 (January 1898): 27.

Schwab, Gustav H. "A Practical Remedy for the Evils of Immigration." *Forum* 14 (February 1893): 805–14.

Senner, J. H. "Immigration from Italy." *North American Review* 162 (September 1896): 649–57.

[Shaw, S. Adele]. "The New Immigration Commissioner." *Survey* 45 (March 1921): 914–15.

Simpkins, Francis B. *Pitchfork Ben Tillman, South Carolinian.* Baton Rouge: Louisiana State University Press, 1944.

Smith, David A. "From the Mississippi to the Mediterranean: The 1891 New Orleans Lynching and Its Effects on the United States Diplomacy and the American Navy." *Southern Historian* 19 (1998): 60–85.

[Smith, Geddes]. "Taking the Queue out of Quota: An Interview with W. W. Husband, Commissioner General of Immigration." *Survey* 15 (March 1924): 667–69.

Solomon, Barbara M. *Ancestors and Immigrants: A Changing New England Tradition.* 1956. Reprint. Boston: Northeastern University Press, 1989.

Sorin, Gerald. *Tradition Transformed: The Jewish Experience in America.* Baltimore: Johns Hopkins University Press, 1997.

Stebner, Eleanor J. *The Women of Hull House: A Study of Spirituality, Vocation, and Friendship.* Albany: State University of New York Press, 1997.

Stephenson, George M. *A History of American Immigration, 1820–1924.* Boston: Ginn and Company, 1926.

Stocking, George W., Jr., ed. *The Shaping of American Anthropology, 1883–1911: A Franz Boas Reader.* New York: Basic Books, 1974.

Straus, Oscar S. *Under Four Administrations.* Boston: Houghton Mifflin, 1922.

Taylor, Sandra C. *Advocate for Understanding: Sidney Gulick and the Search for Peace with Japan.* Kent, Ohio: Kent State University Press, 1984.

Thelen, David P. "Social Tensions and the Origins of Progressivism." *Journal of American History* 56 (September 1969): 323–41.

Trigger, Bruce G. "Early Native North American Responses to European Contact: Romantic versus Rationalistic Interpretations." *Journal of American History* 77 (March 1991): 1195–1215.

U.S. Commissioners of Immigration. *Report of the Commissioners of Immigration Upon the Causes Which Incite Immigration to the United States.* Volume 1 of *Reports of the Commissioners.* Washington, D.C.: U.S. Government Printing Office, 1892.

———. [Herman J. Schulties], *Report on European Immigration to the United States of America and the Causes Which Incite the Same, with Recommendations for the Further Restriction of Undesirable Immigration and the Establishment of a National Quarantine* (Washington, D.C.: U.S. Government Printing Office, 1893).

U.S. Congress. *Biographical Directory of the American Congress.* Washington, D.C.: U.S. Government Printing Office, 1928.

———. *Congressional Record.* Washington, D.C.: U.S. Government Printing Office, 1888–1924.

———. House. *Guide to Research Collections of Former Members of the United States House of Representatives.* Washington, D.C.: U.S. House of Representatives, 1988.

———. House. Committee on Immigration. *Hearings before the Committee on Immigration and Naturalization,* H230-15. 66th Congress, 1st session (June 1919): 1–88 and H230-2. 66th Congress, 2nd session (May 1920): 1–30.

———. Senate. Committee on Immigration. *Reports* and *Documents. Serial Set,* 1888–1924.

———. *Statutes at Large of the United States of America, From December 1901 to March 1903.* Washington, D.C.: U.S. Government Printing Office, 1904.

U.S. Department of Commerce, Bureau of the Census. *Fourteenth Census of the United States Taken in the Year 1920.* Washington, D.C.: U.S. Government Printing Office, 1922, 3:47–48.

———. *Historical Almanac of the United States, Colonial Times to 1970.* Bicentennial edition. Washington, D.C.: U.S. Government Printing Office, 1975.

U.S. Department of Labor. Bureau of Immigration. *Annual Report of the Commissioner General of Immigration to the Secretary of Labor.* Washington, D.C.: U.S. Government Printing Office, 1921–1924.

U.S. Immigration Commission. *Reports of the Immigration Commission.* 41 volumes. Washington, D.C.: U.S. Government Printing Office, 1911.

U.S. Industrial Commission. *Reports of the Industrial Commission: Including Testimony, with Review and Digest, and Special Reports.* 1901. Reprint, New York: Arno, 1970.

Vought, Hans. "Division and Reunion: Woodrow Wilson, Immigration, and the Myth of American Unity." *Journal of American Ethnic History* 13 (Spring 1994): 24–50.

Walker, Francis A. "Immigration." *Yale Review* 1 (August 1892): 124–45.

———. "Restriction of Immigration." *Atlantic Review* 77 (June 1896): 822–29.

———. "Restriction of Immigration." Pp. 2:437–51 in *Discussions in Economics and Statistics,* ed. Davis R. Dewey. New York: Henry Holt and Company, 1899.

Ward, Robert. "An Immigration Restriction League." *Century* 49 (February 1895): 639.

Washburn, Charles G. "Memoir of Henry Cabot Lodge." *Proceedings of the Massachusetts Historical Society* 58 (April 1925): 324–76.

Weber, John B., and Charles S. Smith. "Our National Dumping Ground." *North American Review* 154 (April 1892): 424–38.

Weisberger, Bernard A. *Many People, One Nation.* Boston: Houghton Mifflin, 1987.

Weyl, Walter E. "It Is Time to Know." *The Survey* 28 (April 1912): 65–67.

Whelply, James. "International Control of Immigration." *World's Work* 8 (September 1904): 5254–59.

Who Was Who In America. Chicago: Marquis Publications, 1968.

Williams, Vernon J. *Rethinking Race: Franz Boas and His Contemporaries.* Lexington: University of Kentucky Press, 1996.

Willis, John C. *Forgotten Time: The Yazoo Mississippi Delta after the Civil War.* Charlottesville: University of Virginia Press, 2000.

Wilson, Woodrow. "Character of Democracy in the United States." *Atlantic Monthly* 64 (November 1889): 577–88.

———. *A History of the American People.* New York: Harper and Brothers, 1901.

Wunderlin, Clarence E., Jr. *Visions of a New Industrial Order: Social Science and Labor Theory in America's Progressive Era.* New York: Columbia University Press, 1992.

Zeidel, Robert F. "Hayseed Immigration Policy: 'Uncle Joe' Cannon and the Immigration Question." *Illinois Historical Journal* 88 (autumn 1995): 173–88.